& MODEL FIRE STATION TOYS

"A really unusual book that deserves to be in the library of anyone who collects model fire apparatus or fire stations. Extensively researched and very well put together. Don't let this one go by!"
—John A. Calderone (editor, *Fire Apparatus Journal* magazine)

"If you love toy firehouses, you'll love this collectible book on the subject!"
—Charlie Mack (author, *The Encyclopedia of Matchbox Toys*)

"Another outstanding addition to his series of books. Andrew has outdone himself with this compendium of firehouse models, as well as support scale fire apparatus and information about the original buildings used for the models."
—Mike Legeros (longtime model fire apparatus collector and fellow drummer)

"...a factual, comprehensive guide to this hobby... a book you will not regret purchasing and can't put down once you have it. ⭐⭐⭐⭐⭐"
—Jimmy Martinez (firefighter/EMT and creator of a 16,000-piece LEGO custom-made *EMERGENCY!* firehouse)

"...truly one of a kind—packed full of pictures and details. This book is a must-have for anyone interested in the fire service."
—Dave Audlin (former firefighter and avid collector—and another fellow drummer)

"...an outstanding publication about the different replicas of firehouses, looks great!"
—Donald Jimerson (Deputy Chief, Village of Phoenix Fire Department, south Chicago)

"I love the fact that the stations match up with collectible fire trucks. The history of the First Due Firehouse Replicas stations and the different models for each house was like reading a history book of the cities and the real firehouses. I keep going back and forth between pages with my grandkids, looking at the pictures and sharing information on the trucks they have. Great job on the book Andrew, this is one that collectors will treasure."
—Riley O'Brien (ex-firefighter/paramedic & model fire apparatus collector)

& MODEL FIRE STATION TOYS

by
Andrew Benzie

Andrew Benzie Books
Martinez, California

<u>On the Cover:</u>
Los Angeles County Fire Department Engine 51/Squad 51
  "EMERGENCY!" Firehouse (hand-painted resin),
  Code 3 Collectibles, USA, 2001, 1:64
  (see page 70)

<u>Engine 51 on Duty:</u>
Crown Firecoach (Code 3 Collectibles #12957, 2001, 1:64)
Ward LaFrance (Code 3 Collectibles #12391, 2002, 1:64)

<u>Squad 51 on Duty:</u>
Dodge 300 (LJN, 1975, 1:72)
Dodge 300 (Hot Wheels #26273, 1999, 1:64)
Dodge 300 "LA Sands County" (M2 #32500, 2023, 1:64)
Dodge 300 (Code 3 Collectibles #13940, 2001, 1:64)
Dodge 300 (Iconic Replicas #50-0338, 2022, 1:50)
Dodge 300 (Fire Replicas #FR165-51, 2024, 1:50)
Dodge 300 (Dinky Toys #267, 1979-80, 1:43)

<u>Firefighters on Duty:</u>
Firefighters I/II (American Diorama, Mijo Exclusives, 2020/22, 1:64)

FIREHOUSE REPLICAS
& MODEL FIRE STATION TOYS

by
Andrew Benzie

for information about other books in this series:
www.ModelFireEngines.com

join our Facebook group where you can learn about upcoming releases and share photos of your own models:
www.facebook.com/groups/firstdue

Published by Andrew Benzie Books: www.andrewbenziebooks.com

Copyright © 2024 Andrew Benzie. All rights reserved. No part of this publication may be reproduced, distributed, or transmitted in any form or by any means, or stored in a database or retrieval system without prior written permission of the author. This book is derived from the author's independent research.

First Edition v1.12: September 2024
ISBN: 978-1-950562-49-7 (paperback) ISBN: 978-1-950562-48-0 (hardcover)

Photography, cover design, and book design by Andrew Benzie.
Created by human intelligence—this book contains no artificial ingredients.

Andrew Benzie Books
Martinez, California

*Dedicated to those who call a firehouse their home—
thank you for your noble service.*

CONTENTS

PREFACE i

INTRODUCTION iii

PART ONE:
MODEL FIRE STATION TOYS 1

Ives Fire Engine House 1
Hubley Fire Dept. Fire Apparatus Scale Models 1
Kingsbury Fire Station 8 1
Arcade Engine Co. No. 99 1
Marx General Alarm Fire Department Headquarters 1
Marx Automatic Fire House 1
Keystone Fire Department and Burning Building 2
Plasticville Fire House Kit (O/HO) 3
Marx Fire House 3
Wyandotte Toytown Fire Dept. 4
The Lucky Toys Joy Town Fire Station 5
Mettoy Joytown Firehouse 5
Dinky Toys Fire Station Kit 6
Matchbox Fire Station (Red Roof) 8
Matchbox Fire Station (Green Roof) 9
Matchbox Emergency Station 10
Matchbox Big MX Complete Fire Rescue Site 11
Matchbox World's Smallest Fire Station Mini Playset 12
Matchbox Car•Go Fire Station 12
Matchbox Motor City Electronic Rescue Station 12
Matchbox Fire & Rescue Center 12
Matchbox Fire Station with Auto-Motion Features 12
Matchbox Pop Up Adventure Set Fire Station 13
Matchbox Motor City Fire Station 13
Matchbox Go! Action Rescue Town 13
Matchbox Roll 'n Rescue Fire Station 13
Matchbox Hero City Fire Station Playset 13
Matchbox Fire Station Adventure Set 13
Matchbox Fire Station Take-Along Playset 13
Matchbox Pop Up Adventure Set Fire Rescue 13
Matchbox Action Drivers Fire Station Rescue 13
Tootsietoy Fire Station 14
Parker Brothers/Pastime Products Fire House 16
Fleetwood Toys *"EMERGENCY!"* Firehouse 17
LEGO Fire Station 18
LEGO Fire Brigade 18
LEGO Fire Station 18
LEGO Fire House 18
LEGO Engine Company No. 9 18
LEGO Fire Station 18
LEGO *Ghostbusters* Firehouse Headquarters 19
LEGO Winter Village Fire Station 19
LEGO Fire House-I 19
LEGO Fire Control Center 19
LEGO Flame Fighters 19
LEGO Blaze Brigade 19
LEGO Firefighter's HQ 19
LEGO Fire Station (X6) 19
LEGO Fire Station with Fire Truck 19
Tomica Electro Fire Station 20
Tomica Fire Station 21
Tomica U-Mate Fire Station 22
Tomica U-Mate Hospital 22
Tomica U-Mate Fire Station 23
Tomica Fire Station 24
Tomica Kabaya Fire Station and Hospital 24
Tomica Hypercity Rescue Fire Station 25
TomyTec Diorama Collection Fire Station 25
Majorette Majokit Fire Station Construction Playset 26
Majorette Majokit Emergency Center Set 26
Majorette Mini Majo-Kit Fire Brigade 27
Majorette Firefighter Firehouse 27
Majorette Creatix Rescue Station 27
Majorette/Jada Creatix Rescue Station 27
Starlux Caserne de Pompiers (for Solido models) 28
Starlux Centre de Secours (for Solido models) 29
Solido Jeu de Société Party Game 29
Starlux City Intervention Set 29
Siku Volvo F12 Transporter w/Fire Station 30
SIKUWorld Fire Station Set 31
SIKUWorld Fire Station 31
Corgi Classics Model Fire Depot 32
Corgi Juniors Fire Station Set 34
Corgi Juniors Coastal Rescue Station 35
M.T.H. Operating Firehouse (Grey/Red) 36
Lionel Fire Station 36
Model Power Fire House 37
Model Power Fire Department 37
Tyco US1 Electric Trucking Fire Station 38
Tonka Builder Playset Fire Engine House 39
Tonka Big Fire Department Playset 39
Hot Wheels Firefighter Sto & Go 40
Hot Wheels Sto & Go Emergency Station 40
Hot Wheels World Fire Station w/Elevator 40
Hot Wheels Rescue Center 40
Hot Wheels World Fire Station w/Pop Up Flames 40
Hot Wheels Raceway Fire Station 40
Hot Wheels Sto & Go *Baywatch* Rescue Station 41
Hot Wheels Planet Micro Urban Firefighting Scene 41
Hot Wheels Downtown Fire Station Spinout Playset 41
Hot Wheels Spin City Fire Station Spinner Tower 41
Hot Wheels City Super Loop Fire Station 41
Galoob Micro Machines City Scenes Fire Station 42
Galoob Micro Machines Fire Dept. 43
Galoob Micro Machines Travel City Firehouse 43
Galoob Micro Machines Blaze & Roar Fire Station 43
Galoob Micro Machines Double Action Fire Station 43
Galoob Micro Machines Firehouse City 43
Galoob Micro Machines Fire & Rescue Playset 43
Boley Dept. 1-87 First Alarm Fire Station 44
Boley Dept. 1-87 First Alarm Fire Station (Prototype) . . . 45
Road Champs Fire-House Playset 46
American Diorama 4 Bay Fire Station 48
Funrise City Force Center Fire Station (1:64/1:32) 50

PART TWO: FIREHOUSE REPLICAS 53

Code 3 Collectibles
- FDNY E10/L10 "The Tenhouse" 54
- FDNY E82/L31 "La Casa Grande" 56
- FDNY E235/B57 "The Eye of Bed-Stuy" 58
- FDNY L79/B22 "North Shore Truckin'" 60
- Boston E24/L23 "Grove Hall" 62
- Washington, D.C. E10/L13 "House of Pain" 64
- Chicago E17/L46 *"Backdraft"* 66
- Chicago E78/A6 "The Pride of Wrigleyville" 68
- Los Angeles County E51/S51
  "EMERGENCY!" 70
- Burning Building and Firefighter Figures 72
- FDNY Rescue Company 3D Patch Set 72
- Old Glory American Flag Assortment 73

First Due Firehouse Replicas
- FDNY E1/L26 "Midtown Madness" 74
- FDNY E7/L1/B1 "Duane Street Circus" 76
- FDNY E9/L6/SAT1
  "Chinatown Dragonfighters" 78
- FDNY E40/L35 "The Cavemen" 80
- FDNY E58/L26 "Fire Factory" 82
- FDNY E59/L30 "Harlem Zoo" 84
- FDNY E73/L42 "La Casa Caca"/
  "La Casa Elefante" 86
- FDNY E75/L35/B19 *"Animal House"* (Old)
  Valiant Service Edition 88
- FDNY EMS Station #19 "University Heights"/
  "Da Boogie Down Bronx" 89
- FDNY E75/L35/B19 *"Animal House"* (New) 90
- FDNY E201/L114/B40 "Emerald Isle" 92
- FDNY E207/L110/B31/Super Pumper System
  "Tillary St. Tigers" 94
- FDNY E242 "The Pride of Bayridge" 96
- FDNY E273/L129 "The Mouse House" 98
- FDNY L8 *"Ghostbusters"* 100
- FDNY S1 "The One and Only" 102
- FDNY S288/HazMat 1
  "Fortuna Favet Fortibus" 104
- FDNY R2 "The Bulldog" (New) 106
- FDNY R3 "Big Blue" 108
- FDNY R5/E160 "Blue Thunder"/"The Hillbillies" . . 110
- Oceanic VFDNY H&L Co. No.1 E1/BFU1 112
- Yonkers E313/T73 "Far East" 114
- Buffalo E2/L9/B56 116
- Syracuse Fire Station 1 118
- West Haverstraw Hose Co#2
  E23/R23 "House of Blues" 120
- Philadelphia E50/L12 "Northern Knights" 122
- Boston E30/L25 124
- Chicago E18 "Devil Dogs" 126
- Chicago E42/T3/S1 "Iron Ring" 128
- Chicago E113 130
- Chicago E124/T38 "Hole In the Wall Gang" 132

First Due Firehouse Replica *(cont'd)*
- Denver E3 "Pride of the Points"/
  "Eye of the Storm" 134
- Orlando E2/L2 "The Pride of Parramore" 136
- LAFD E18 "Knollwood" 138
- LAFD E39/T39/B10 "The Big House" 140
- LAFD E51 "LAX" 142
- SFFD E3/T3 144
- SFFD E15/T15 *"Towering Inferno"/"Ocean's 15"* 146
- Honolulu E5/L5 "Kaimuki" 148

Bernard's Fire Station
- FDNY E231/L120 "Watkins Street" 150
- FDNY R1 "Outstanding" (New) 152
- FDNY R2 "The Bulldog" (Old) 154

Twin Whistle Sign & Kit Co.
- FDNY S18 "South of the Park" 156
- FDNY E5 "14th Street Express" 156
- FDNY E249 "Camp Rogers Rats" 156
- FDNY E286/L135 "Myrtles Turtles" 156
- FDNY S61/B20 "Taking in a Job Near You" 157
- FDNY S252 "In Squad We Trust" 157
- FDNY S288/HazMat 1 "Fortuna Favet Fortibus" . . . 157
- FDNY R1 "Outstanding" (Old) 157
- FDNY R4/E292 "Winfield Cougars" 158
- Hose Tower Kit 158
- New Jersey Fire Tower 158

Swiss Dog Studios
- Chicago-Style Four-Bay Firehouse 159

Iconic Replicas
- Los Angeles County E51/S51 *"EMERGENCY!"* 160

APPENDIX: MISCELLANEOUS FIRE DEPARTMENT MODELS 161

- How to Build a Firehouse Replica 161
- Rip Van Winkle Hose Company 169
- Town of Mamaroneck Fire Department 170
- 1:87 Scale Firehouses 172
- FDNY LEGO Firehouses 174
- FDNY LEGO Headquarters 180
- Los Angeles County E51/S51 *"EMERGENCY!"*
  LEGO Firehouse 182
- Firehouse Dioramas 184
- Mack Fire Engine Assembly Plant 186
- FDNY Fleet Services "The Shops" Facility 188

INDEX 196

BIBLIOGRAPHY 198

ABOUT THE AUTHOR 199

OTHER BOOKS IN THE SERIES . . 199

*Fire Station Kit (plastic), Dinky Toys,
England, 1957-65, 1:43*

*Model Fire Depot Kit (cardboard),
Corgi Classics, England, 1997, 1:50*

PREFACE

I first began collecting die-cast model fire engines when I was six years old, though I didn't realize it at the time. My parents emigrated from London prior to my birth in Berkeley, California during the summer of 1968—and little known to me, this meant every few years I would return to see my grandparents in England—the joyous land of **Corgi** and **Dinky Toys**.

I still remember purchasing my Corgi American LaFrance open cab tiller truck with my grandparents at the world-famous Harrods department store in London. With its string-activated extendable ladder, this model quickly assumed the role of *first due* in my fictional fire department. I still own this replica today—it has served its citizens well over the years.

As a child, my local combination bicycle/toy store (The Handlebar) had two large glass cases which displayed more Corgi and Dinky Toys than I could have ever imagined. Of the many remarkable models these two companies produced, I spent most of my time dreaming about the fire engines and rescue units found in their small full-color catalogs which featured hand-drawn artistic depictions of the vehicles and their moving parts.

When I was a teenager I was lucky enough to participate in a trip to Europe with my schoolmates. In addition to taking in the scenery and culture, I also found time to visit several toy stores. I ended up with a few very special replicas in my suitcase on the way home, including my new prize possession—the **Siku Volvo F12 Transporter with Fire Station**.

While taking art classes in high school I decided to create my first model firehouse. This large 1:50 scale structure had four apparatus bay doors in the front and three on the side. The walls were made of cardboard which I hand-colored with ink markers. Since I was also taking an electronics class, I learned how to install interior and exterior 9-volt lighting as well as a working siren.

Volvo F12 Transporter w/Lowboy Trailer (metal) &
Fire Station No.3 (plastic), Siku, West Germany, 1985-1989, 1:55

That first firehouse model was followed by three increasingly more detailed replicas over the next few years. These firehouses were loosely based on my local department's fire stations in the suburban/rural Orinda-Moraga Fire Protection District.

One of my firehouse replicas (and the accompanying apparatus models) was featured at an art show at Saint Mary's College in Moraga as part of my high school art class display. Unfortunately, these replicas didn't stand the test of time and only a few photographs remain of these creations.

FDNY Engine 10/Ladder 10 "The Tenhouse" (hand-painted resin), Code 3 Collectibles, USA, 2004, 1:64

The author's first firehouse replica (cardboard), c.1983, 1:50— note the switches on the roof which activate the lights and siren

During the late 1990s and 2000s I collected numerous **Code 3 Collectibles** fire apparatus models along with their companion series of detailed 1:64 scale hand-painted resin firehouse replicas, including their "Burning Building" produced in 2001. All of Code 3's firehouse releases are presented in this book.

In 2017 I published the first books in my *Model Fire Engines* series. These three books focus on fire apparatus models (and firehouses) produced by **Conrad**, **Siku**, and **Tomica**. I hope to release more books in this series in the future.

The author's second and third firehouse replicas (foam core, plastic, bamboo skewers, straws), c.1984-86, 1:50

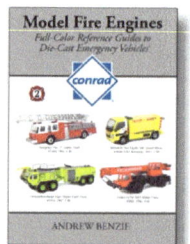 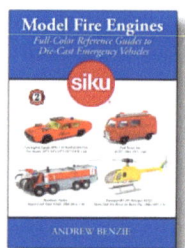 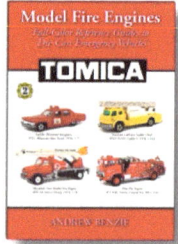

The first three books in the author's "Model Fire Engines: Full Color Guides to Die-Cast Emergency Vehicles" series, Andrew Benzie Books, 2017, Revised 2nd Editions (with appendices) published June 2024

In 2021 I designed and built a series of 1:64 scale firehouse replicas to house my extensive collection of Code 3 models. These buildings were designed to augment the nine firehouses released by Code 3 and "continue where they left off." I decided to offer a limited number of these hand-built firehouse replicas for sale to fellow collectors under the name **First Due Firehouse Replicas**. We currently offer replicas of 38 firehouses from all over the United States.

The author posed with his fourth firehouse replica (foam core/mixed media) at Saint Mary's College art show, Moraga, California, c.1987, 1:50

Code 3 Collectibles promotional flyer, 2000

FDNY Engine 59/Ladder 30 "The Harlem Zoo" (foam core/mixed media), First Due Firehouse Replicas, USA, 2023, 1:64

I began work on this publication in March 2023. The process began by selecting which firehouse replicas to include, photographing each firehouse (along with the apparatus quartered inside), and doing research on each model to determine years of production, scale, and any other tidbits of information I could find to pass along to enthusiasts. Please let me know of any errors, they will be corrected in future versions of the book.

The *Firehouse Replicas & Model Fire Station Toys* book you now hold in your hands was actually the first title I intended to publish in this series. However, things often don't go quite as planned—and in this case for the better. So I'm now very happy to present to you my collection of model fire station toys and firehouse replicas—I hope you enjoy reading the book as much as I did putting it together.

—Andrew Benzie, September 2024

First Due Firehouse Replicas website banner showing the first three releases

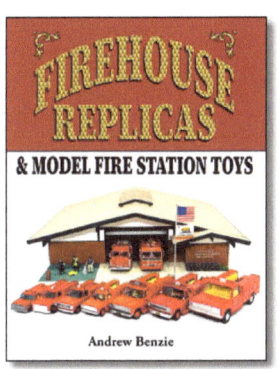

Firehouse Replicas & Model Fire Station Toys, Andrew Benzie Books, 2024

INTRODUCTION

The goal of this book is to present my collection of firehouse replicas and model fire station toys in a fashion which will be both enjoyable and educational to you, the reader. To that end, I decided to break this book up into two sections—**Part One** will focus on model fire station toys produced from the 1940s onward, and **Part Two** will focus on detailed models replicating real firehouses produced from the early 2000s to present day.

Please send any feedback or comments to andrew@andrewbenzie.com. If you enjoy this book, please consider leaving a positive review on Amazon. You can find the latest releases from First Due Firehouse Replicas at *www.ModelFireEngines.com* or on Facebook at *www.facebook.com/groups/firstdue*.

The author's model fire station toys display

The author's firehouse replicas display

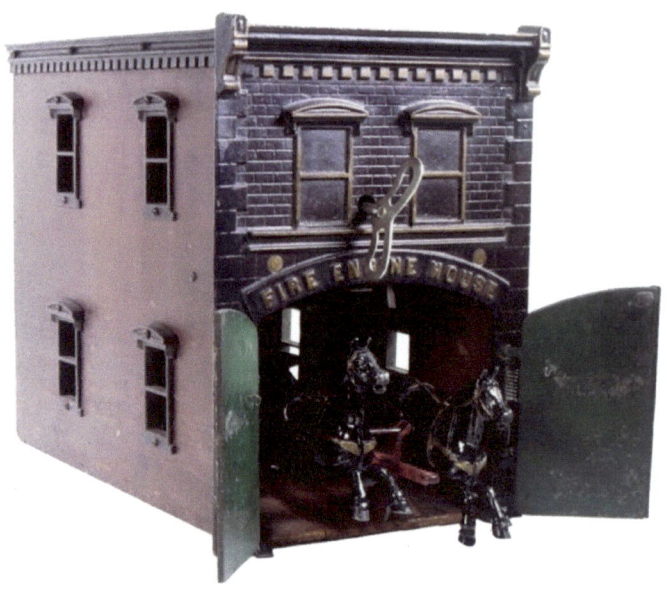

Fire Engine House (cast iron and wood) including apparatus (cast iron),
Ives, USA, 1890s

Fire Station 8 (steel) including pumper (metal),
Kingsbury, USA, 1930s

Hubley Fire Dept. Fire Apparatus Scale Models (metal),
Hubley, USA, 1948

Engine Co. No. 99 (wood) with apparatus (cast iron),
Arcade, USA, 1940s

Note: The model fire station toys listed in Part One as "including apparatus" were sold with the accompanying fire apparatus models—
for those listed as "with apparatus" the fire apparatus models shown were sold separately

PART ONE: MODEL FIRE STATION TOYS

The history of model fire station toys dates back to the late-19th century when toymakers began producing miniature versions of firefighting equipment including horse-drawn fire engines and ladder trucks.

One of the earliest known model firehouses was produced by the American toymaker **Ives** in the 1890s. This cast-iron firehouse features an interior clockwork mechanism which, when activated, rings a bell, opens the bay doors, and sends the horse-drawn apparatus on its way. Other companies such as **Kingsbury** also produced metal firehouses in the early to mid-20th century.

By the 1940s tin became a popular material for model firehouses and other toys. These tin toys (including those produced by **Marx**) were often painted in bright colors and feature intricate mechanical details such as operational apparatus bay doors.

Cardboard and particle-board have also been common construction materials for model fire station toys. These buildings were often sold in flat boxes with some assembly required. Manufactures producing paper/wood-based products include **Corgi Classics**, **Corgi Juniors**, **Keystone**, and **Starlux**.

In the post-World War II era, plastic became the material of choice for most model firehouses which were designed to be both durable and affordable. Notable toy fire station manufacturers from this era include **Dinky Toys**, **Matchbox**, **Tomica**, and **Tootsietoy**. Over the years a variety of plastic model fire stations have been marketed directly to model railroad enthusiasts such as those produced by **Boley**, **M.T.H.**, **Model Power**, and **Plasticville**.

Since the late 1950s, three of the world's largest toy companies (**Hot Wheels**, **Matchbox**, and **LEGO**) have added an astounding number of model fire stations to their product lines. The sheer number of releases by these three companies alone demonstrates the worldwide popularity of model fire station toys.

Model fire station toys continue to be popular among both children and collectors. Modern model firehouses are often highly detailed and feature realistic designs including working doors, authentic fire trucks and other firefighting equipment—even lighting and sound effects. Model fire station toys can be a fun and educational way for children to learn about firefighting and fire safety, and they are also highly valued by collectors as a way to preserve the history of firefighting and collectible toys.

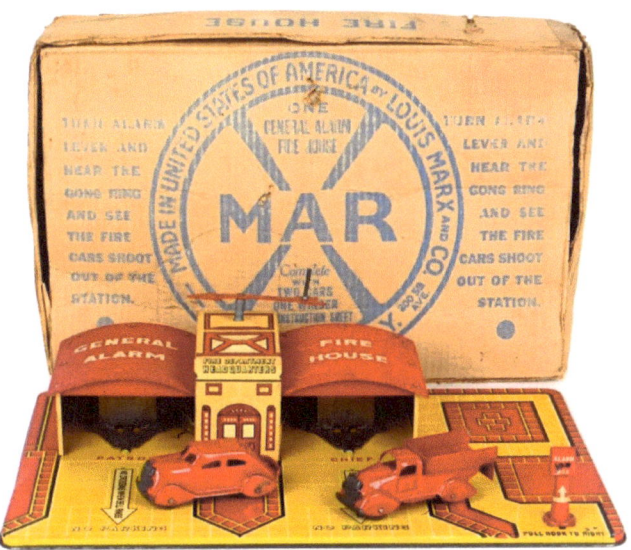

General Alarm Fire Department Headquarters including apparatus (tin), Marx, USA, 1938

The firehouse features a firefighter "Training School" in the back of the building

Automatic Fire House including friction fire chief car (tin), Marx, USA, 1949

*Fire Department and Burning Building (particle board)
including pumper and ladder truck (plastic), Keystone, USA, 1950s*

Fire Department and Burning Building
Keystone #1-165, 1950s

Keystone Toys (Boston, Massachusetts) produced this **Fire Department** set in the 1950s. Included with the two-bay firehouse are the burning building (with functioning hydrant and hose) and the hose and ladder company apparatus. The colonial-style red brick design is similar to many real firehouses located throughout the northeastern United States in the 1950s.

The firehouse is constructed from painted Masonite boards and the apparatus bay doors are metal and plastic. When the crank on the side of the firehouse is turned a fire bell rings and the two bay doors open. There are spring-loaded devices at the rear of each bay which, when activated, propel the apparatus out the doors at a high rate of speed.

The unique burning building features two "fires" which can be extinguished (turning them sideways) by drawing water from the hydrant into the pumper then spraying the flames. The ingenious design allows the water to be recycled back into the reservoir where it can reflow through the hydrant and pumper.

Keystone also released a three-bay version of this firehouse (with an additional chief bay). The example shown here still has its original cardboard tag which states "Everything Works! Fire Bell Rings! Door Opens Automatically! Cars Rush Out! Hydrant Works! Hose Shoots Water! Puts Out Fire! Uses Same Water!"

What child in the 1950s wouldn't want to have one?

The popularity of Keystone Toys declined as plastic toys became more prevalent in the toy market. The company ceased production in 1958, and their toys have since become highly sought-after collectibles among vintage toy enthusiasts.

Plasticville Fire Dept. Engine Co 7, Ladder Co 8
Plasticville Fire House Kit #45610, 1950s

Plasticville (originally a subsidiary of **Bachman Bros., Inc.**, Philadelphia, Pennsylvania) has been producing a popular line of products and structures for model railroad enthusiasts since 1947. Many Plasticville items are still produced today from their original molds.

Plasticville buildings are usually a simple design made of walls which snap together permitting them to be assembled without glue. This firehouse (like most Plasticville structures) is styled after 1950s United States suburban buildings—the product line has changed little since the late 1950s. The kits were sold in both O and HO scale.

In 1984, Plasticville was taken over by **Kader Industries** of Dongguan, China and production moved to China shortly thereafter.

Fire House Kit (plastic) including American LaFrance pumper and ladder truck (plastic), Plasticville, USA, 1950s, O scale

Fire House Kit (plastic), Plasticville, USA, 1950s, HO scale with fire engine and ladder truck (metal), Model Power, USA, 1970s (not included with firehouse)

HO (half-O) scale vs. O scale firehouses

Fire House (plastic) including apparatus and figures (plastic), Marx, USA, 1950s, O scale

The **Louis Marx Company** (New York City) produced a line of "Marxville" plastic buildings during the 1950s in direct competition to Bachman's popular Plasticville kits. This design is remarkably similar to **Keystone's Fire Department**.

Toytown Fire Dept. Engine Co. No. 51/ Ladder Co. No. 74, Wyandotte, 1950s

Wyandotte Toys (Wyondotte, Michigan) **Toytown Fire Dept. Engine Co. No. 51 & Ladder Co. No. 74** was produced by the **All Metal Products Company**, an American toy manufacturer which operated from the early 1920s through the mid-1950s. The company was known for producing a wide range of pressed steel toys under the Wyandotte brand name.

Wyandotte toys were popular for their durability, realistic designs, attention to detail, and quality craftsmanship. The company often incorporated moving parts, realistic features, and intricate designs into their toys, making them appealing to both children and collectors.

The Toytown firehouse shown here is constructed out of lithographed metal and includes a plastic American LaFrance ladder truck. The firehouse's spring-loaded apparatus bay door is activated by the push of a small lever located on the lower right front of the building. The Wyandotte Toys logo is printed on the bottom of the toy.

To keep costs down, the company used scrap and surplus materials whenever possible, often manufacturing their toys from scrap metal obtained from local auto factories. In 1948, die-cast and plastic toys were added to the Wyandotte line, allowing it to compete with other companies who sold inexpensive dime store-type toys at lower prices than the Wyandotte pressed metal toys.

The All Metal Products Company faced financial challenges in the 1950s, which led to its eventual closure in 1957. The decline in popularity of pressed steel toys and the rise of plastic toys contributed to the company's struggles.

Today, Wyandotte toys are highly sought-after collectibles, and since they were primarily made of metal, many continue to survive in good condition today.

Fire chief and fire engine (metal), Tootsietoy, USA, 1960s (not included with firehouse)

Toytown Fire Dept. Engine Co. No. 51/Ladder Co. No. 74 (tin) including American LaFrance ladder truck (plastic), Wyandotte, USA, 1950s

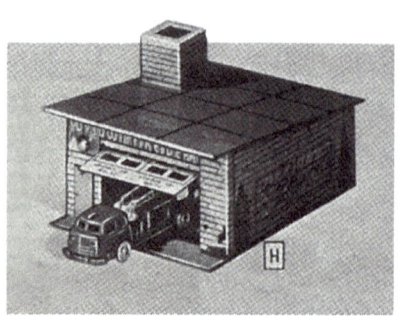

Sears catalog showing the original plastic American LaFrance ladder truck, 1950s

Joy Town Fire Station
The Lucky Toys #7028A, 1970s

The Lucky Toys (Hong Kong) produced a large number of die-cast, plastic, and electronic products for the toy and hobby markets beginning in the 1950s.

This 1:64 scale plastic **Joy Town Fire Station** was sold as a set with three fire vehicles—each containing a friction motor to power the rear wheels. The fire chief car is missing from this example, but you can see this car on the box. The two fire engines (Maxim and Land Rover pumpers) look nearly identical to smaller scale metal units released by **Matchbox** in 1966.

Joy Town Fire Station (plastic) including Maxim and Land Rover pumpers (plastic), The Lucky Toys, Hong Kong, 1970s, 1:64

Of interesting note, a similarly named tin **Joytown** fire station and accompanying apparatus models were sold by the **Mettoy Toy Company** in 1949. Mettoy would go on to create their famous **Corgi Toys** line in 1956.

Mettoy Joytown Fire Station including apparatus (tin), England, c. 1949

Fire Station Kit
Dinky Toys #954, 1957-65

Dinky Toys (England) was the brand name for a range of die-cast model vehicles produced by the British toy company **Meccano Ltd.** from the early 1930s in both Liverpool, England and Bobigny, France. Dinky Toys were among the most popular die-cast vehicles ever made—pre-dating many other well-known companies including **Corgi**, **Matchbox**, and Mattel's **Hot Wheels**.

The firm sold a variety of popular models based on real-world cars, trucks, military vehicles, airplanes, and boats. Their detailed models often include working parts, opening doors, and flashing lights. France ceased production in 1972, and England closed their factory on Binns Road in 1979. Since then, the name changed owners several times, eventually ending up in the hands of **Mattel** (USA).

This rare 1957-1965 Dinky Toys fire station was sold as an unassembled kit which includes a large clear overhead plastic skylight, two sideways-sliding nylon apparatus bay doors, and has room for two 1:43 scale vehicles.

Dinky Toys Appliances on Duty:
ERF Fire Tender #266, 1976-80, 1:43
Ford Transit Fire Appliance #271, 1975-77, 1:43
Land Rover Fire Appliance #282, 1974-80, 1:43
Superior Cadillac Ambulance #288, 1967-71, 1:43
(not included with firehouse)

Fire Station Kit (plastic) with appliances (metal), Dinky Toys, England, 1957-65, 1:43

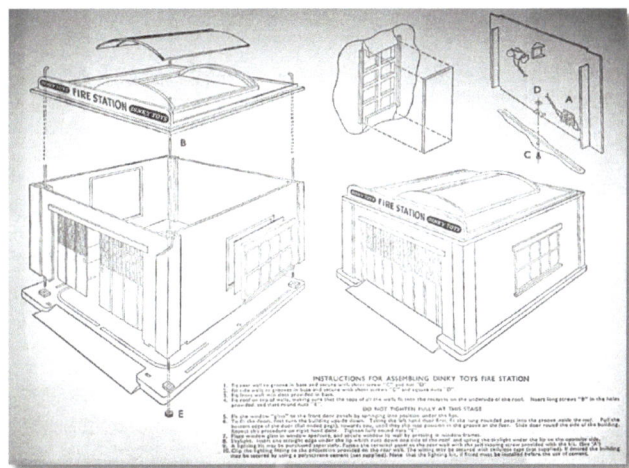

Assembly instructions located on the underside of the box top

With this exciting and easy-to-assemble Kit, you can quickly erect a fine up-to-date Fire Station for your Dinky Toys Fire Fighting vehicles. Transparent windows and roof, and sliding nylon doors, add effective touches of realism.

Contents of the Dinky Toys Fire Station Kit

Matchbox is a toy brand introduced by **Lesney Products** (London, England) in 1953. The original die-cast Matchbox toys were packaged in boxes similar to those in which matches were sold. The brand eventually grew to encompass a broad range of toys including larger-scale die-cast models, plastic model kits, slot car racing, and action figures.

Due to the popularity of **Mattel's** new competing line of **Hot Wheels** cars, Matchbox introduced their **Superfast** series in 1969 which included wider and faster low-friction wheels.

During the 1970s Matchbox began to switch to the more conventional plastic and cardboard blister packs which were used by other die-cast toy brands (including Hot Wheels). By the 2000s the box-style packaging was reintroduced for the collector market.

In May 1992 Matchbox was purchased by **Tyco Toys** which in turn was bought by Mattel in 1997, controversially uniting Matchbox with its longtime rival Hot Wheels under the same corporate banner.

Fire Station Set (Red Roof)
Matchbox #MF-1, 1963-67

Matchbox produced their plastic **#MF-1 Fire Station (Red Roof)** in England from 1963 through 1967. Features include two inward-opening plastic bay doors and an interior fire pole.

The firehouse was sold in three versions—**#MF-1** (the firehouse only), and the **#G-5** and **#G-10** gift sets which include four die-cast models. The list price for the **#MF-1** was $3.

This example (like most from this era) has a yellowed area along the bottom where the glue has interacted with the plastic over the years creating a discoloring.

<u>Matchbox Apparatus on Duty:</u>
Bedford Lomas Ambulance No. 14, 1962
Daimler Ambulance No. 14, 1958
Ford Fairlane Fire Chief No. 59, 1964
Mercedes-Benz Ambulance No. 3, 1968
Merryweather Marquis Fire Engine No. 9, 1960

Fire Station Set (Red Roof)
(plastic) with apparatus (metal),
Matchbox, England, 1963-67

Fire Station Set (Green Roof)
Matchbox #MF-1, 1964-67

Matchbox released this **#MF-1 Fire Station (Green Roof)** in 1964. The plastic firehouse was packaged as a pre-assembled building with all graphics applied. The building contains a department office, an upstairs dormitory, and the main apparatus bay with space for three vehicles.

This rare green roof fire station was originally intended to be **Ambulance Station #MA-1** as shown in the 1964 Matchbox catalog below. For unknown reasons it was instead released as an alternate fire station version with different graphics than that of the original **#MF-1 Red Roof** release.

Matchbox catalog showing the upcoming green roof "Ambulance Stn. MA-1," 1964

Fire Station Set (Green Roof) (plastic) with apparatus (metal), Matchbox, England, 1964-67

<u>Matchbox Apparatus on Duty:</u>
Cadillac Ambulance No. 54, 1965
Foamite Crash Tender No. 63, 1964
Ford Galaxy Fire Chief No. 59, 1965
Maxim "Denver" Pumper No. 29, 1966

Emergency Station
Matchbox #587902, 1976

This classic **Emergency Station** was released by **Matchbox** way back in 1976. I still remember this one from when I was a child. With a press of the green switch on the roof, the apparatus bay floor tilts up which in turn opens the (rubber band-powered) doors and sends the vehicles inside flying out to their next call. Repeatedly pushing the red switch on the roof winds up a mechanical siren-sounding device hidden inside the roof. This well-designed simple firehouse is certainly from a different era.

Matchbox Apparatus on Duty:
Carmichael Commando Fire Unit #57F, 1982
Carmichael Commando Police Rescue #57F, 1982
Generic (Chevrolet) Ambulance 3 #75, 1977
International Ambulance #1178, 2019
Super GT Fire #17/18, 1985
Super GT Rescue #17/18, 1985
(not included with firehouse)

Emergency Station (plastic) with apparatus (metal), Matchbox, England, 1976

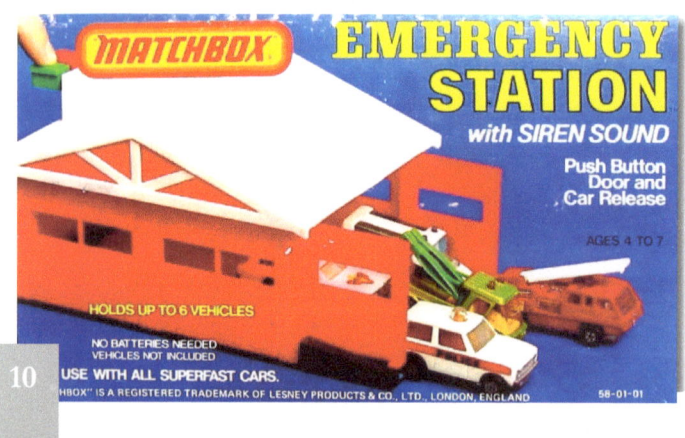

Big MX Complete Fire Rescue Site
Matchbox #62-05-06, 1972

Matchbox revealed their new **Big MX** series of six modified **King Size** castings in 1972. Each vehicle includes drive points which can be operated by using the included battery-powered activator drill.

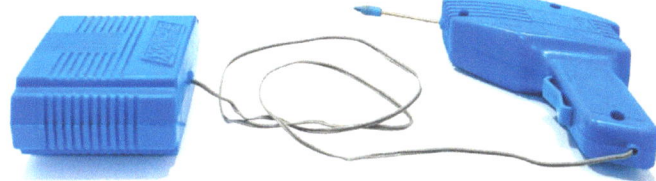

The final release in the series was the **Fire Rescue Site** which includes a modified **#K-15 Merryweather Fire Engine** lettered for Kent Fire Brigade, the power activator with battery pack, three plastic sections or roadway, a four-story burning building, one firefighter figure, and three women to rescue.

The activator's Phillips head can be inserted in to the three drive points on the truck to control positioning and extension of the ladder. The goal is to control the firefighter at the end of the ladder (held on by a plastic clip) to rescue the women by aiming his outstretched arm through their clasped hands.

Big MX Complete Rescue Site (plastic) including fire truck (metal), Matchbox, England, 1972

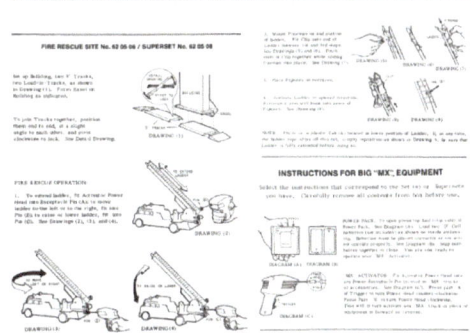

World's Smallest Fire Station #1684
Mini Playset #1
Matchbox #35400, 1990

Matchbox produced this model fire station in 1990 as part of their **World's Smallest Matchbox** lineup of toys. The set includes three tiny rescue vehicles (a fire chief, rescue, and utility truck) and the plastic fire station which can be attached to the other releases in the series. The firehouse can be folded up (which includes a storage area for all three units) for transport.

At the time, this release was a clear response from Matchbox to both **Galoob's** popular **Micro Machines** series and **Hot Wheels' Planet Micro** lineup.

Car•Go Fire Station
Matchbox Hero City
#2708420312, 2004

This unique firehouse design from **Matchbox Hero City** includes a nozzle at the end of an articulating boom, a winch with rope and hook, and **Highway Rescue Fire Truck #MB01**. The lower apparatus bay doors swing open to allow a ramp to unfold. Designed for kid's road trips—fits in a drink holder!

World's Smallest Fire Station #1684, Mini Playset #1 (plastic) including apparatus (plastic), Matchbox, England, 1990, ~1:150

Car•Go Fire Station (plastic) including fire truck (metal), Matchbox, USA, 2004

<u>Other **Matchbox** firehouse releases</u>:

Matchbox Motor City Electronic Rescue Station #MC660, 1992
Matchbox Fire & Rescue Center #50720, 1995
Matchbox Fire Station with Auto-Motion Features #50722-1, 1996
Matchbox Motor City Fire Station #50671.20, 1996
Matchbox Go! Action Rescue Town #37079, 1999
Matchbox Roll 'n Rescue Fire Station #88449, 2000
Matchbox Hero City Fire Station Playset #88436, 2003
Matchbox Fire Station Adventure Set #J4759, 2005
Matchbox Fire Station Take-Along Playset #89425, 2005
    Matchbox Pop Up Adventure Set Fire Rescue #N6076, 2008
    Matchbox Action Drivers Fire Station Rescue #HBD76, 2021

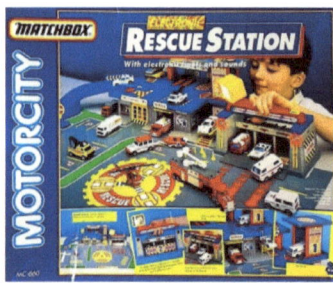
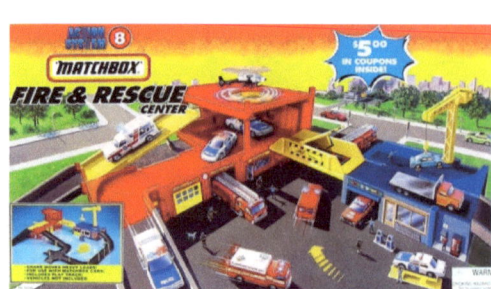

Pop Up Adventure Set Fire Station
Matchbox #K6972, 2006

The toymakers at **Matchbox** worked overtime on this firehouse. An ingenious design allows this case to magically unfold and transform into not only a firehouse, but an entire firefighting scene. Includes fire pole, plastic "water" rockets and cannons, and **Highway Rescue Fire Truck #MB01**.

Pop Up Adventure Set Fire Station (plastic) including fire truck (metal), Matchbox, USA, 2006

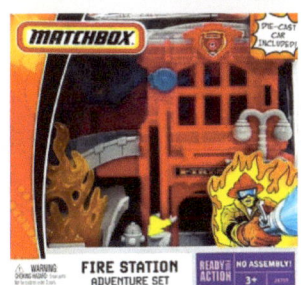

Tootsietoy (Chicago, Illinois) began manufacturing die-cast toy cars and other toy vehicles in the early 1920s, though the company's origins date from about 1890. By the early 1920s the name "Tootsie" was being used as a brand name and "Tootsietoy" was registered as a trademark in 1924. The "Tootsie" moniker was derived from one of the founder's granddaughters whose name was "Toots."

Tootsietoy made metal prizes for Cracker Jack boxes in the 1930s, and later provided die-cast pieces for the popular Monopoly board game. Tootsietoy, which is now owned by **J. Lloyd International, Inc.**, is still based in Chicago and makes about 40 million cars per year.

Fire Station
Tootsietoy #1810, 1960s

This plastic **Tootsietoy** fire station includes a set of metal American LaFrance fire apparatus, a badge, a pair of ladders, a stretcher, a life net, two axes, and a fire pole. It is similar to a firehouse produced by **Matchbox** around the same time. I've had the pumper and the ladder truck since I was a child.

Fire Station (plastic) including American LaFrance pumper, ladder, and tower (metal), Tootsietoy, USA, 1960s

1810 TOOTSIETOY FIRE STATION. Modern two-story fire station complete with swinging doors and slide pole. Fire fighting equipment includes a snorkel truck, pumper truck, panel truck, fire chief's car, emergency jeep, aerial ladder truck, fire chief's badge, emergency net, two ladders, fire axes and stretcher. Full color illustration forms a stage setting backdrop. Overall size of box 7½ x 9 x 18½. ½ dz. to master carton. Weight 10 lbs.

Fire House: The Build and Play Set
Parker Brothers/Pastime Products #951, 1961

Pastime Products (a division of **Parker Brothers**, Salem, Massachusetts and Des Moines, Iowa) produced this firehouse playset in 1961. It sold for $2 and was packaged in a flat box containing four pre-cut cardboard sheets including the firehouse walls, apparatus bay door, a ladder, and three firefighter figures. Once separated from the sheets, the walls could be easily assembled into the firehouse by matching up the appropriate letters printed on the corner of each wall.

The apparatus bay door opens by lifting the bell tower wall upwards. Once this piece is removed, the fire chief and pumper are ready to roll into action. These two units (included with the set) were produced by **Tootsietoy** (Chicago, Illinois).

The side of the box states: "the build and playset / *contains fire house, all cars and play figures shown on cover* / to assemble: match letter to letter / stimulating activity / fun for boys and girls / *designed by Arnold Arnold.*" Other **Arnold Activity Sets** produced at the time include a **Bridge Set** and a **Service Station Set**.

Fire House: The Build and Play Set (cardboard), Parker Brothers/Pastime Products, including fire chief and fire engine (metal), Tootsietoy, USA, 1961

EMERGENCY! Rescue Squad with Firehouse
Fleetwood Toys #421-101, 1970s

Fleetwood Toy Corporation (New York City) specialized in inexpensive rack toys based on numerous licensed trademarks including *Marvel Comics*, *Buck Rogers*, *The Love Boat*, *CHiPs*, *BJ and the Bear*, *the A-Team*, and *EMERGENCY!*.

Fleetwood's **EMERGENCY! Rescue Squad with Firehouse** set includes a fold-out cardboard firehouse of the famous Los Angeles County Fire Station #51 along with three plastic vehicles—a helicopter, a fire chief, and a pumper which strongly resembles the Maxim "Denver Pumper" #29C produced by **Matchbox/Lesney** from 1966-1970. Fleetwood also sold various other *EMERGENCY!* sets including **Air Rescue**, **Paramedic Kit**, **Stamp Set**, **Rescue Light**, and a **Survival Kit**.

Los Angeles County Fire Department Fire Station #51 EMERGENCY! Rescue Squad with Firehouse (cardboard), including helicopter, fire chief, and fire engine (plastic), Fleetwood Toys, USA, 1970s

Fleetwood Toys EMERGENCY! themed products

Based on sales, **LEGO®** is the largest toy manufacturer in the world. One of Europe's biggest companies, **The Lego Group** is a privately held company based in Billund, Denmark. The company began manufacturing their world-famous interlocking toy bricks in 1949.

LEGOs are produced in Denmark, Hungary, Mexico, and China. Annual production of the bricks averages 36 billion, or about 1,140 elements per second.

As of 2015, 600 billion LEGO parts have been produced. Films, games competitions, and eight Legoland amusement parks have been developed under the brand.

Numerous LEGO firehouse sets have been released over the years culminating with their iconic 4,634-piece *Ghostbusters* Firehouse Headquarters released in 2016.

Fire Station
LEGO #1308, 1957

LEGO's Fire Station #1308 was the first LEGO fire station ever produced. It was released in 1957 and consists of 109 pieces including a red HO scale Bedford fire engine. This firehouse includes a white 1 x 8 brick with the words "FIRE STATION" imprinted (in various languages). This fire station was repackaged in 1958 as **Fire Station #308**.

Fire Brigade
LEGO #10197, 2009

LEGO's Fire Brigade is the first LEGO fire station released under their **Creator** line. This incredibly detailed model of a 1932 firehouse includes a fire engine, fire-dog, numerous firefighting tools, helmet racks, a ping-pong table, bell tower, and a fire pole.

Fire Station including fire engine (plastic), LEGO, Denmark, 1957

Fire Brigade including fire engine (plastic), LEGO, Denmark, 2009

Other **LEGO** firehouse releases:

Fire Station #374, 1970
Fire House #570, 1973
Engine Company No. 9 #590, 1978
Fire Station #6382, 1981
Fire House-I #6385, 1985
Fire Control Center #6389, 1990
Flame Fighters #6571, 1994
Blaze Brigade #6554, 1997
Firefighter's HQ #6478, 2000
Fire Station #7240, 2005
Fire Station #7495, 2007
Fire Station #7208, 2010
Fire Station #60004, 2013
Fire Station #60110, 2016
Fire Station #60215, 2019
Fire Station with Fire Truck #60414, 2024

*Note: See the **Appendix** for a collection of custom-built LEGO firehouses representing FDNY and Los Angeles County Fire Department*

Ghostbusters Firehouse Headquarters
LEGO #75827, 2016

LEGO's *Ghostbusters* Firehouse Headquarters is the most impressive of the many LEGO firehouse released over the years. With over 4,600 pieces, this amazing three-story firehouse includes the laboratory containment unit, darkroom, apparatus bay, office, kitchen, sleeping quarters, bathroom and recreation rooms. The walls of the building fold outwards to reveal the interior elements.

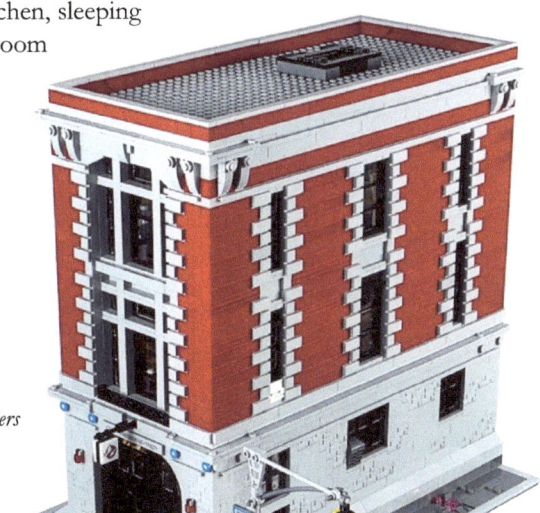

Ghostbusters Firehouse Headquarters (plastic), LEGO, Denmark, 2016

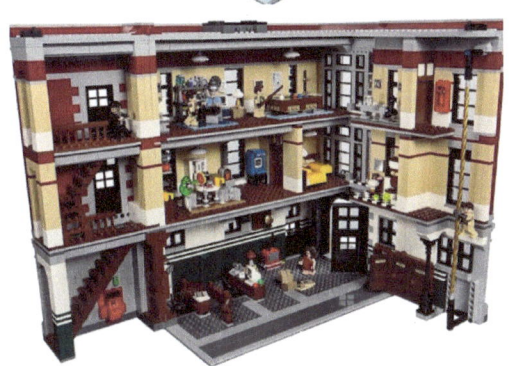

Winter Village Fire Station
LEGO #10263, 2018

LEGO's Winter Village Fire Station is the ninth release in LEGO's **Creator Expert Winter Village** line. This vintage-style firehouse celebrates the holiday season with an ice-skating pond, a sled, presents, and a Christmas tree.

Winter Village Fire Station including fire engine (plastic), LEGO, Denmark, 2018

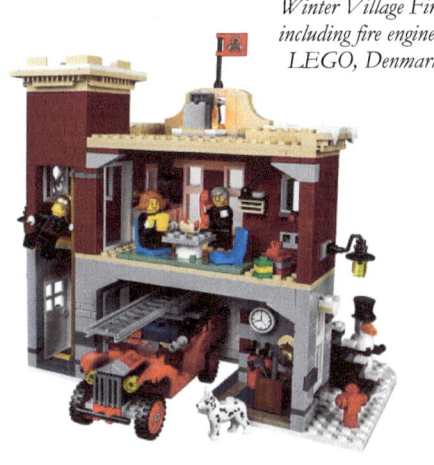

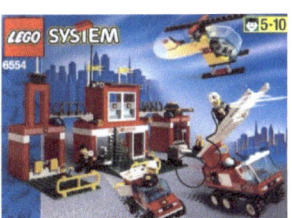

Electro Fire Station
Tomica #56643, 1979

Tomica's forty-five-year-old **Electro Fire Station** is constructed of plastic and cardboard and includes a battery-powered siren and flashing light on the roof. The push of a button tilts the apparatus bay floor up sending the units speeding on their way.

<u>Tomica Apparatus on Duty:</u>
Isuzu Snorkel Fire Truck #68, 1985, 1:110
Nissan Diesel UD Condor Chemical Fire Engine #94, 1977, 1:90
Nissan Skyline 2000GT #82, Special Tomica, 1995, 1:64
(not included with firehouse)

Electro Fire Station (plastic/cardboard) with apparatus (metal), Tomica, Japan, 1979

Tomy (Tokyo, Japan) was founded in 1924 by Eijira Tomiyama, and the company's **Tomica** line of die-cast vehicles was introduced in 1970 as a result of the surge of interest in die-cast cars led by **Matchbox** and **Mattel's Hot Wheels**.

Tomica models were originally based exclusively on domestic Japanese vehicles and varied in scale to achieve an overall length of around 3 inches. To compete in the global market, the **Pocket Cars** line was introduced in 1974.

Tomica models were almost exclusively produced in Tomy's local factory in Tokyo until 1993. By July 1997 all regular line Tomica cars were made in China, and in 2009 production began to move to Vietnam.

As of 2015, four out of every five Japanese children under the age of eight own at least one Tomica. There are currently 140 models in the lineup with a new model added on the third Saturday of each month.

Fire Station
Tomica #25356, 1987

Tomica released this fire station in 1987. The plastic parts come unassembled and require the application of a variety of stickers from the included sheet. The model contains an upper floor office and the main garage with covered parking for five pieces of apparatus. The left bay includes a plastic roll up door.

The set also includes a firefighter figure, a hose, a stairway with hose tower, and a ground ladder. With the help of a 9-volt battery, the roof light flashes and the siren wails.

Tomica Apparatus on Duty:
American LaFrance Ladder Chief #F33, 1978, 1:143
Dodge Coronet #F10, 1976, 1:74
Hino/Morita Dutro Ambulance #119, 2004, 1:74
Hino/Morita Dutro Fire Engine #41, 2003, 1:72
Hino Super Dolphin Transporter with Bulldozer #56, 2005, 1:102
Nissan Diesel/Quan Water Tender #57, 2006, 1:110
Toyota Hiace Ambulance #36, 1988, 1:66
(not included with firehouse)

Fire Station (plastic) with apparatus (metal), Tomica, Japan, 1987

U-Mate Fire Station
Tomica #45013, 2004

At first glance **Tomica's** unique **U-Mate Fire Station** appears as a simple unadorned plastic box but when unfolded reveals a firehouse hidden within. Both the roof and front wall are attached with hinges and can be folded up to form a carrying case. Includes **Hino Fire Engine #29**.

U-Mate Hospital
Tomica #45102, 2004

Tomica's U-Mate Hospital is a nice companion piece to their U-Mate Fire Station. Like that release, the roof and front wall fold on hinges to reveal a hospital inside. Includes **Toyota Estima #87** lettered for Tokyo Fire Department.

U-Mate Fire Station (plastic) including apparatus (metal), Tomica, Japan, 2004

U-Mate Hospital (plastic) including apparatus (metal), Tomica, Japan, 2004

U-Mate Fire Station
Tomica #45110, 2005

Tomica produced two versions of this **U-Mate** building in 2005—a blue police station and a red fire station. The kit requires assembly and the application of a sheet of stickers. This unique fire station toy design includes a plastic roof and base with cardboard walls sandwiched in between. Includes rooftop helipad and **Isuzu Snorkel Fire Truck #68**.

U-Mate Fire Station (plastic/cardboard) including apparatus (metal), Tomica, Japan, 2005

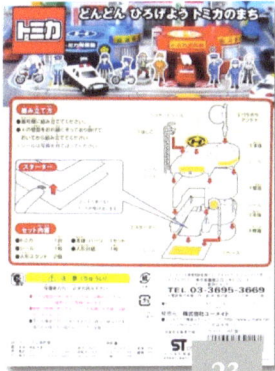

Fire Station
Tomica #79571, 2008

In the 2000s **Tomica** produced a large number of plastic buildings with interconnecting sidewalks to link them together. Their 2008 **Fire Station** release includes the two-bay firehouse (with flashing lights and siren), neighboring hospital, four sections of sidewalk, and three firefighters who are seated in the upstairs office.

Fire Station (plastic) with apparatus (metal), Tomica, Japan, 2008

Kabaya Fire Station and Hospital
Tomica #52038, 2013

Tomica's Kabaya Fire Station and Hospital is nearly identical to their previous 2008 **Fire Station** release, but in a smaller scale measuring around 1:150. The three buildings shown here were sold as individual products, each including one vehicle.

Kabaya Fire Station and Hospital (plastic) including apparatus (plastic), Tomica, Japan, 2013, 1:150

Rescue Fire Station
Tomica Hypercity #70555, 2014

Tomica's popular **Hypercity** received a new firehouse in 2014. Similar to their previous releases, this firehouse features interconnecting sidewalks, flashing lights, sirens, and a firefighter figure. Includes **Toyota Harrier #HR-01** rescue vehicle.

Fire Station
TomyTec Diorama Collection #082, 2010s

At 1:150 scale, this is one of the smallest firehouses in this book. Measures just 5" x 4" x 4". The plastic fire apparatus models were sold separately.

*Rescue Fire Station (plastic) including apparatus (metal),
Tomica Hypercity, Japan, 2014*

*Fire Station (plastic) with apparatus (plastic),
TomyTec Diorama Collection, Japan, 2010s, 1:150*

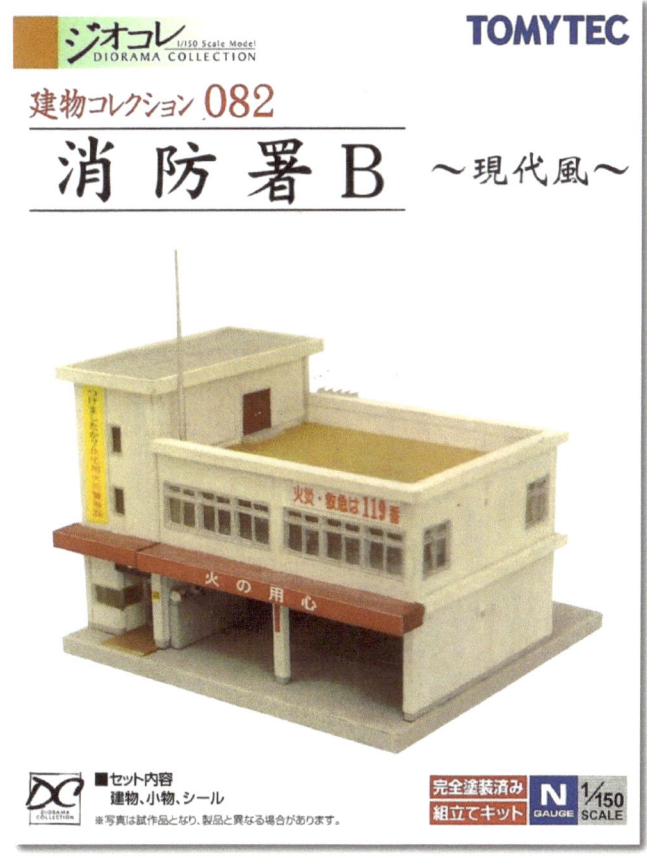

Majorette (France) is a manufacturer of miniature die-cast model cars which was founded by Emile Veron in 1961. Sometimes referred to as "The Matchbox as France," the company has produced a variety of die-cast fire-related models representing American LaFrance, Chevrolet, Ford, Jeep, Land Rover, Range Rover, Ward LaFrance, and others.

Majorette purchased the **Solido** company in 1980, and in 2010 both firms became part of the **Simba-Dickie** group.

Majokit Fire Station Construction Playset Majorette #7601.71, 1980s

This 1:64 scale **Majorette Majokit Fire Station Construction Playset** includes over 150 pieces, a Range Rover fire engine with water tank trailer, a helicopter, and four firefighter figures. The plastic Majokit parts snap together to form towns and cities for Majorette or other similar size model vehicles.

Majokit Fire Station Construction Playset (plastic) including apparatus (metal), Majorette, France, 1980s, 1:64

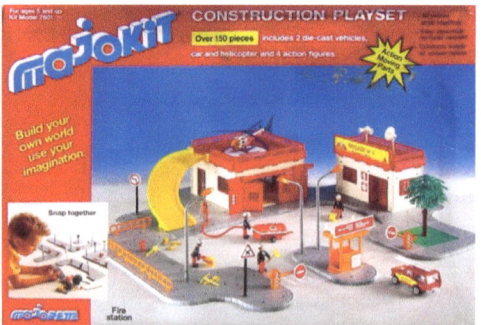

Majokit Coffret Poste de Secours (Emergency Center) Set, Majorette #020021, 1983

Majorette's Majokit Emergency Center includes five die-cast emergency vehicles along with the rescue station itself. The two unique apparatus bay doors swing open and slide to each side.

Majokit Coffret Poste de Secours (Emergency Center Set) (plastic) including apparatus (metal), Majorette, France, 1983, 1:64

"Build your own empire with Majokit— collect them all, use your imagination to create layouts as shown below"

Mini Majo-Kit Fire Brigade
Majorette, 1980s

Twelve **Mini Majo-Kits** were produced by **Majorette** in the 1980s. Each set includes a segment of sidewalk, street signs, and other related items. This **Fire Brigade** set includes a hydrant.

Firefighter Firehouse
Majorette #05/11, 2010s

This **Majorette Firefighter Firehouse** features a garage with functioning roll-up door (operated by sliding the handy belt clip on the roof) and includes a **Renalt Megane II #07/11** "Feuerwehr" car.

*Mini Majo-Kit Fire Brigade
with Firefighter Figures (plastic), Majorette, France, 1980s*

*Firefighter Firehouse (plastic) including apparatus (metal),
Majorette, France, 2010s, 1:64*

Creatix Rescue Station
Majorette #3467452070611, 2020s

This feature-packed **Majorette Creatix Rescue Station** includes a **Renault Master Transporter #239C** fire brigade van and a helicopter landing pad on the roof.

Creatix Rescue Station
Majorette/Jada #2120500271JA, 2020s

This **Majorette/Jada Toys Creatix Rescue Station** features 65-pieces, tower with lift, fuel pump, fire hydrant, garage, four S.O.S. die-cast vehicles, and a helicopter with helipad. This rescue station can be combined with modules from other Creatix sets to expand your Majorette world.

*Creatrix Rescue Station (plastic)
including apparatus (metal),
Majorette, France, 2020s, 1:64*

*Creatrix Rescue Station (plastic)
including apparatus (metal),
Majorette/Jada, France/USA, 2020s, 1:64*

Solido is a French manufacturing company which produces die-cast scale models of cars, military vehicles, and commercial vehicles. Solido was established in 1930 by Ferdinand de Vazeilles in the western Paris suburb of Nanterre, France. The company was one of the first European firms to champion the virtues of "unbreakable" die-cast metal.

In 1953, de Vazeilles bequeathed the company, then called **Solijouets SA,** to his son Jean René. By 1960, de Vazeilles' three children, Jean, Charlotte, and Colette were running the company. At the end of the 1970s, facing a financial crisis, Solido merged with the **Jouet Francais Group**. The new company was called **Heller-Solido SA**—the de Vazeilles family no longer controlled the Solido company. By the end of 1980, Heller-Solido SA went into liquidation and was purchased by **Majorette**.

Caserne de Pompiers *(Fire Station)*
(for Solido Models)
Starlux #BA.30.101, 1980s

Starlux (France) was one of the largest toy soldier manufacturers in existence from 1947 through the late 1990s. In the early 1980s the company produced a series of wooden building sets designed to be paired with **Solido** die-cast vehicles.

This extremely rare **Caserne de Pompiers** (fire station) release includes the three-bay drive-through "Centre De Secours" firehouse, a yellow particle board base (which folds in half), two wooden buildings (with opening plastic pedestrian doors), a fire tower (with ladder and four-way diaphone), two plastic gas pumps, and several firefighting figures. I purchased this item on eBay (with the original box) in the 1990s—I haven't seen another example since. For these photos I attempted to recreate the scene portrayed on the cover of the box below.

From the box (translated from French to English):
The gas pumps and the stretcher-bearers and wounded group are included in the barracks. The other figurines, vehicles and helicopter represented on this model are sold separately. The vehicles and the helicopter are reproduced with the kind permission of the SOLIDO Company. STARLUX S.A -B.P. 36 - CHAMIERS - 24021 PÉRIGUEUX

<u>*Solido Apparatus on Duty:*</u>
- Alouette III Helicopter #3814, Securite Civile, 1986, 1:55
- Berliet Camiva 4X4 Fuex de Forets #3354 + Guinard Moto Pompe #360, 1980-81, 1:50
- Berliet Camiva 770 KE Premier Secours #350, Ville de Paris, 1972-80, 1:50
- Berliet Camiva 770 KE Voiture Echelle EPA 30 #352, 1973-80, 1:50
- Berliet Camiva GBC 34 Vehicule Lance Mousse #351, Aeroport de Paris, 1972-80, 1:50
- Land Rover 109 #1034, Sapeurs Pompiers Moselle, 1980-82, 1:43
- Renault 4L Fourgonnette #1325, Ville de Paris, 1983-87, 1:43
- Renault 18 #1318, Ville de Paris, 1982-87, 1:43

(not included with firehouse)

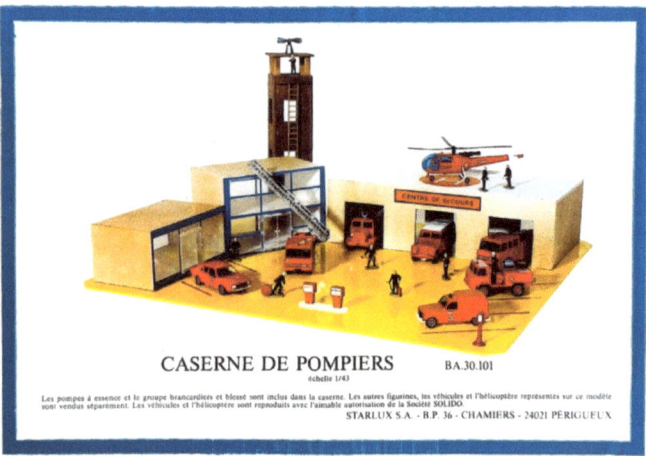

Caserne de Pompiers (wood/plastic), Starlux with apparatus (metal), Solido, France, 1980s, 1:43

Centre de Secours *(Rescue Center)*
Starlux, 1980s

Centre de Secours (wood/plastic) including figures (plastic), Starlux, France, 1980s, 1:43

Jeu de Société *(Board Game)* Party Game
Solido, 1974

Solido (France) produced this "new and exciting" fire department-themed party game in 1974. According to page 11 of the 1974 Solido catalog, this game includes "4 vehicles in kit form plus 1 boxed game, size 505 x 395 mm." The photograph shows a deck of cards and four lanes of apparatus approaching a burning building. Loads of pre-Internet fun!

Jeu de Société Party Game (mixed media), Solido, France, 1974, 1:43 from Solido Catalog, p.11, 1974

City Intervention Set
Starlux #806142, 2020s

A revived **Starlux** (France) company produced this **City Intervention** Set in the 2020s which includes an assortment of plastic fire apparatus, various warning signs, and a two-bay firehouse with opening doors.

City Intervention Set including apparatus (plastic), Starlux, France, 2020s, 1:72

Siku Volvo F12 Transporter
w/Lowboy Trailer & Fire Station No. 3
Siku #4015, 1985-1989

This unique mobile model fire station was produced by **Siku** (Germany) in 1:55 scale from 1985 through 1989. The most interesting feature of firehouse being it was sold as an unassembled kit with its many contents meticulously loaded on a **Volvo F12 Lowboy** trailer. The set includes an instruction sheet detailing how to construct the firehouse once delivered on site.

The three-bay firehouse is composed of plastic parts—the apparatus bay doors swing out and slide into their open position. The set includes both "Fire Station #3" and "Feuerwache" interchangeable plastic signs for the lowboy trailer.

I purchased this model new while on a trip to Germany as teenager so it holds a very special place in my collection. I still have the box and all the original parts.

Volvo F12 Transporter w/Lowboy Trailer (metal) & Fire Station No.3 (plastic), Siku, West Germany, 1985-1989, 1:55

Note: You can download and print the Siku Fire Station instructions here: www.ModelFireEngines.com/download.html

Siku (founded 1921 in Germany by Richard Sieper) produced their first model fire engine (#121, 1:60 scale) out of plastic in 1950 and began making Zamak (zinc-alloy) die-cast models in 1963 for the **V Series** ("V" for "vehrkehrs," or "traffic" model).

The **Super Series** models (1:55 scale) debuted in 1975 and have been popular with collectors ever since. The smaller **Club Series** (usually 1:87) was introduced in 1990 and was merged into the Super Series in 1993.

The **Super Classic** range of classic old-timer fire engines (1:50 scale) was added in 2005 to complement the contemporary models in the Super Series. **SIKUWorld** was launched in 2013 and consists of plastic buildings and street tiles including two model fire stations.

High quality production, attention to detail, and working parts are hallmarks of Siku models. Siku owns the well-known HO scale plastic model producer **Wiking**.

Fire Station Set
SIKUWorld #5502, 2015

Taken from Siku promotional material:
The new fire service play set is excellently prepared for the next alarm call in **SIKUWorld!** The fire engine is ready to spring into action at the fire station. The blue alarm light on the roof is flashing. Only the doors need opening and it's on the road to the next call-out. A helicopter landing pad is marked out on the fire station's roof for airborne emergencies. The air pocket on the building shows the pilot the wind direction for an optimal approach. The set can be integrated into the flexible SIKUWorld system, or used individually, one platform has a sloping driveway.

Fire Station
SIKUWorld #5508, 2020

Taken from Siku promotional material:
The fire brigade is ready for action immediately, the roller door is raised, and the fire brigade vehicle is soon on the way. Nee-naa, nee-naa: The integrated Light & Sound module with flashing LEDs and six different sounds change the playroom into a fire scene. The **SIKUWorld** is growing thanks to the new fire station. The two-floor building can be assembled by following the clearly illustrated instructions. From the assembly parts, individual buildings can be created in L or U form, or the parts can be built up into a multi-story building.

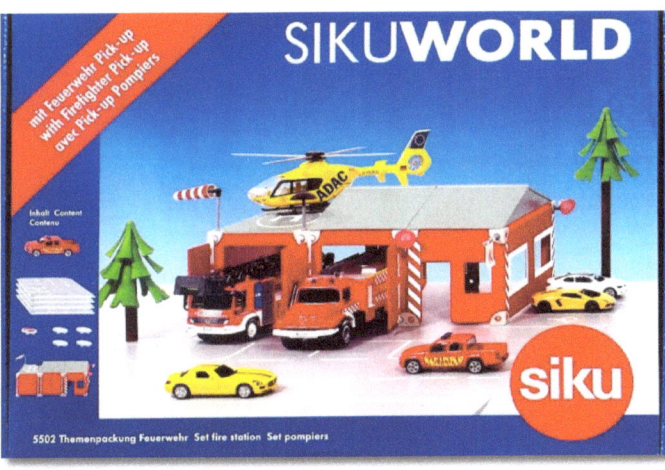

Fire Station Set (plastic) with apparatus (metal), SIKUWorld, Germany, 2015, 1:55

Fire Station (plastic) with apparatus (metal), SIKUWorld, Germany, 2020, 1:55

Corgi Toys is the brand name of a range of die-cast toy vehicles originally produced by **The Mettoy** ("Metal Toy") **Company** (Northampton, England) founded in 1933. Corgi Toys were introduced in 1956 in direct competition to **Meccano's Dinky Toys** which had dominated the British market for many years.

In 1989, the Corgi brand was sold to **Mattel**, and in 1995 Corgi regained its independence as a new company, **Corgi Classics Limited**. Both Corgi and Corgi Classics Limited brands were acquired by **Hornby** in 2008. Corgi was named after the Queen's favorite dog breed.

*Model Fire Depot (cardboard)
with apparatus (metal),
Corgi Classics, England, 1997, 1:50*

Model Fire Depot
Corgi Classics #31802, 1997

Corgi Classics released their **Model Fire Depot** in 1997, it was produced for them by **Metclafe Models**. The kit contains sheets of pre-cut cardboard and clear plastic windows along with a set of instructions detailing how to assemble the four-bay firehouse.

The kit includes an office area on the left side of the building. It can easily be modified into a two-bay firehouse, or multiple kits can be combined together to allow access for longer vehicles such as tractor-drawn aerials.

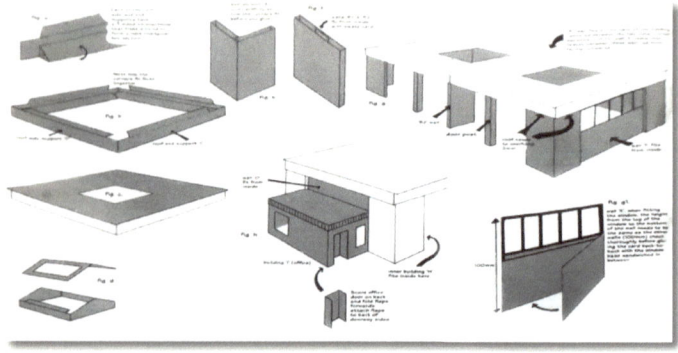

Instructions for assembly are included in the box

Corgi Apparatus on Duty:
American LaFrance Tractor-Drawn Aerial, Jersey City #97398, 1995
Dodge Monaco Fire Chief, Chicago Fire Dept. #06002, 2002
Emergency-One Ladder, Demo #54901, 1999
Emergency-One Rescue, Demo #52201, 1997
Emergency-One Rescue, Long Lake Vol. Fire Dept. #52203, 1998
Mack B Tractor-Drawn Aerial, Chicago Fire Dept. #52701, 1995
Mack CF Pumper, Chicago Fire Dept. #90232, 2002
Mack CF Pumper, Jersey City #52001, 1995
Seagrave J Quad Pumper, Chicago Fire Dept. #50803, 2002
Volkswagen Van Fire Marshall, Bureau of Fire Safety #98475, 1995
(not included with firehouse)

Fire Station Set
Corgi Juniors #3053, 1978

This **Corgi Juniors Fire Station Set** was produced in 1978 and includes the unassembled firehouse along with a **Ford Gran Torino Fire Chief**, an **ERF Fire Tender**, and an **ERF Simon Snorkel Fire Engine**.

The pre-cut firehouse walls and roof require removal from two included fiberboard sheets. The base is made of molded black plastic with grooves to hold the walls in place.

The back of the box includes a "London Store," two "Petro Chemicals" tanks, and an assortment of flames which can be cut out and assembled to create a firefighting scene.

The reason for the Ford Gran Torino's off-center roof beacon is this casting was originally designed to replicate *Starsky & Hutch's* undercover police car.

Fire Station Set (cardboard) including fire chief, snorkel, and fire engine (metal), Corgi Juniors, England, 1978

The rear of the box includes various items which can be cut out to create a firefighting scene

Husky was launched by **The Mettoy Company** (Northampton, England) in 1964 to compete with **Lesney's** popular **Matchbox** line of die-cast vehicles. The Husky models had plastic bases which made them lighter than their Matchbox counterparts. In 1970 Husky was rebranded to **Corgi Juniors**.

Coastal Rescue Station No.15 (plastic) including apparatus (metal) and figures (plastic), Corgi Juniors, England, 1976

Coastal Rescue Station No.15
Corgi Juniors #3022, 1976

This plastic **Corgi Juniors Coastal Rescue Station** was produced in 1976. Along with the rescue station, the set includes a playmat, six plastic figures, and six die-cast rescue vehicles.

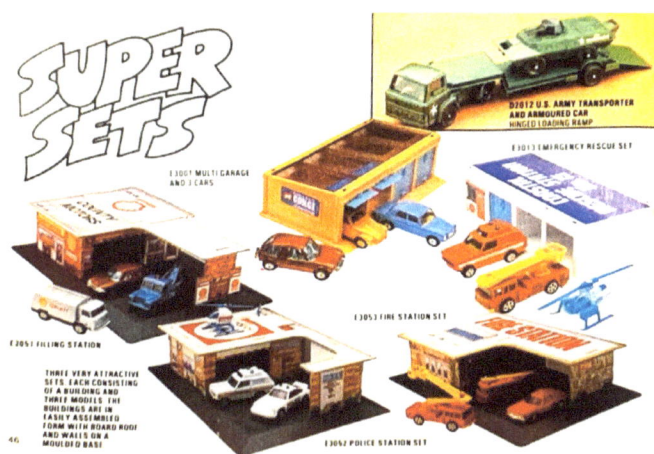

*Corgi Juniors Super Sets:
Gas Station, Police Station, Fire Station,
Multi Garage, and Coastal Rescue Station*

Operating Firehouse (Grey/Red)
M.T.H. Electric Trains #30-9157, 2005

M.T.H. Electric Trains (Elkridge, Maryland), also known as **Mike's Train House**, has been a family-owned and operated business since 1980. They provide authentic train sets, parts, and accessories for hobbyists of all levels.

M.T.H.'s **RailKing** firehouse is designed to enhance O scale (1:48 scale in the U.S.) model railroad layouts. The fully assembled and fully painted firehouse includes a lighted interior, flashing exterior lights, and digital sound effects.

When the activation switch is pressed, the apparatus bay door opens, a firefighter slides down the fire pole, and the fire engine cranks up and rolls out of the firehouse on its way to the next emergency. The included Mack B pumper is based on a previous **Corgi** 1:50 scale release but has two additional metal pins protruding from the base to drive/steer it down the road.

Firehouse dimensions are 16 5/8" x 15 3/8" x 12 3/8". This product has been produced in multiple color variations since the mid-1990s. The grey version of the firehouse is lettered "City Fire Department" while the apparatus is designated as **Columbia, MD Engine Company 208**. The red version of the firehouse is lettered "City Fire Department" while the apparatus is designated as **Columbia, MD Engine Company 234**.

Operating Firehouse (Red) (plastic) including fire engine (metal), M.T.H. Electric Trains, USA, 1990s-2020s, O scale

Lionel (first established in New York City) has produced their world-famous line of model trains since 1900. Other than the color scheme, their **Fire Station #22291-50**, lettered "Company No. 2," is identical to **M.T.H.'s Operating Firehouse**.

Fire Station (plastic) including fire engine (metal), Lionel, USA, 2022, O scale

Operating Firehouse (Grey)
(plastic) including fire engine (metal),
M.T.H. Electric Trains, USA, 1990s-2020s, O scale

*Hydrant and dalmatian are
included with the firehouse*

Model Power (Edison, New Jersey) was founded in 1970 by Michael Tager. This family-owned company produced a popular line of model trains and accessories for over 50 years. During that time, they produced two plastic firehouses (**#409** & **#1511**) which were available as kits or as fully-assembled models.

Fire Department (plastic),
Model Power, USA, 1970s, HO scale

Fire House (plastic),
Model Power, USA, 1970s, N scale

Fire Station with Switch Track and Storage Yard
Central City Fire Co. No. 1,
Tyco US1 Electric Trucking #3456, 1983

This unique plastic firehouse was produced by **Tyco** (Woodbury Heights, New Jersey) as part of their **US1 Electronic Trucking** range which provides an alternative to traditional slot car racing sets by focusing on driving heavy vehicles around various playset pieces along a road-styled track. An assortment of trucks is able to pick up and deliver loads from various "action accessories" without intervention from the operator.

The vehicles can run in reverse due to having guide pins at both the front and rear of the chassis.

The firehouse (#3456) includes the switch track (with storage yard siding) and a **Mack MR Fire Engine** (#3911). This firehouse was also available as part of the larger *Fire Alert!* set (#3214). This example includes two Ford Mustang fire chief cars from Tyco's 1990 **Race & Chace U-Turn** series (#7087). All units include bell and siren sounds and flashing lights.

Bingo players have a chance to win $1,000 on Thursday nights at this firehouse

*Fire Station with Switch Track and Storage Yard
Central City Fire Co. No. 1 (plastic) with apparatus (plastic),
Tyco US1 Electric Trucking, USA, 1983, HO scale*

Tonka (founded in 1946 as **Mound Metalcraft** in Mound, Minnesota) is an American brand and former manufacturer best known for making steel toy truck models of construction equipment. Tonka was acquired by **Hasbro** in 1991, and relocated to Hasbro's facilities in Pawtucket, Rhode Island.

In 1998 Hasbro began a licensing deal with **Funrise Toys** to manufacture and distribute Tonka trucks. Early releases include trucks fitted with electronics for lights and sounds. In 2001 **Maisto International** acquired the rights to use the Tonka name in a line of 1:64 scale models.

Builder Playset Fire Engine House 23
Tonka #5047, 1979

This plastic **Fire Engine House 23** was produced in 1979 by **Tonka** as part of their **Builder Playset** series which also includes a **Custom Van Shop**, a **Service Station**, a **Pizza Shop**, and a **Post Office**.

The building was sold unassembled in a cardboard box along with a sheet of stickers to apply to the walls. A **Tonka Scrambler** truck with a fire pump skid load is included, and the firehouse features opening side and apparatus bay doors.

Big Fire Department Play Set
Tonka #11112, 2001

This truly "multi-brand" firehouse was manufactured and distributed by **Maisto** in 2001 under license from **Hasbro** who owned the rights to the **Tonka** brand name and includes a fire engine based on a 1966 **Matchbox** Denver pumper.

According to the box, this firehouse includes a "real fire dept. look, a loading ramp, a movable figure, and vehicle storage."

Big Fire Department Play Set (plastic) including fire engine (metal), Tonka, USA, 2001

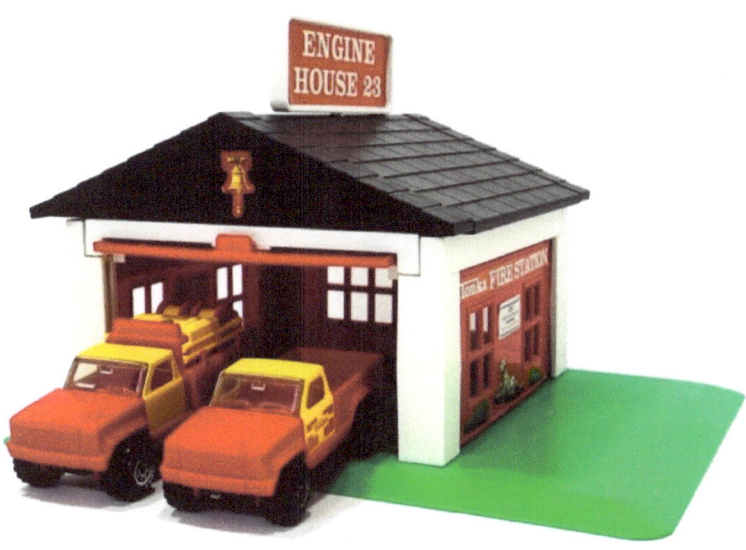

Builder Playset Fire Engine House 23 including apparatus (plastic), Tonka, USA, 1979

Hot Wheels is a popular American brand of scale model cars introduced by **Mattel** on May 18, 1968. The series was a huge success and completely disrupted the industry for small die-cast car models from 1968 onward, forcing the competition at **Matchbox** and elsewhere to redesign their product lines.

Hot Wheels was the primary competitor of Matchbox until Mattel bought Matchbox owner **Tyco** in 1997.

Firefighter Sto & Go
Fire Station and Burning Building
Hot Wheels #2683, 1988

Hot Wheels (El Segundo, California) produced this **Firefighter Fire Station and Burning Building** in 1988 representing **Danville Fire Station 8**. The plastic set includes "1 burning building, 1 fire station, fire hose extinguisher, fire ladder, fire hydrant, 2 cones, barricade sign board, label sheet and instructions."

The fire station and burning building fit together—"everything stores inside—it's portable," or can be separated for play action. The bell tower lowers for transport, and the extendable "A.C.E." sign can be used as a carrying handle. The set comes with three vehicles including **Engine 51** and **Squad 51**.

The burning building's unique design features a side lever which when pressed pumps air to raise the "flames." To fight the fire, the valve on the nozzle of the rubber extendable fire hose can be pressed to release the air pressure and lower or "extinguish" the flames.

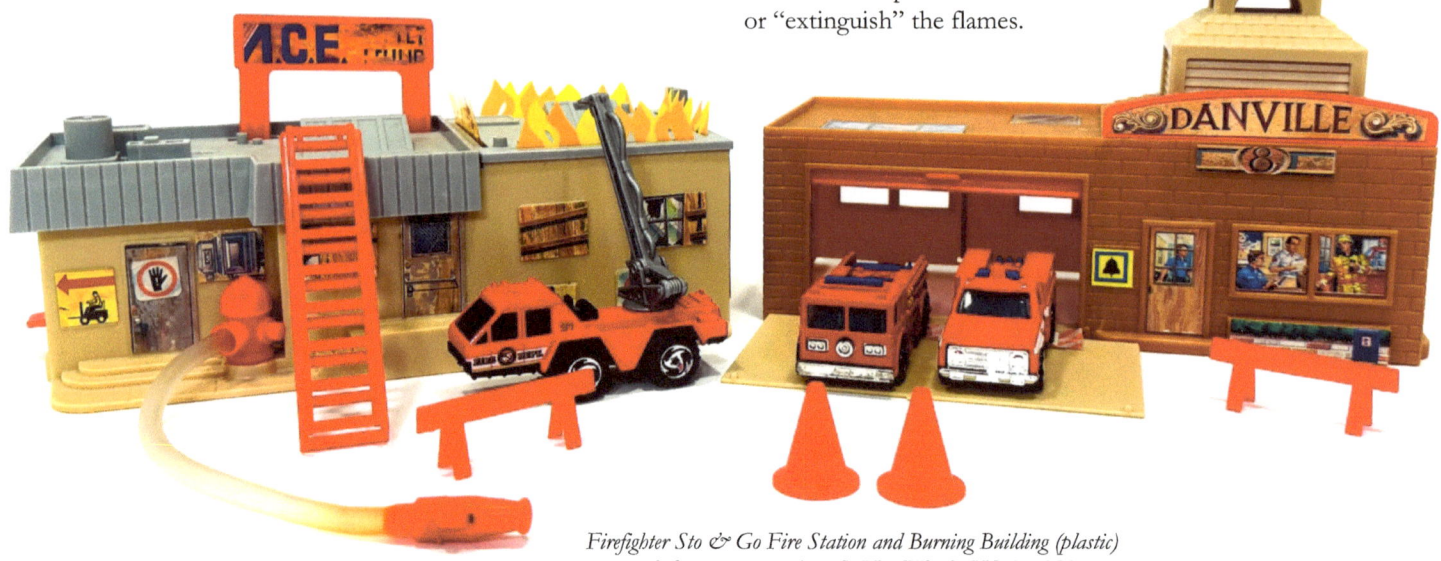

Firefighter Sto & Go Fire Station and Burning Building (plastic) including apparatus (metal), Hot Wheels, USA, 1988

<u>Hot Wheels Apparatus on Duty</u>:
Engine 51 (Fire-Eater, 1988)
Squad 51 (Rescue Ranger, 1988)
Snorkel 31 (Fire Stopper, 1988)

<u>Other **Hot Wheels** Firehouse Releases</u>:
Sto & Go Emergency Station #7612, 1988
World Fire Station w/Elevator #19309, 1997
Rescue Center #88217, 2000
World Fire Station w/Pop Up Flames #89857, 2000
Raceway Fire Station #4733, 2008

Sto & Go
Baywatch Lifeguard Rescue Station
Hot Wheels #65625, 1995

This ***Baywatch*** **Rescue Station** was produced by **Hot Wheels** in 1995 as part of their **Sto & Go** series. The set includes the plastic rescue station & dock, a lifeguard figure & tower (with umbrella), a fuel pump & car repair lift, and a boat dock. The set also includes a generic die-cast 4x4 pickup, a plastic rescue speedboat & helicopter, and a rubber shark.

Sto & Go Baywatch Lifeguard Rescue Station (plastic) including apparatus (plastic/metal), Hot Wheels, USA, 1995

Firefighting Scene, Urban Rescue Series #1,
Hot Wheels Planet Micro #18716, 1997

This **Hot Wheels Planet Micro Urban Rescue** firefighting rescue scene consists of a plastic base, two firefighter figures, an American LaFrance pumper & tractor-drawn aerial ladder truck, and a Westland Lynx helicopter.

Firefighting Scene, Urban Rescue Series #1 (plastic) including apparatus (plastic/metal), Hot Wheels Planet Micro, USA, 1997

Downtown Fire Station #68 Spinout Playset, Hot Wheels, USA, 2017

Spin City Fire Department #68 Car Spinner Tower, Hot Wheels, USA, 2019

City Super Loop Fire Station #68, Hot Wheels, USA, 2022

Lewis Galoob Toys, Inc., founded in 1957, was a toy company headquartered in South San Francisco, California. The company is best known for their **Micro Machines** lineup which account- ed for 50% of the company's sales in 1989. American toy giant **Hasbro** purchased Galoob for $220 million in 1998.

Fire Station
Galoob Micro Machines City Scenes #6468, 1989

Micro Machines was a line of toys originally made by **Galoob** (now part of **Hasbro**) from the mid-1980s through the 1990s. The Micro Machines lineup includes various realistic plastic vehicles and playsets slightly larger than N scale.

Fire Station including apparatus (plastic), Galoob Micro Machines City Scenes, U.S.A, 1989

The **City Scenes** light-up firehouse was produced in 1989 and includes two vehicles. The Datsun fire department pickup is designated "SFFD Fire & Rescue 702."

The rear wall of the firehouse can be folded down to reveal the double-AA battery compartment which powers a single interior bulb. Through ingenious use of an interior system of clear hard plastic walls, this lamp successfully lights up the apparatus bay as well as the many firehouse windows, each depicting an interior firehouse scene.

Fire Dept. Engine Co. 15
Galoob Micro Machines, 1989

This **Engine Co. 15** airport-style firehouse features one apparatus bay, two helipads, and a control tower. The apparatus bay door can be opened by turning the round knob on the far left.

Fire Department Firehouse No. 7
Galoob Micro Machines Travel City #6410, 1988

Galoob produced this **Micro Machines Travel City** firehouse in 1988. The set includes the firehouse, two vehicles, and a carrying case which serves as a base when unfolded.

Fire Dept. Engine Co. 15 with apparatus (plastic), Galoob Micro Machines, USA, 1989

Fire Department Firehouse No. 7 including apparatus (plastic), Galoob Micro Machines Travel City, USA, 1987

The popularity of Galoob's Micro Machines no doubt led to the release of **Matchbox's World's Smallest Mini Playsets** and **Hot Wheels' Planet Micro** lines in the 1990s.

<u>Other **Micro Machines** Firehouse Releases</u>:

Blaze & Roar Fire Station #6480, 1990
Double Action Fire Station #75111, 1995
Hiways & Byways Firehouse City #64547, 1997
Fire & Rescue Playset #MMW0033, 2020

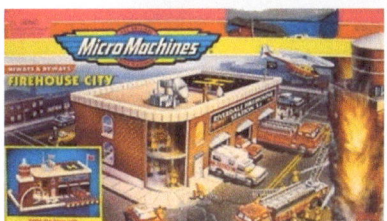

Boley was incorporated in Chino, California in 1981, and introduced their **Dept. 1:87** line of models in 1998. The die-cast metal and plastic vehicles are popular with HO model railroad enthusiasts. Manufacturers represented include GMC, International, Oshkosh, Seagrave, Spartan, and others.

Four firehouses were planned for Boley's **First Alarm Fire Series**, however only one made it into production. A prototype was made of a second single-bay FDNY firehouse but was never sold. **Bill Craven** designed both firehouses for Boley—you can see his custom **Rip Van Winkle** firehouse designs the **Appendix**.

The Boley 1:87 line of vehicles was purchased by **Walthers** in 2012 and is now part of their **Scene Master Series**.

Fire Station, Boley Dept. 1-87
First Alarm Fire Series #2601/#2602/#2603, 2007

This plastic 1:87 scale fire station and the accompanying apparatus models were produced by **Boley** under their **Dept. 1:87** and **First Alarm Fire Series**. The firehouse includes two opening front apparatus bay doors, a non-opening rear door, and a hose tower on the side. This model is available in three color variations:

#2601 Brick
#2602 Grey
#2603 Red

(apparatus models not included with firehouse)

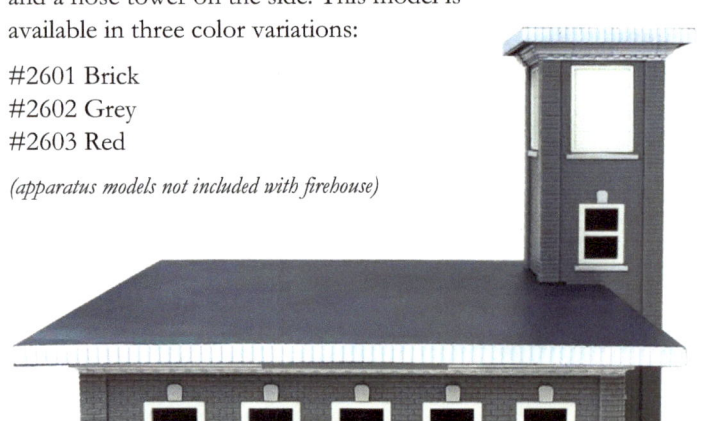

Fire Station (grey, plastic), Boley Dept. 1-87 First Alarm Fire Series, USA, 2007, HO scale

Fire Station (brick, plastic) with apparatus (metal), Boley Dept. 1-87 First Alarm Fire Series, USA, 2007, HO scale

Fire Station (red, plastic) with apparatus (metal), Boley Dept. 1-87 First Alarm Fire Series, USA, 2007, HO scale

FDNY Fire Station (Prototype) Boley Dept. 1-87 First Alarm Fire Series

A second Boley release (based on an FDNY firehouse) progressed as far as the prototype stage, but unfortunately never made it into production. You can see both Bill Craven's and Boley's prototype models below.

Boley introduces a 1930s style 2-bay fire station for its First Alarm fire series. Designed for your affordable layouts and dioramas, this fully assembled 2-storey fire station featuring opening doors, imitated glass windows, and a hose drying tower.

This classic two-story single bay New York City style firehouse will be a great addition to any layout or fire collection. Small changes will be added, as we are trimming the building in white limestone. This is the second of a series of four firehouses released within the next two years.

Bill Craven designed the two foam-core prototype models above for Boley based on real firehouses in Rhode Island and New York City

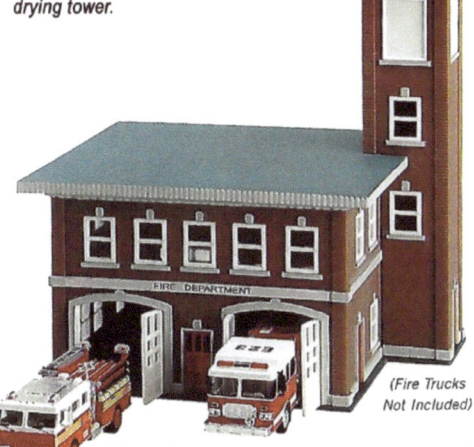

This nostalgic northeastern style has been a blue print for the later built modernized stations. (Fire Trucks Not Included)

Fire Station (FDNY Prototype), Boley Dept. 1-87 First Alarm Fire Series, USA, HO scale

The **Road Champs Company** was originally founded by Jack Robbins as **JRI Inc.** in Bala Cynwyd, Pennsylvania in the 1970s as a distributor of die-cast toys. The company focused on 1:64 scale American vehicles later adding 1:43 scale models to their lineup. In 1997 Road Champs was purchased by **JAKKS Pacific**—the final Road Champs series was released in late 2001.

In the early 1990s, Road Champs introduced red *(Deluxe Series w/metal base, 1990)* and lime green *(Sounds of Power w/plastic base & siren sound, 1991)* versions of an American LaFrance snorkel lettered for Chicago F.D. Truck 17 (1:72 scale).

Their following popular **Fire Rescue Series** featured International and HME fire engines, heavy rescues, and telesquirts representing U.S. fire departments including Boston, Louisville, New Orleans, St. Louis, Philadelphia, and Washington, D.C.

In what appears to be a direct move to capitalize on the popularity of the then new 1:64 scale **Code 3 Collectibles** series of fire engines, Road Champs released their short-lived **Fireman Series** in 1999 consisting of a detailed replica screwed to a hard plastic base and packaged in a clear soft plastic dome. The box states, "Dedicated to our Courageous Firefighters" and lists a large lineup of cities scheduled for future releases (including a phone number stating "Call us to reproduce your company fire truck").

Only two models were produced (an International pumper for New Orleans and an HME pumper for Washington, D.C.) before the series was canceled. It is believed the series was dropped due to legal action threatened by Code 3 Collectibles related to copyright infringement.

Fire-House Playset (plastic),
Road Champs, USA, 1994, 1:64

The interior of this firehouse includes a fire pole

Fire-House Playset
Road Champs #7770, 1994

Road Champs produced this 1:64 scale model **Fire-House Playset** in 1994. The set includes pre-cut sticker sheets of windows, doors, and other interior and exterior firehouse graphics to apply to the plastic walls, roofs, and doors.

The two halves of the building can be joined together on a hinge to create either one long firehouse with both front and rear apparatus bay doors, or a side-by-side firehouse with five apparatus bay doors in front and an open rear. The building includes a rooftop helipad and a bell tower and was also sold as a police station version (molded in blue plastic).

Washington D.C. Apparatus on Duty:
Engine (HME, Road Champs Fireman Series #42009, 1999, 1:64)
Engine (International, Road Champs #64605, 1990s, 1:64)
Truck 16 (Seagrave, Code 3 #12659, 1998, 1:64)
Telesquirt (HME, Road Champs #64605, 1990s, 1:64)
Rescue (International, Road Champs #64605, 1990s, 1:64)
(not included with firehouse)

American LaFrance Snorkels, Chicago Fire Department Truck 17, Road Champs Deluxe Series/Sounds of Power Series, USA, 1990/1991, 1:72

International Fire Engine, New Orleans Fire Department, Road Champs Fireman Series, USA, 1999, 1:64

4 Bay Fire Station
American Diorama #77731, 2010

American Diorama produced this large **4 Bay Fire Station** in 2010. This firehouse features eight functional apparatus bay doors and a detachable front apron. The roof of the building is removable for easy access to the interior and two battery boxes—a total of four AA batteries power four groups of three LEDs which light the interior. Each apparatus bay includes two sliding yellow exhaust removal hoses (which in real life would magnetically attach to the exhaust pipes of the apparatus). Only 300 of these very rare firehouses were produced—dimensions are 20½" x 16" x 6½".

4 Bay Fire Station (polyresin, mixed media), American Diorama, USA, 2010, 1:64

Firefighters I, II, and Paramedic Figures (metal) American Diorama, Mijo Exclusives, 2020-22, 1:64

American Diorama (El Monte, California) produces quality hand-painted items made from polyresin and die-cast metal. The company handles all production from product designs, sampling, and tooling to mass production from their factory in Mainland China. Custom (OEM) projects are welcomed by the company.

American Diorama also produces a large variety of die-cast metal figures in 1:18, 1:24, 1:43, and 1:64 scales. The 1:64 figures shown throughout this book came from their **Mijo Exclusive Firefighter (I & II)**, **Paramedic**, and **HazMat** sets. For more information, see www.americandiorama.com.

<u>Miami/Metro-Dade Apparatus on Duty:</u>
Engine 3 (Pierce Quantum, Del Prado #142, 2006, 1:80)
Engine 20 (American LaFrance, Code 3 #12865, 2006, 1:64)
Engine 30 (Pierce Quantum, Code 3 #12760, 1999, 1:64)
Telesquirt 2 (Pierce Quantum, Code 3 #12920, 2001, 1:64)
Ambulance Rescue 2 (Freightliner, Code 3 #12084, 2004, 1:64)
Helicopter 3 & Helipad (Bell 412, Code 3 #12602, 2001, 1:64)
Crash Truck 7 (Oshkosh T-3000, Code 3 #12154, 1999, 1:64)
Battalion 2 (Dodge Ram 3500, customized Greenlight, 1:64)
Battalion 5 (GMC Suburban, Code 3 #12375, 1999, 1:64)
(not included with firehouse)

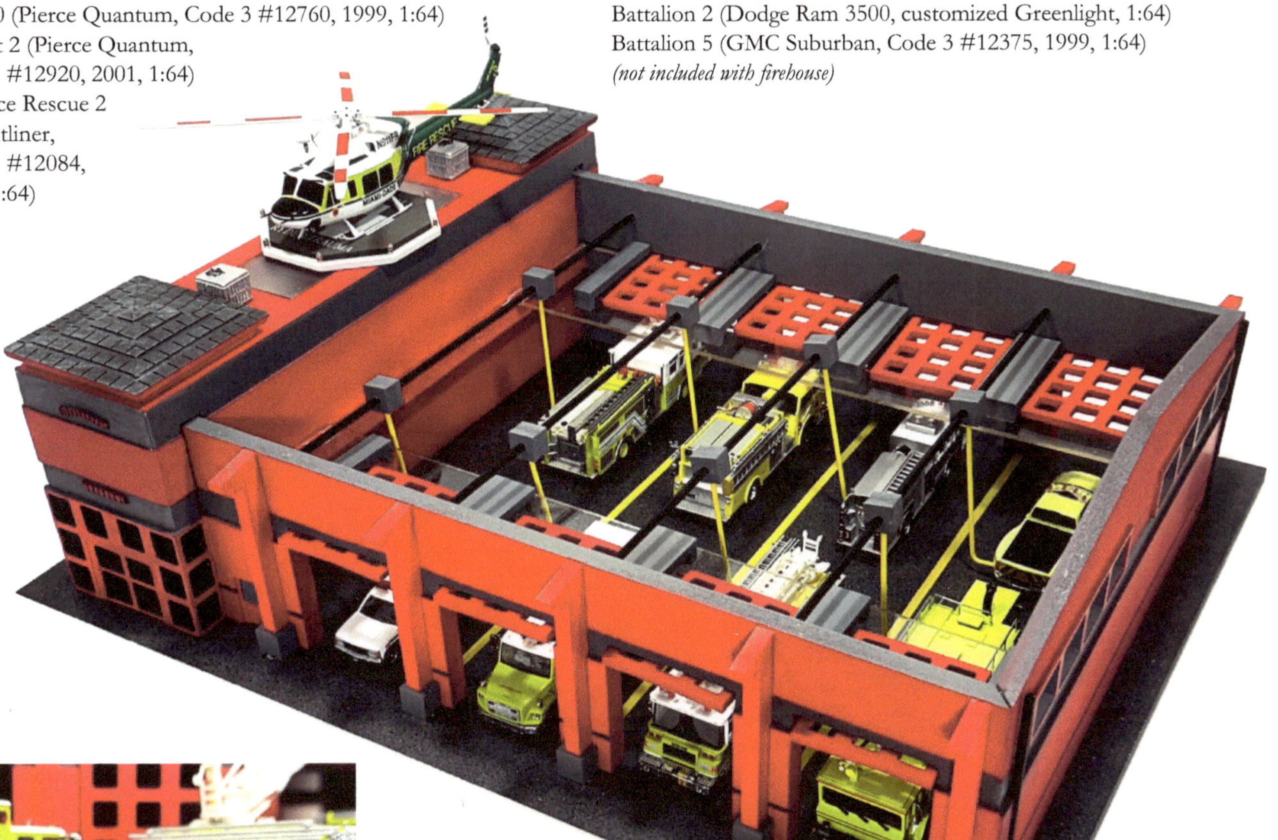

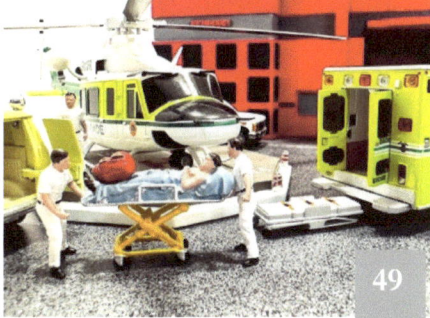

Funrise Toy Corporation was established in 1987 in Van Nuys, California by Arnie Rubin who would go on to found **Code 3 Collectibles** ten years later. On June 8, 2007, Funrise Toy Corp. became a subsidiary of **Matrix Holdings Ltd.**

City Force Center Fire Station
Funrise #02781 (1:64/1:32), 1994

This **Funrise** (*pre-Code 3 Collectibles*) firehouse was designed as a children's play toy and was sold along with a series of plastic rescue vehicles which, like the firehouse, include battery-operated flashing lights and sounds. Firehouse sounds include dispatches to various emergencies in the Los Angeles area.

City Force Center (plastic) including apparatus (plastic), Funrise, USA, 1994, 1:64/1:32

Other Funrise "City Force Center" emergency vehicles available

This firehouse includes three emergency vehicles, four firefighter figures, and a fire hydrant

This firehouse was produced in both 1:64 and 1:32 scales. Later 1:64 scale versions were sold without the lights and sounds, with signs above the apparatus bay doors in place of the buttons. All versions feature plastic roll-up apparatus bay doors.

In order to display three Code 3 LAFD 88 units (including a T.D.A.), the expanded firehouse below was constructed by joining two Funrise City Force Center Fire Stations together.

<u>Los Angeles City Apparatus on Duty:</u>
Engine 88 (Seagrave, Code 3 #02450, 1997, 1:64)
Engine 88 (Pierce, Code 3 #12664, 1999, 164)
Ladder 88 (Ladder Towers Incorporated, Code 3 #12892, 2001, 1:64)
(not included with firehouse)

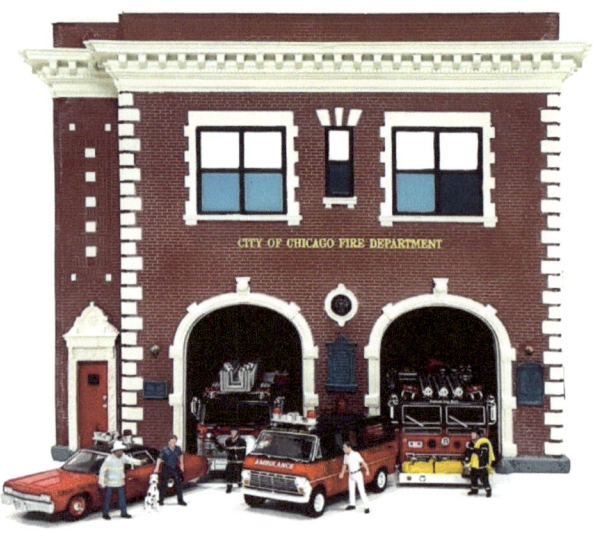

Chicago Fire Department Engine 17/Ladder 46 "Backdraft"
(hand-painted resin), Code 3 Collectibles, USA, 2000, 1:64

FDNY Engine 75/Ladder 35/Battalion 19 "Animal House" (New)
(foam core, mixed media), First Due Firehouse Replicas, USA, 2022, 1:64

FDNY Ladder 8 "Ghostbusters" (foam core, mixed media),
First Due Firehouse Replicas, USA, 2022, 1:64

SFFD Engine 15/Truck 15 "Towering Inferno"/"Oceans's 15"
(foam core, mixed media), First Due Firehouse Replicas, USA, 2022, 1:64

Note: The firehouses above are each associated with blockbuster Hollywood movies

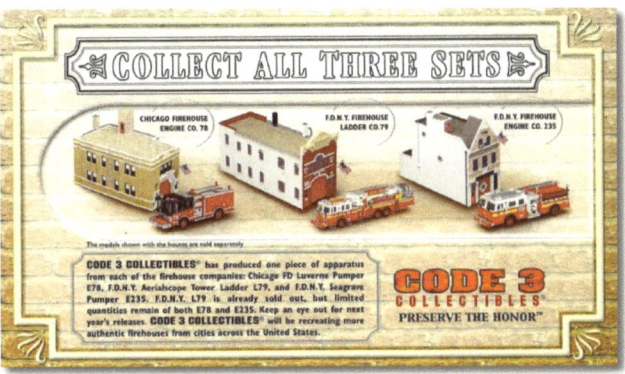

Code 3 Collectibles promotional flyer advertising their new line of 1:64 scale firehouses representing Chicago Engine 78, FDNY Ladder 79, and FDNY Engine 235, 2000

PART TWO:
FIREHOUSE REPLICAS

By the early 2000s, the quality and efficiency of toy manufacturing had improved to the point at which companies were able to produce extremely realistic highly-detailed replicas of real buildings. Since the following releases depict real-life firehouses, I refer to them as firehouse replicas rather than the model fire station toys we explored in **Part One**.

Code 3 Collectibles (1997-2011) raised the bar for both model fire apparatus and firehouse collectors when they released their first 1:64 scale models in 1998. Between August 2000 and December 2004, Code 3 released a series of hand-painted resin firehouses representing nine famous firehouses throughout the United States. This highly-collectible series includes replicas of firehouses from New York City, Boston, Chicago, Washington, D.C., and Los Angeles County. They also released a detailed replica of a burning building which was designed to display two Code 3 replicas in action at the scene of a house fire.

In January 2022, **First Due Firehouse Replicas** introduced their first scale firehouse replicas. Their goal is to continue where Code 3 left off, and to produce a series of accurate, detailed, photo-realistic 1:64 scale model firehouses suitable for collectors to acquire, enjoy, and display their collection. To date, First Due Firehouse Replicas has released over 35 model fire stations based on real buildings in New York City, Boston, Chicago, Philadelphia, Los Angeles (city and county), and many other cities.

Other companies producing accurate scale firehouse replicas include **Bernard's Fire Station**, **Twin Whistle Sign & Kit Co.**, and **Iconic Replicas**. As well as generic offerings, these companies have produced firehouse replicas of buildings in New York City, Chicago, Boston, Pittsburgh, and Los Angeles.

I hope you enjoy the firehouse replicas presented here in **Part Two**. These very special buildings not only provide a vital service to their communities, but they often offer a unique perspective on the history of the cities in which they serve.

Note: While every effort has been made to provide current accurate information about the firehouses and companies included in Part Two, in order to maintain historical collectible authenticity, information provided by Code 3 promotional material has been left as it was originally printed

Code 3 Collectibles was an American company based in Woodland Hills, California which produced high-quality die-cast metal replicas of emergency vehicles from 1997 through 2011. The company was founded by Arnie Rubin who had previously established **Funrise Toy Corporation** which manufactured and marketed toys for **Tonka**.

Although the company sold a series of police cars and *Star Wars* replicas, Code 3 was known mainly for their high-quality accurate 1:64 scale models of fire trucks and emergency vehicles.

From 2000 to 2004 the company produced a series of hand-painted resin firehouses along with the apparatus quartered inside. Most releases include a printed booklet featuring a description of each firehouse and the neighborhood served.

On August 19, 2011, Code 3 announced it was ceasing all production. The final model produced was a Seagrave raised-roof Marauder II Aerialscope lettered for FDNY Ladder 46. Today Code 3 Collectibles replicas are still highly sought-after by enthusiasts, collectors, and fans of emergency services.

FDNY Engine 10/Ladder 10 "The Tenhouse" (hand-painted resin), Code 3 Collectibles, USA, 2004, 1:64

Code 3 Collectibles Collectors Club Newsletter Volume 8, Number 4, Fourth Quarter 2004

FDNY Engine 10/Ladder 10 "The Tenhouse"
Code 3 Collectibles #13109

Release Date: December 2004   Edition Size: 10,000

Taken from the booklet included with the firehouse replica:

This recently renovated firehouse in lower Manhattan has been known as the "Tenhouse" since 1984 as both Engine Company 10 and Ladder Company 10 are located together here. This is one of only two FDNY fire stations in which the engine company and ladder company have the same number. The two FDNY companies in "Tenhouse" are two of the original paid fire companies in NYC, however, they have only been quartered together since 1984.

Located directly across the street from Tower 2 of The World Trade Center, the fire station did not sustain any damage at the WTC bombing of 1993. They were not so fortunate on 09/11/01 when the fire station had both heavy exterior and interior damage. The fire station at 124 Liberty Street was repaired, renovated, and modernized with a multi-million-dollar refit, celebrated with an official re-opening on Nov. 1, 2003.

The first alarm areas of Engine and Ladder 10 consist of high-rise office buildings, historic churches, piers, etc. Engine Company 10 is one of only seven FDNY engine companies using pumpers with special 1,000 g.p.m. high-pressure pumps.

Location: 124 Liberty Street, Manhattan, New York, NY

Years in Service: 1980-2001, 2003-present

Companies Quartered:
Engine 10 (organized 1865, quartered 1980-2001, 2003-present)
Ladder 10 (organized 1865, quartered 1984-2001, 2003-present)

Apparatus Quartered:
Engine 10 (Seagrave, Code 3 #12834, 2004)
Ladder 10 (Seagrave, Code 3 #12724, 2003)
Chemical Protective Clothing (CPC) 10 (Ford F-150, Greenlight with custom body and graphics)

Note: The apparatus bay doors of this replica have been updated to reflect the current "American flag" design. You can download and print the replacement doors artwork here: www.ModelFireEngines.com/download.html

FDNY Engine 82/Ladder 31 "La Casa Grande"
Code 3 Collectibles #13108

Release Date: February 2004   Edition Size: 3,000

Taken from a Code 3 Collectibles flyer:

Famous Firehouse in the Bronx

FDNY Firehouse L31/E82 is the single best known FDNY firehouse due in large part to Dennis Smith's book, *Report from Engine Co. 82*. Code 3 Collectibles' talented artisans have captured the essence of this historical three-story house in a limited edition 1:64 scale detailed miniature. This hand painted model has simulated brick work and roof tiling with opening double-bay doors, complete with details like raised lettering naming the station's apparatus and a building plaque with the names of the builders, architects, and dates. This reproduction is a great complementary piece to FDNY E82 and L31 die-cast replicas.

Location: 1215 Intervale Avenue, The Bronx, New York, NY

Years in Service: 1904-present

Companies Quartered:
Engine 82 (organized 1905, quartered 1905-present)
Engine 85 (organized 1967, quartered 1967-1971)
Ladder 31 (organized 1907, quartered 1907-present)
Tactical Control Unit 712 (organized 1969, to become Ladder 59, quartered 1969-1971)
Battalion 3 (quartered 1956-1968)
Battalion 20 (quartered 1906-1930)
Battalion 27 (quartered 1969-1978)
Division 7 (quartered 1948-1949, 1951-1956)
Searchlight 3 (quartered 1951-1967)
Hydrant Service Unit 7 (quartered 1951-1957)

Apparatus Quartered:
Engine 82 (Seagrave, Code 3 #12190, 2000)
Engine 82 (Mack CF, Code 3 #12335, 2004)
Ladder 31 (Seagrave, Code 3 #12190, 2000)
Ladder 31 (Mack CF, Code 3 #12513, 2004)
Battalion 27 (Plymouth Belvedere Wagon, customized Greenlight)

FDNY Engine 82/Ladder 31 "La Casa Grande" (hand-painted resin), Code 3 Collectibles, USA, 2004, 1:64

*Code 3 Collectibles Collectors Club Newsletter
Volume 7, Number 1, First Quarter 2004*

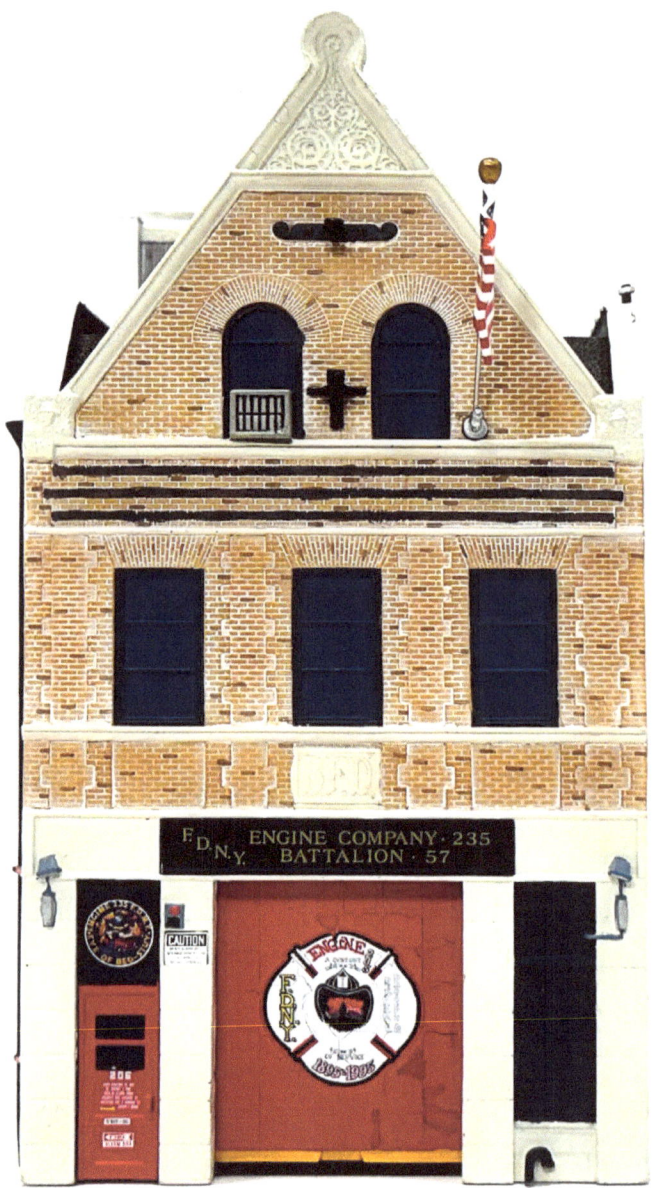

Location: 206 Monroe Street, Brooklyn, New York, NY

Years in Service: 1895-present

Companies Quartered:
Engine 235 (organized 1895, quartered 1895-present)
Battalion 57 (organized 1969, quartered 1969-2009)
Squad 3 (organized 1955, quartered 1955-1966)
Gasoline Fuel Wagon 3 (organized 1923, quartered 1923-1957)

Apparatus Quartered:
Engine 235 (Seagrave, Code 3 #12302, 1998)
Battalion 57 (GMC Suburban, Code 3 with custom decals)

Code 3 Collectibles flyer promoting FDNY Engine 235 firehouse, 2000

FDNY Engine 235/Battalion 57
"The Eye of Bed-Stuy"
Code 3 Collectibles #13100

Release Date: October 2000   Limited Edition

Taken from the booklet included with the firehouse replica:
History Of Engine 235 Fire Department of New York by Michael Boucher

Over 100 years ago, Engine 235 was not known as 235, and was not part of the Fire Department of New York. It was the 35th engine company placed in service by the City of Brooklyn, the fourth largest city in the country at the time. The Brooklyn Fire Department was organized on September 15, 1869, with a paid force of thirteen engine and six ladder companies. They replaced fifty-three volunteer fire companies that protected only half of what is Brooklyn today. The rest of Brooklyn was made up of small towns that had their own fire departments and were annexed by Brooklyn in 1894.

Engine 35 was placed in service on July 1, 1895, in new quarters at 206 Monroe Street. Also on the same day, Engine 36 was placed in service in the East New York section of Brooklyn. Both companies were added to fill in the gaps in fire protection. Engine 35 filled the hole between Engine 9 to the north, Engine 22 to the east, Engine 14 to the south and Engine 19 to the west.

The 25-feet wide by 100-feet deep lot was purchased on August 28, 1894, from the Bedford Bank of Brooklyn for $3,000. The new building cost $16,365 to build. The three-story firehouse had a single door for the exit of the apparatus. On the first floor, a house watch desk was located to the right of the apparatus door, and an entrance doorway was located to the left. A one-story addition for the horse stalls was attached to the rear. Behind the station was a one-story building to store the feed and hay for the horses. On the second floor were the captain's quarters and office, the rest of the floor was the bunkroom and lockers, the third floor contained a sitting and recreation room.

Engine 235's first horse-drawn apparatus was a new 1895 LaFrance 3rd size steamer that could pump around 500-600 gallons per minute. In 1917, the company received a new 1917 Robinson 700 g.p.m. piston pumping engine, thus ending the era of horse-drawn engines. Over the years, Engine 235 has used apparatus built by American LaFrance, International, Mack, Seagrave, and Ward LaFrance. Today the company responds with a 1994 Seagrave that can pump 1,000 gallons per minute.

Today, Engine 235 shares its quarters with Battalion 57. Battalion 57 was organized on November 29, 1969 to help cover the heavy workload of the area.

Engine 235 was the first company to be trained for CFR-D when the Fire Department took over Emergency Medical Services in 1995. The first day, Engine 235 responded to 25 EMS runs and two "All Hands" fires in a 24-hour period.

Engine 235 has been faithfully protecting the citizens of Brooklyn for over 100 years, regardless of the number, whether 35, 135 or 235. As the community changed from rural to densely populated, the dedication of the members in the firehouse on Monroe Street has never changed. No matter what the need is, whether air in a bicycle, a safe haven for a child, a cut finger, or a battle with the "Red Devil," Engine 235 can be and will be counted on to serve with pride and dedication.

FDNY Engine 235/Battalion 57 "The Eye of Bed-Stuy" (hand-painted resin),
Code 3 Collectibles, USA, 2000, 1:64

FDNY Tower Ladder 79/Battalion 22
"North Shore Truckin'"
Code 3 Collectibles #13101

Release Date: September 2000   Limited Edition

*FDNY Ladder 79/Battalion 22
"North Shore Truckin'" (hand-painted resin),
Code 3 Collectibles, USA, 2000, 1:64*

Taken from the booklet included with the firehouse replica:
History Of Ladder 79 Fire Department of New York by Michael Boucher

The West New Brighton section of Staten Island along the Kill Van Kull was settled before the Revolutionary War. The first factories sprang up in the early 1820s and the area grew with a small commercial center around Broadway and Richmond Terrace. The name of West New Brighton was picked for the new Post Office that was built in the 1870s. The first organized fire company was Cataract Engine 2, located at the end of Van Street off Richmond Terrace. It went into service on August 19, 1844 and served until being replaced by the paid department in 1905. On April 2, 1874, the fire companies along the north shore of Staten Island formed the North Shore Fire Department. The department grew to a total of six engines, nine hose companies and seven ladder companies before disbanding. Staten Island had 56 volunteer fire companies protecting the island before 1905.

On January 1, 1898, New York City, which included the Bronx, Brooklyn, and Long Island City along with parts of Queens County and Staten Island, merged into the five boroughs of New York City. New York City, Brooklyn and Long Island City had paid fire departments with the rural areas of Queens County and Staten Island being protected by volunteer companies. The law stated that the City of New York would continue the services of the volunteer departments until such a time that a paid force could be placed in service with buildings, equipment, and men. Until such time, each volunteer would be paid $1,000 per year for the upkeep of the equipment and horses.

In 1905, the New York City Fire Department began to expand into the outlying areas of the boroughs. The city bought the lot and building located at 1189 Castleton Avenue from Medora Ladder 3 on October 19, 1905, for a cost of $10,250 and designated this station as Ladder Co. 104.

On Jan. 1, 1913, Ladder 104 was renumbered to Ladder 79. After many moves, Battalion 22 was quartered at Ladder 79 and the two have responded to all calls from this station ever since.

In 1916, the quarters of Ladder 79 and Battalion 22 were remodeled for a cost of $3,600. New cement floors were placed in the cellar and the apparatus floors. The wooden apparatus floor was no longer suitable for the heavier motorized apparatus and was costly to maintain. The stable walls of the one-story extension were expanded to accommodate a second floor above as a recreational room.

Ladder 79 is known as the "North Shore Truckin' Company." In 1906, Ladder 79 (104) responded to 11 runs with 8 workers. During 1999, Ladder 79 responded to 1,301 runs with 803 workers. Battalion 22 answered 2,932 alarms during 1999 making them the 8th busiest battalion in the city with 2,358 hours worked. Ladder 79 and Battalion 22 have been working the north shore of Staten Island for the last 95 years. During this time, they have been dedicated to providing the best fire protection to the citizens of Staten Island. No matter how small the problem or size of the raging fire, Ladder 79 and Battalion 22 have met the challenge with distinction.

<u>Location:</u> 1189 Castleton Avenue, Staten Island, New York, NY

<u>Years in Service:</u> 1905-present

<u>Companies Quartered:</u>
Ladder 79 (organized 1905, quartered 1905-present)
Battalion 22 (organized 1905, quartered 1930-2017, 2017-present)
Division 6, 7, 8, 10 (quartered 1905-1930)

<u>Apparatus Quartered:</u>
Tower Ladder 79 (FWD/Saulsbury Aerialscope, Code 3 #12730, 2000)
Battalion 22 (GMC Suburban, Code 3 #12403, 1998)

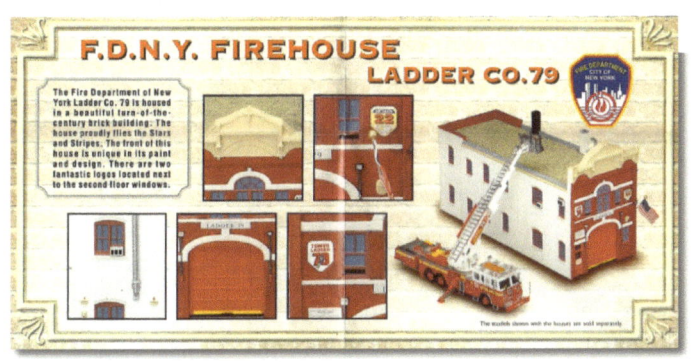

Code 3 Collectibles flyer promoting FDNY Ladder 79 firehouse, 2000

The Fire Department of New York Ladder Co. 79 is housed in a beautiful turn-of-the-century brick building. The house proudly flies the Stars and Stripes. The front of this house is unique in its paint and design. There are two fantastic logos located next to the second floor windows.

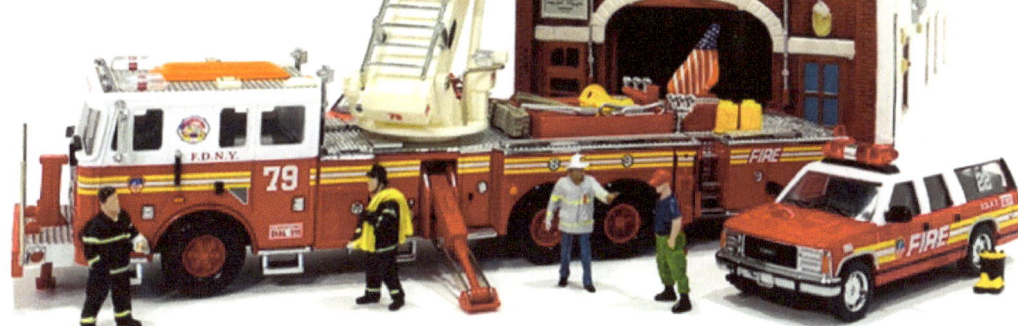

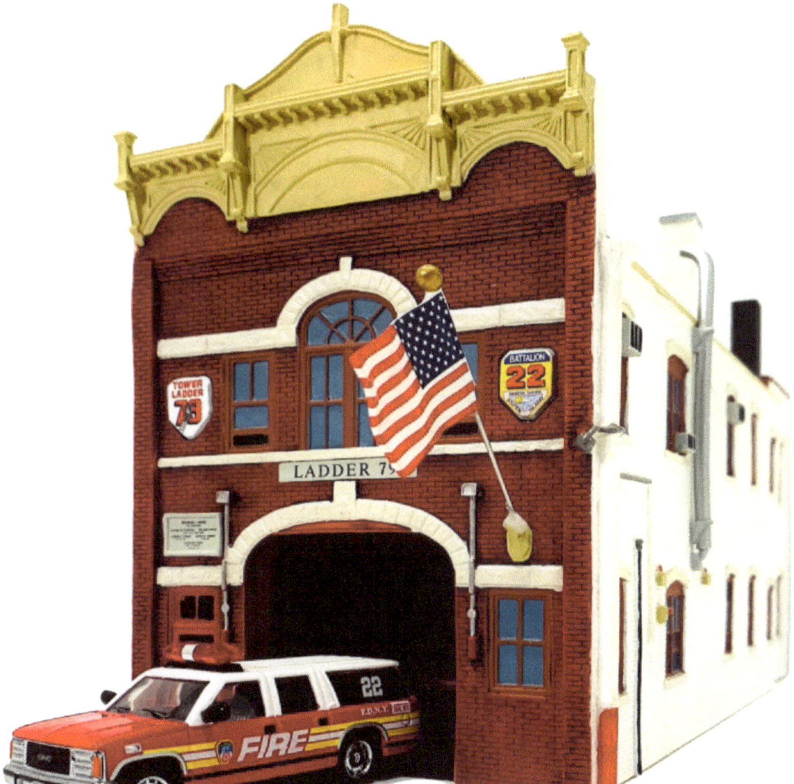

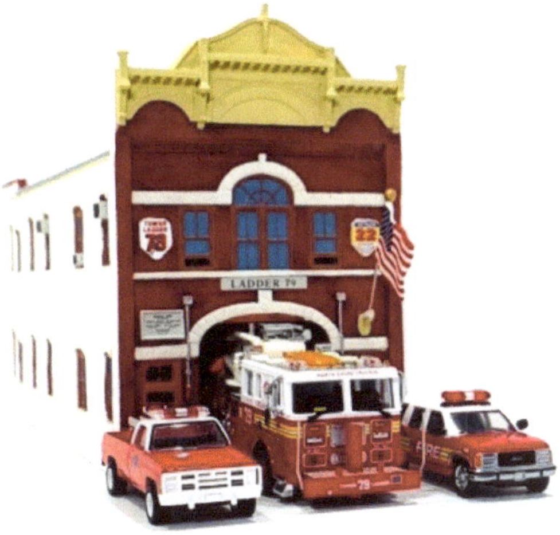

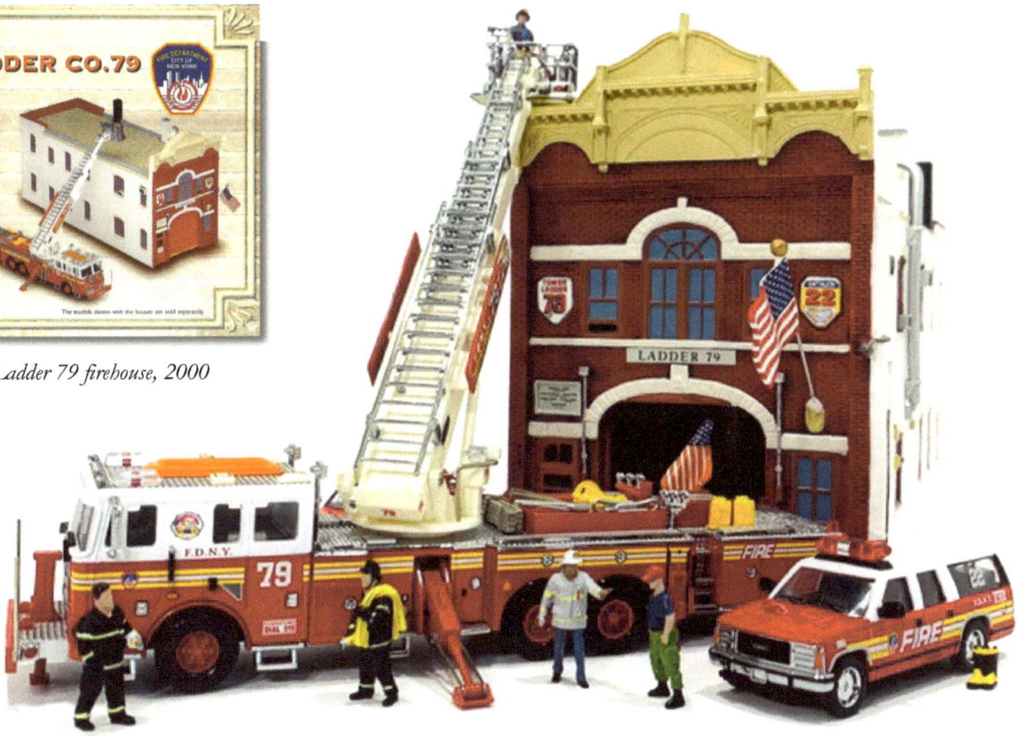

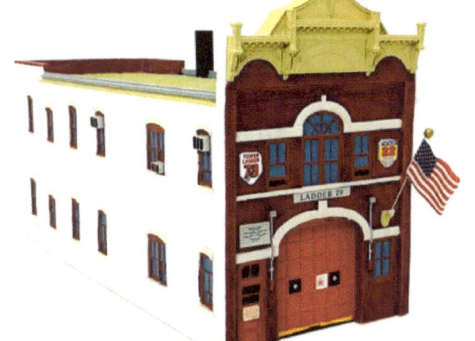

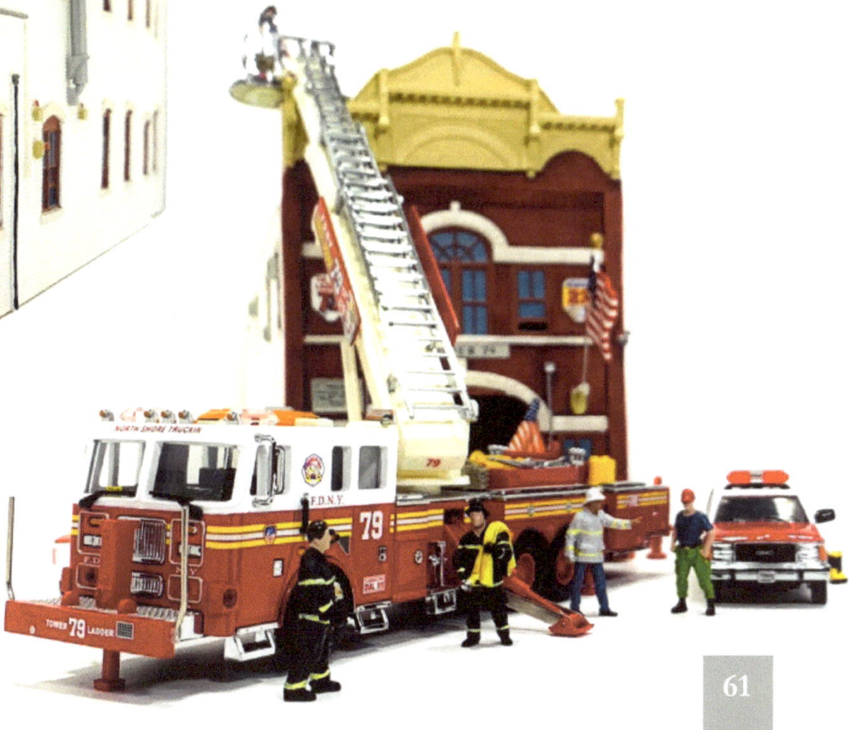

Note: *The apparatus bay doors of this replica have been updated to reflect the current "American flag" design. You can download and print the replacement doors artwork here: www.ModelFireEngines.com/download.html*

Boston Fire Department Engine 24/Ladder 23 "Grove Hall" (hand-painted resin), Code 3 Collectibles, USA, 2001, 1:64

Boston Fire Department
Engine 24/Ladder 23 "Grove Hall"
Code 3 Collectibles #13105

Release Date: June 2001   Limited Edition

Taken from the booklet included with the firehouse replica:

The firehouse at 36 Washington Street, Grove Hall, Dorchester was opened on November 8, 1898, and occupied by a newly organized fire company. This company was Combination Ladder 6, and it was equipped with a new Fire Extinguisher Manufacturing Company horse-drawn truck. This was a combination City Service ladder truck, which was also equipped with chemical tanks.

In April 1905, the name was changed to Ladder Co. 23. When the firehouse was built, it was equipped with nice arched doorways and nice Dutch doors. In later years, the doors were widened and the front windows were changed.

On August 9, 1910, a major fire occurred off Albany Street that eventually spread to the Fire Department Repair Shop. Some apparatus was removed but others were lost. Ladder Co. 23's truck was destroyed. They were assigned a new American LaFrance horse-drawn city service truck in December 1910.

On May 14, 1913, Chemical Co. 5 was organized at 36 Washington Street and they were equipped with a new American LaFrance motorized combination chemical and hose wagon. They remained in service until they were disbanded on October 13, 1922.

On August 20, 1923, Ladder Co. 23 was assigned a new American LaFrance City Service ladder truck that was equipped with a 35-gallon chemical tank. This unit replaced the horse-drawn ladder truck.

On October 23, 1922, the department was divided into 3 divisions again and the 3rd Division was moved from Ladder Co. 4 on Dudley Street to the quarters of Ladder Co. 23 in Grove Hall where they would remain until February 4, 1947.

The 3rd Division was again reorganized on January 19, 1949 and returned to Ladder Co. 23.

A major reorganization of the entire fire department took place on March 31, 1954. The 3rd Division was again disbanded, and the city would operate with two fire divisions.

Lighting Plant 2 was established and placed at the quarters of Ladder Co. 23 on October 9, 1947. They were equipped with a new Mack truck with a body built by Lacey of Medford, Mass. They only remained at Grove Hall until January 21, 1948, when they moved downtown to Bowdoin Square. On the same day, Lighting Plant 3 moved to Grove Hall from Bowdoin Square. All three of the Lighting Plants ran identical 1947 Mack/Lacey units.

The department photographer was established in 1946, and the office and darkroom were located on the top floor at Grove Hall. When a new firehouse was built on Neponset Ave., Dorchester in 1959, the photographer moved to the newer quarters.

Lighting Plant 3 remained in Grove Hall until they were placed in reserve on May 1, 1956.

On October 25, 1972, Rescue Co. 2 was reestablished and the "RPU" became a straight rescue company. Rescue Co. 2 moved to a new firehouse on Blue Hill Avenue on Aug. 16, 1973.

On the next day, Engine Co. 24 moved from their firehouse on Warren Street, which was about ¾ of a mile away, to Grove Hall and their 100-year-old firehouse was closed.

During the winter months of 1996, both companies moved out as a new floor and other improvements were made. Ladder Co. 23 moved in with Engine Co. 52 and Ladder Co. 29 on Blue Hill Avenue, and Engine Co. 24 moved in with Engine Co. 16 on Gallivan Blvd.

At the present time, Engine Co. 24 is assigned a 1999 Emergency-One 1,250 pump and Ladder Co. 23 is assigned a 1997 Emergency-One 110' rear mount aerial.

Location: 36 Washington Street, Boston, MA

Years in Service: 1898-present

Companies Quartered:
Chemical Engine Company 5 (quartered 1913-1922)
Engine Company 13 (quartered 1960-1967)
Rescue-Pumper Company (quartered 1967-1972)
Engine Company 24 (quartered 1972-present)
Combination Ladder Company 6 (quartered 1898-1905)
Ladder Company 23 (quartered 1905-present)
Rescue Company 2 (quartered 1972-1973)
Lighting Plant 2/3 (quartered 1947-1948/1948-1956)

Apparatus Quartered:
Engine 24 (Emergency-One Cyclone II, Code 3 #12340, 2000)
Ladder 23 (Emergency-One, Code 3 #12960, 2004)
Ambulance 6 (Ford F-350, Code 3 #12105, 1999)
Division 7 (GMC Suburban, Code 3 #12402-0007, 1998)
Safety/Special Operations H1 (GMC Suburban, Code 3 #12402-0001, 1998)

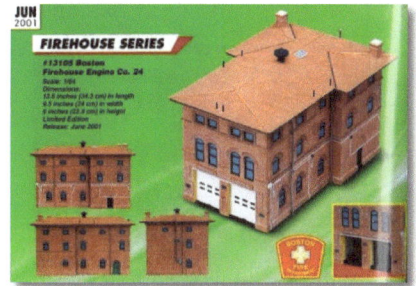

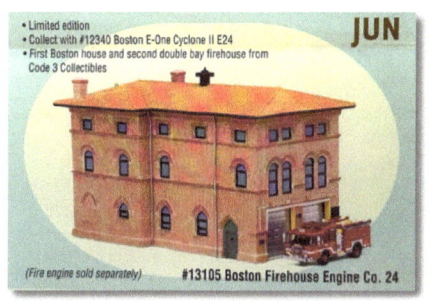

Code 3 Collectibles flyers promoting Boston Engine 24/Ladder 23 firehouse, June 2001

Washington, D.C. Fire and EMS
Engine 10/Truck 13 "The House of Pain"
Code 3 Collectibles #13106

Release Date: October 2001   Limited Edition

Taken from the booklet included with the firehouse replica:

In 1895, the population of Northeast Washington, D.C. was growing and the need for fire prevention was evident. On July 2, 1905, Engine Company No. 10 was organized; the firehouse was located at 1341 Maryland Avenue, N.E.

Over the years the community changed. Commercial establishments popped up on H Street and Florida Avenue. The need for a ladder truck in the are was evident. On December 9, 1925, Truck Company No. 13 was organized—the firehouse was located at 1342 Florida Avenue, N.E., only three blocks from the quarters of Engine Company No. 10.

In 1940, due to the recommendation of the National Board of Fire Underwriters, the department consolidated several companies. On June 4, 1940, Engine Company No. 10 moved three blocks north to the quarters of Truck Company No. 13. For many years, the two companies maintained a steady pace of being one of the busiest firehouses in the city.

In 1991, Engine Company No. 10 became the busiest engine company in the nation responding to 9,947 runs. Also, during 1991, Truck Company No. 13 was rated the second busiest truck company in the nation. During that year the firehouse was given the name "The House of Pain."

The firehouse earned this name because of the large number of runs the both the engine and truck companies responded on each day. As a result of being one of the busiest fire companies in the city, Engine Company No. 10 and Truck Company No. 13 has become one of the most sought-after firehouses in the city for assignment.

In 1994, the company broke all records for a 24-hour period when Engine Company No. 10 responded on 47 runs. From 1991 to 2000, Engine Company No. 10 was rated the busiest engine company in the nation and responded to 75,526 runs.

Washington, D.C. Fire and EMS Engine 10/Truck 13
"The House of Pain" (hand-painted resin),
Code 3 Collectibles, USA, 2001, 1:64

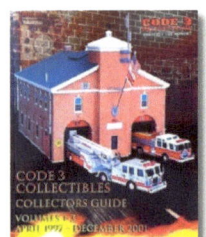  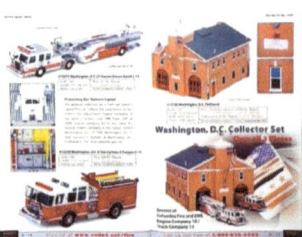 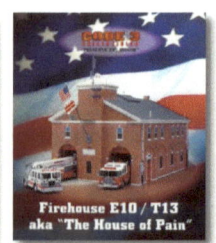 

Code 3 Collectibles Washington, D.C. Fire and EMS promotional material, 2001

Code 3 Collectibles Collectors Club Christmas Card, 2001

<u>Location:</u> 1342 Florida Avenue NE, Washington, D.C.

<u>Years in Service:</u> 1925-present

<u>Companies Quartered:</u>
Engine 10 (organized 1895, quartered 1940-present)
Truck 13 (organized 1925, quartered 1925-present)
Ambulance 10

<u>Apparatus Quartered:</u>
Engine 10 (Emergency-One, Code 3 #12339, 2001)
Truck 13 (Ladder Towers Incorporated, Code 3 #12672, 2001)
Ambulance 10 (Ford F-350, Code 3 with custom decals)
EMS 28 (GMC Suburban, Code 3 #12374, 1999)
Battalion Chief (Ford LTD Crown Vic, Greenlight #29999, 2018)

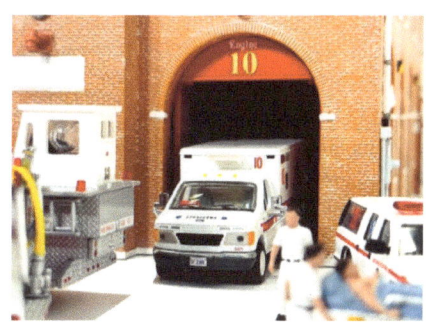

Chicago Fire Department Engine 17/Ladder 46 "Backdraft" (hand-painted resin), Code 3 Collectibles, USA, 2000, 1:64

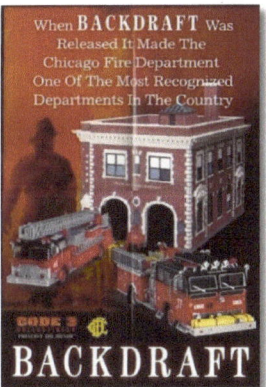 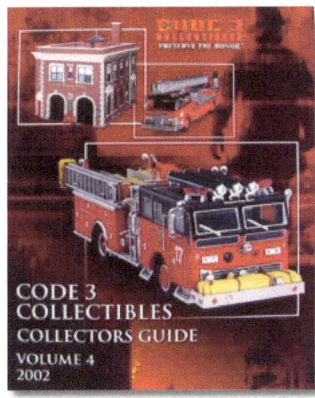

Code 3 Collectibles promotional material, Chicago Backdraft firehouse, 2002

Chicago Fire Department
Engine 17/Ladder 46 *"Backdraft"*
Code 3 Collectibles #13107

Release Date: October 2002   Limited Edition

Taken from the booklet included with the firehouse replica:
This Chicago Firehouse goes Hollywood
Code 3 Collectibles is proud to bring its collectors this limited-edition Chicago Firehouse replica of the firehouse used in Ron Howard's film *Backdraft*. This highly-detailed model features intricate architectural moldings, opening double-bay doors and even a bench in front of the station. Collect with #12392 Chicago Ward La France Pumper E-17 and #12495 Chicago Mack CF Rear Mount L-46 as a set!

Trivia on the Movie in the Making
When Ron Howard filmed *Backdraft* he made the Chicago Fire Department one of the most recognized departments in the country. The C.F.D. loaned Universal Studios several pieces of apparatus for their new movie. It is very unusual for Hollywood to use actual authentic apparatus. Most movies using fire apparatus are filmed on the West Coast and use privately owned trucks painted to reflect the city they are meant to represent.

The most recognized engine from the movie would be Engine 17. Engine 17 started service with the Chicago Fire Department in July 1970. This 1970 Ward LaFrance Pumper was first assigned to Engine Co. 8. The pumper was later assigned to Engine 18. In 1987, it was refurbed with a Ranger cab and E-One body before it was given to Ron Howard's production group in July of 1990. Ron Howard used Engine 18 (portrayed as Engines 17 & 51 in the movie) until February of 1991. After the filming of the movie, the apparatus was given to Engine 69 were it remained in-service until 1995 when it was disposed of.

Three different ladder trucks were used as the famous Truck 46 in filming *Backdraft*. A 1972 Mack CF with a 100' Pirsch Ladder was customized by Ron Howard by adding updated headlights, a siren, warning lights and customizing some bodywork. The tiller was a 1976 International Harvester Tractor-Drawn Ladder with a CFA Clintonville Trailer and 100' Seagrave Ladder. The American LaFrance 100' truck was assigned to Truck 36 before the movie and after the movie was a shop spare. A 1978 American LaFrance Century Pumper was marked in the movie as Engine 67 & 25. The Engine was originally Engine 46 of the Chicago Fire Department and after filming was returned to the department as Engine 80. Engine 24 was also an American LaFrance Century Pumper. It was marked 24, 27 and 17 in the movie. It was Engine 34 of the C.F.D. before filming and Engine 28 after.

Along with using authentic apparatus, Ron Howard also used Chicago's firehouses to retain the authenticity in his movie. The firehouses used in filming were Engine Co. 65 (which was Engine 17 and Ladder 46 in the movie), Engine Co. 8 (which was Robert DeNiro's Engine Co. 51 office in the movie), and training drills were filmed at Engine Co. 49.

<u>Location:</u> 3002 W. 42 Street, Chicago, IL

<u>Years in Service:</u> 1929-present

<u>Companies Quartered:</u>
Engine 65 (organized 1891, quartered 1929–present)
Truck 52 (organized 1929, quartered 1929–present)
Ambulance 69 (organized 2014, quartered 2014–present)

<u>Apparatus Quartered:</u>
Engine 17 (Ward LaFrance, Code 3 #12392, 2002)
Ladder 46 (Mack CF, Code 3 #12495, 2002)
Ambulance (Ford Club Wagon, Greenlight #30242, 2021)
Battalion Chief (Dodge Monaco, Greenlight #42700, 2014)

Chicago Fire Department
Engine 78 "The Pride of Wrigleyville"
Code 3 Collectibles #13103

Release Date: August 2000   Limited Edition

Taken from the booklet included with the firehouse replica:
History Of Engine Co. 78
Chicago Fire Department by Jim Regan

Engine 78 of the Chicago Fire Department was organized on December 31, 1894, in an area of the city formerly known as the Town of Lakeview. The company's First Captain was George B. Miller. Equipment consisted of an Ahrens steam Fire engine capable of pumping 650 gallons per minute drawn by two horses and a separate horse-drawn hose wagon carrying 650 feet of 2½" hose. Partial motorization came in 1912 when Engine 78 received a Harder Chemical and Hose Wagon which they operated until 1915.

During November 1915, Engine 78 moved into a new Fire station located at 1052 West Waveland Avenue where they have remained in service for the last 84 years. This firehouse was the first in Chicago designed for motorized fire apparatus and no stable for the horses was provided. New construction was occurring across the street which would affect the neighborhood for all time. A modern ballpark was being erected to house the Whales of the Federal League, and since 1916 the Cubs of the National League.

Over the years, many visiting companies have made 78's quarters their home. Squad 4 was the first tenant, followed by various divisions and marshals, including the 3rd Division in 1929. Ambulance 6 was organized here in 1928 and has remained with Engine 78 ever since.

The neighborhood protected by Engine 78 saw some rough times during the 1960s and '70s but it never was ravaged by the arson epidemic that did great damage to its immediate neighbor to the north, Uptown. Today, the area is in resurgence and is being "gentrified" as older buildings are rehabbed and restored. The area is now known as "Wrigleyville," obviously due to its proximity to Wrigley Field, right across the street from 78.

Engine 78, "The Pride of Wrigleyville" is currently manned by three platoons of firefighters led by Captain Patrick Maloney and two lieutenants. They operate a 1997 HME/Luverne 1,500 gallon-per-minute pumper that has a 500-gallon water tank. The company protects the diverse area of Chicago's north lakefront from Diversey Avenue to Lawrence Avenue including many high-rise apartment buildings, commercial areas, and light industry. During 1998, the company responded to 2,298 runs of which 1,422 were for fire responses.

Location: 1052 West Waveland Avenue, Chicago, IL

Years in Service: 1915-present

Companies Quartered:
Engine 78 (organized 1894, quartered 1915-present)
Ambulance 6 (organized 1928, quartered 1928-present)
Squad 4 (organized 1919, quartered 1919-1925)
Division 3 (organized 1929, quartered 1929-1948)

Apparatus Quartered:
Engine 78 (Luverne, Code 3 #12318, 2000)
Engine 78 (Ford C-8000, Hallmark with custom decals)
Engine 78 (Mack B, Corgi #98450, 1995, 1:50)
Ambulance 6 (Ford E-350, Code 3 #12065, 2001)
Ambulance 6 (Cadillac, customized Johnny Lightning)
Battalion 12 (Chevrolet Caprice, Greenlight #30243, 2021)

Chicago Fire Department Engine 78 "The Pride of Wrigleyville" (hand-painted resin),
Code 3 Collectibles, USA, 2000, 1:64

Note: The apparatus bay door of this replica has been updated to reflect the current design. You can download and print the replacement door artwork here: www.ModelFireEngines.com/download.html

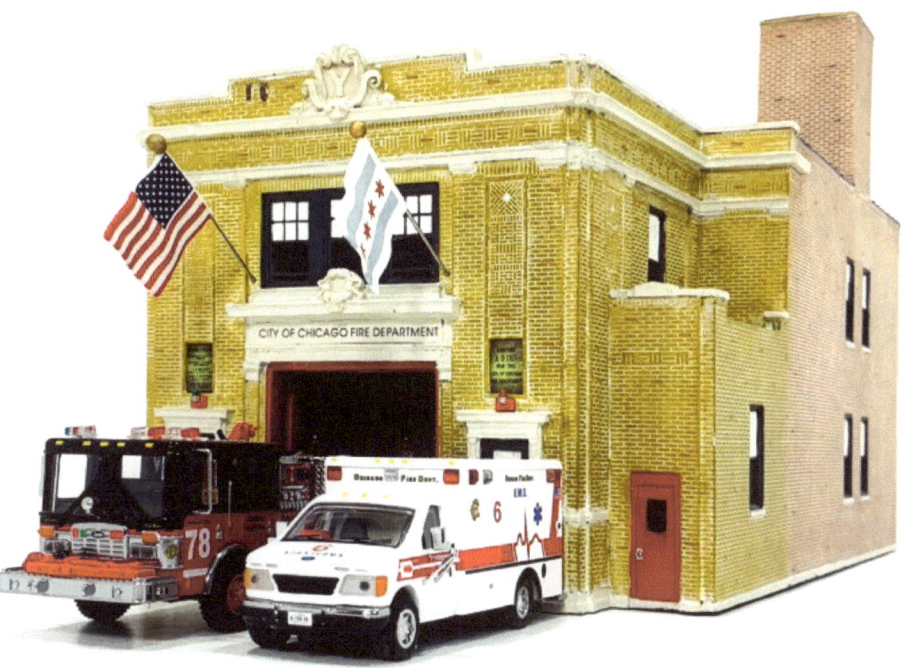

Code 3 Collectibles Collectors Guide Volume #3, 2001

*Los Angeles County Fire Department Engine 51/Squad 51 "EMERGENCY!"
(hand-painted resin), Code 3 Collectibles, USA, 2001, 1:64*

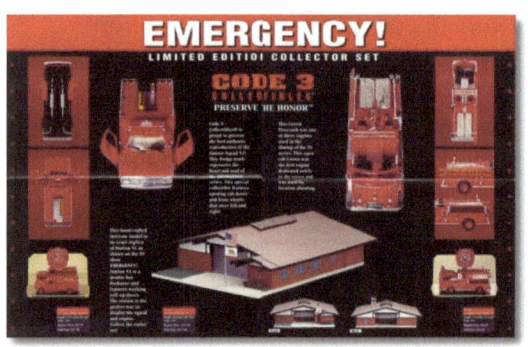
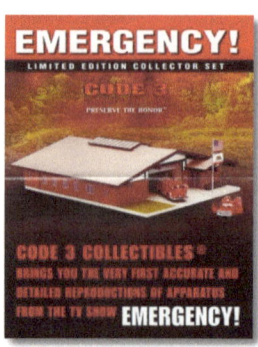

Code 3 Collectibles Los Angeles County EMERGENCY! firehouse promotional material, 2001

Los Angeles County Fire Department
Engine 51/Squad 51 *"EMERGENCY!"*
Code 3 Collectibles #13104

Release Date: April 2001   Limited Edition

Taken from a Code 3 Collectibles flyer:
This hand-crafted intricate model is an exact replica of Station 51 as shown on the TV show *EMERGENCY!* Station 51 is a double-bay firehouse and features working roll-up doors. The station is the perfect way to display the squad and engine. Collect the entire set!

Code 3 Collectibles is proud to present the first authentic reproduction of the famous Squad 51. This Dodge truck represents the heart and soul of the *EMERGENCY!* series. This special collectible features opening cab doors.

The Crown Firecoach was the first engine used in the filming of the TV series. The open cab Crown was the first engine dedicated solely to the series and was used to shoot on location.

The Ward LaFrance Engine 51 is the 2nd most recognized vehicle from the hit show *EMERGENCY!* It is currently in service at Yosemite National Park. Collect Ward 51 with the rest of the *EMERGENCY!* set.

Ex-Engine 51 proudly served Yosemite National Park from this tiny firehouse on the valley floor—it has since been restored and is now on display at the Los Angeles County Fire Museum

<u>Location:</u> 2049 E 223rd Street, Carson, CA

<u>Years in Service:</u> 1966-present

<u>Companies Quartered:</u>
Engine 127
Quint 127
Foam 127

<u>Apparatus Quartered:</u>
Engine 51 (Ward LaFrance, Code 3 #12391, 2002)
Engine 51 (Crown, Code 3 #12957, 2001)
Squad 51 (Dodge 300, Code 3 #13940, 2001)

Burning Building and Firefighter Figures
Code 3 Collectibles #13099

Release Date: March 2001   Limited Edition

Code 3 Collectibles released their limited-edition hand-painted resin model of a "Burning Building" in March of 2001. The set includes nine firefighter figures captured in various poses as they battle to save both life and property in this detailed 1:64 scale scene. The included instruction sheet indicates where to place each figure (in pre-drilled holes) throughout the diorama.

The replica includes a single-lane roadbed in front of the building which can be used to display two emergency vehicles on scene—in this case we chose Rescue Engine 33 and Tower Ladder 33 from Kentland Volunteer Fire Company in Prince Georges County, Maryland.

<u>Apparatus on Scene:</u>
Kentland Pierce Dash Rescue Engine 33 (Code 3 #12895, 2002)
Kentland FWD/Baker Aerialscope 75' Tower
   Ladder 33 "Sally" (Code 3 #12734, 2001)
(not included with burning building)

Taken from a Code 3 Collectibles flyer:
Just the thing you need to display with your 1:64 scale fire and rescue apparatus replicas. This hand-cast and hand-painted building facade comes with 9 figures. This model captures a typical scene portraying the heroic rescue efforts of these brave firefighters.

Burning Building and Firefighter Figures (hand-painted resin) with apparatus (metal), Code 3 Collectibles, USA, 2001, 1:64

FDNY Rescue Company 3D Resin Patch Set, Code 3 Collectibles #13025, 2004

3D Patch Set, Code 3 Collectibles (resin), USA, 2004

Taken from Code 3 Collectibles promotional material:
These patches capture the bravery and identity of the men and woman who protect our communities. These limited edition, highly-detailed, three-dimensional patches of these famed FDNY rescue companies are truly a site to see! Each one is meticulously hand-cast and hand-painted by our skilled artisans to highlight each company patch in all its glory and bring the artwork to life. Each resin patch is 5 inches wide and 5 inches tall and can be displayed either by hanging on the wall or standing them upright with a built-in stand. You will marvel at the texture and vibrant colors of each patch. Start your collection today of these exquisite 3D patches!

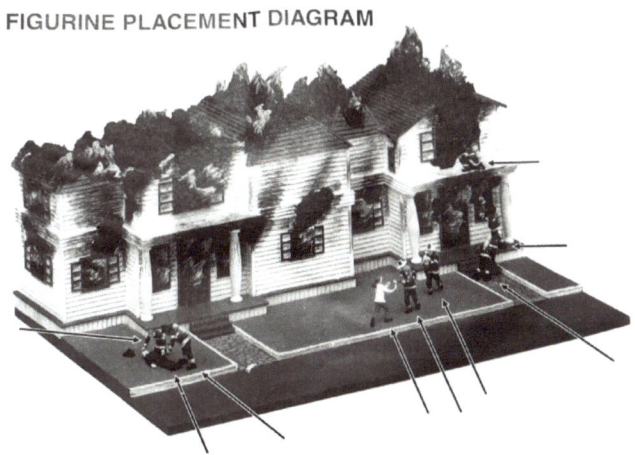

Code 3 Collectibles Burning Building promotional material, March 2001

Old Glory American Flag Assortment, Code 3 Collectibles #12564, 2009

Taken from a Code 3 Collectibles flyer:
This latest release from Code 3 is intended to enhance your entire collection. Fire departments around the country mount the American Flag in an expression of patriotism and a sense of service to the American people they serve in their communities. Now you can add Old Glory to your rigs too. In three styles, full furl, flutter, and parade rest, the flags are rendered in 1:64th scale and can be mounted wherever you want to display them. Twelve flags per set so you can decorate numerous models in your collection.

Old Glory American Flag Assortment, Code 3 Collectibles (rubber/metal), USA, September 2009

First Due Firehouse Replicas (Martinez, California) was established in 2022 to continue where Code 3 left off and to produce a series of accurate, detailed, photo-realistic 1:64 scale model firehouses suitable for collectors to acquire, enjoy, and display their collection. Each firehouse produced is designed to house one or more existing **Code 3 Collectibles** model. Each release is signed and numbered on the base and includes a printed information booklet detailing the history of the building and companies assigned. These museum-quality firehouse replicas are not toys—but rather limited-edition hand-made collectible creations.

FDNY Engine 1/Ladder 24
"Midtown Madness" (foam core, mixed media),
First Due Firehouse Replicas, USA, 2022, 1:64

Engine 1 features a mini–Empire State Building on the roof of the cab while Ladder 24 sports a set of longhorns

FDNY Engine 1/Ladder 24 "Midtown Madness"
First Due Firehouse Replicas #9

Release Date: March 2022

Taken from the booklet included with the firehouse replica:
Code 3 Collectibles produced replicas of both FDNY Engine 1 and Ladder 24 in 2006. Individually these units are known as "Midtown Express" and the "Raging Bulls"—collectively they are referred to as "Midtown Madness"—the ninth release from **First Due Firehouse Replicas**.

The Midtown Madness firehouse is located at 142 West 31st Street, Manhattan, New York City. The building was designed by Lewis & Churchill and has been serving the community since 1946. The firehouse underwent an extensive renovation process from 2002-2004—the updated facility will serve the residents of the districts of Midtown South, Koreatown, and Chelsea for many years to come.

Originally organized as one of the first engines in the paid department, Engine 1 entered service in the former quarters of volunteer Northern Liberty Engine 42 at 1 Centre Street in lower Manhattan on July 31, 1865. Disbanded in 1868, they were reorganized five years later at 165 West 29th Street in Midtown Manhattan on February 17, 1873. They moved to their present quarters which they share with Ladder 24 at 142 West 31st Street on November 3, 1946.

In 2005, Engine 1 was the 5th busiest engine company in Manhattan and 14th in the overall city. They responded to 4,821 alarms in 2005, of which 3,668 were workers. Of these, 1,990 were medical emergencies in which they were 1st in Manhattan and 2nd in the entire City.

Ladder 24 was organized on June 1, 1901, in a large and ornate firehouse at 115 West 33rd Street in Midtown Manhattan. On November 3, 1946, they moved into a new firehouse two blocks south at 142 West 31st Street.

In 2005, Ladder 24 responded to 4,003 alarms, of which 3,005 were workers. They were the 5th busiest ladder company in Manhattan and 10th overall in the entire City for 2005.

Over the years many other units have also been quartered at this firehouse including Division 3, Water Tower 3, Searchlight 21, Department Ambulance 1, and High Ladder 1. Their first alarm district is made up of high-rise commercial office buildings and factories and includes the Empire State Building, Madison Square Garden, Pennsylvania Station, Macy's, and many hotels.

Location: 142 West 31st Street, Manhattan, New York, NY

Years in Service: 1946-present

Companies Quartered:
Engine 1 (organized 1865, quartered 1946–present)
Ladder 24 (organized 1901, quartered 1946–present)
Division 3 (organized 1869, quartered 1946-1951, 1956-1995)
Water Tower 3 (quartered 1946-1957)
Searchlight 21 (quartered 1946-1955, 1959-1972)
Ambulance 1 (quartered 1955-1972)
High Ladder 1 (quartered 1964)

Apparatus Quartered:
Engine 1 (Seagrave, Code 3 #12838, 2006)
Ladder 24 (Seagrave, Code 3 #12854, 2006)
Division 3 (GMC Suburban, Code 3 with custom graphics)

FDNY Engine 7/Ladder 1/Battalion 1 "Duane Street Circus"
First Due Firehouse Replicas #26

Release Date: November 2022

Taken from the booklet included with the firehouse replica:
Code 3 produced replicas of New York City Fire Department Engine 7 and Tower Ladder 1 in August 2007. These companies are two of the oldest in the FDNY, and together they make up the "Duane Street Circus" in lower Manhattan—the twenty-sixth release from **First Due Firehouse Replicas**.

On September 8, 1865, Engine Company 7 (formerly Protector Engine 22 since 1840) was established as one of the first units of the newly-formed paid Metropolitan Fire Department in Manhattan. Their first apparatus included an 1866 Amoskeag 2nd size steamer and an 1865 Amoskeag hose tender.

Due to the ever-growing height of downtown buildings, between 1905-1908 (and again from 1925-1939), Engine 7 operated as a double engine company with each of the two sections having its own pumper and hose wagon. This necessitated construction of a new larger firehouse, and in 1904 three lots were purchased at 100 through 104 Duane Street.

Hook and Ladder No. 1 was established during British rule on July 10, 1772, four years before the Declaration of Independence was signed. After many of its volunteer members marched off to fight in the Revolution, it was reorganized in 1784 and given the name Mutual Hook & Ladder No. 1. This company never lost their organization until the creation of the paid system when Hook and Ladder Company No. 1 was created on September 8, 1865.

The new company used the same location, the same truck, and the same red cap fronts as before, and nine of its twelve members had served in the previous company. It was the only company that was continued with the same number and location, so it can be said Hook and Ladder Company No. 1 has had a continuous existence since June 16, 1784.

Engine 7 and Ladder 1 have been quartered together since the two companies were organized in 1865 at 28 Chambers Street. They moved into their new three-door Beaux-Arts firehouse at 100 Duane Street, Manhattan on New Year's Eve, 1905. The building was clad in boldly rusticated Indiana limestone bands on the upper floors. The 75-foot-wide structure featured three bay doors—two for Engine Company 7 with its two steamers, hose tenders, horses, and 25 members, and the other for Hook & Ladder No. 1 with its ladder wagon, horses, and 17 members.

The esteemed architectural firm of Trowbridge & Livingston's exceptional design earned the structure landmark designation in 1993 and prompted the AIA Guide to New York City to call it "among the most impressive small-scale civic structures of the period."

This firehouse is also the current quarters of the chiefs of the first battalion. Over the years this building has also been home to numerous FDNY special units including Water Tower 1, Searchlight 1, Relay Hose Wagon 1, Smoke Ejector & Foamite Truck 1, the FDNY Office of the Manhattan Borough Command, as well as temporary homes for Engine 10, Ladder 10, Division 1, and Battalion 2.

In 1957 Ladder 1 moved to the center bay to make way for the Fire Department Museum. Eleven pieces of antique apparatus were moved into the right bay, including an 1810

FDNY Engine 7/Ladder 1/Battalion 1 "Duane Street Circus" (foam core, mixed media), First Due Firehouse Replicas, USA, 2022, 1:64

"gooseneck" fire engine. The museum remained open until 1987 when the memorabilia was moved to 278 Spring Street. The fire department's Bureau of Fire Communications then used the space followed by the current Manhattan Borough Command.

Engine 7 is known as *"The Magnificent Seven,"* a reference to the western movie, based on the idea the inside of the firehouse looked like the old west when the department used horses. Ladder 1 is known as, "The Original One," both for being one of the first fire companies in the city and for also being the first Tower Ladder in the FDNY in 1964.

While many other companies were relocated throughout their existence, Ladder Company 1 and Engine Company 7 still remain in their striking 1905 firehouse. Located near the center of NYC government, Engine 7 and Ladder 1's first due area is made up of mainly large commercial buildings as well as City Hall and numerous other government buildings.

Engine 7's 2000 Seagrave pumper was destroyed on September 11, 2001. Amazingly, every member of this firehouse's fifty-five firefighters—including the thirteen on duty that morning and the forty-two who rushed to assist them—survived the attack. This firehouse is featured in the documentary *9/11*.

<u>Location:</u> 100 Duane Street, Manhattan, New York, NY

<u>Years in Service:</u> 1905-present *(as Fire Department Museum: 1957-1987)*

<u>Companies Quartered:</u>
Engine 7 (organized 1865, quartered 1905–present)
Engine 7-2 (quartered 1905-1908, 1925-1939)
Engine 31 (quartered 1967-1970)
Ladder 1 (organized 1784/1865, quartered 1905–present)
Ladder 10 (quartered 1970-1975)
Battalion 1 (organized 1869, quartered 1974-present)
Battalion 2 (quartered 1965, 1967-1974)
Division 1 (quartered 1907-1938, 1941-1956)
Assistant Chief, Manhattan Borough Commander Car 6
Searchlight 1 (organized 1922, quartered 1922-1938)
Relay Hose Wagon 1 (organized 1942,
    quartered 1942-1945)
Smoke Ejector and Foamite Truck 1
    (quartered 1941-1957)
Hydrant Service Unit 1 (quartered 1936-1957)
Mobile Education Unit (quartered 1959-1970)
Photo Unit (used as night quarters 1960s-1970s)

<u>Apparatus Quartered:</u>
Engine 7 (Seagrave, Code 3 #12839, 2007)
Ladder 1 (Seagrave, Code 3 #12738, 2007)
Special Services Ladder 1 (Ford F-450, Greenlight
    with custom body and graphics)
Battalion 1 (GMC Suburban, Code 3 with custom decals)
Assistant Chief, Manhattan Borough Commander Car 6
    (Ford Crown Victoria, Greenlight #29772, 2014)

FDNY Engine 9/Ladder 6/Satellite 1 "Chinatown Dragonfighters"
(foam core, mixed media), First Due Firehouse Replicas, USA, 2023, 1:64

FDNY Engine 9/Ladder 6/Satellite 1 "Chinatown Dragonfighters"
First Due Firehouse Replicas #32

Release Date: May 2023

Taken from the booklet included with the firehouse replica:
Code 3 produced a replica of New York City Fire Department Engine 9 in April 1998 as part of their second series of FDNY Seagrave pumpers (the other releases were Engines 42, 45, 58, and 279). Together Engine 9, Ladder 6, and Satellite 1 are known as the "Chinatown Dragonfighters"—the thirty-second release from **First Due Firehouse Replicas**.

The Chinatown Dragonfighters firehouse is located at 75 Canal Street, Manhattan, New York City. The building was erected in 1968 to better protect the Chinatown section of lower Manhattan. The structure contains a unique "screen" design element which covers nearly the entire second floor facade.

Ladder 6 was first established on September 27th, 1865, at 180 Clinton Street. They relocated two years later to their new firehouse located at 77 Canal Street. Engine 9 was established on September 29th, 1865, as a single engine company at 55 East Broadway. Engine 9 and Ladder 6 moved in together to their new firehouse at 75 Canal Street on May 6th, 1969.

Satellite 1 was organized at Engine 31 in Manhattan, but because the Super Tender was returned to Mack for modifications, Satellite 1 temporarily operated from 26 Hooper Street in Brooklyn with the Super Pumper. After spending time at numerous locations, Satellite 1 moved in with Engine 9 and Ladder 6 on November 22nd, 1975. Satellite 1 is part of the Maxi Water System (ex-Super Pumper System).

The Dragonfighters are part of the FDNY's 4th Battalion (with E15, E28, E31, L11 and L18). Their first due response area includes a variety of commercial and residential buildings, a hospital, and incidents occurring on the Manhattan Bridge.

<u>Location:</u> 75 Canal Street, Manhattan, New York, NY

<u>Years in Service:</u> 1969-present

<u>Companies Quartered:</u>
Engine 9 (organized 1865, quartered 1969-present)
Ladder 6 (organized 1865, quartered 1969-present)
Satellite 1 (organized 1965, quartered 1975-present)

<u>Apparatus Quartered:</u>
Engine 9 (Seagrave, Code 3 #12300, 1998)
Ladder 6 (Seagrave, Code 3 with custom graphics)
Satellite 1 (Peterbilt 520/Ferrara, custom-built by Nghia Takeshi, 2023)

*FDNY Satellite 1 "Chinatown Dragonfighters"
custom-built by Nghia Takeshi, 2023, 1:64*

Note: To learn how this firehouse was constructed, see Building a First Due Firehouse Replica in the **Appendix** on page 161

FDNY Engine 40/Ladder 35
"The Cavemen" (foam core, mixed media),
First Due Firehouse Replicas, USA, 2022, 1:64

"The Cavemen" replica includes
the neighboring Riverside Branch of
The New York Public Library

FDNY Engine 40/Ladder 35 "The Cavemen"
First Due Firehouse Replicas #12

Release Date: April 2022

Taken from the booklet included with the firehouse replica:
The final pumper **Code 3** produced before going out of business in 2011 was a Seagrave Marauder II model representing Engine 40 of the New York City Fire Department—the twelfth release of **First Due Firehouse Replicas**. Only two versions of the Marauder II pumper were released, the other being Engine 63. The final model released was Tower Ladder 46, unfortunately no other ladder versions of the Marauder II cab were ever produced.

"The Cavemen" firehouse is located at 131 Amsterdam Avenue, Manhattan, New York City, and was constructed between 1988 and 1993. This unique firehouse is located beneath a 60-story office building which includes the Riverside Branch of The New York Public Library.

Both companies have been in existence well before the area became known as Lincoln Square in the 1960s. The first due response area of Engine 40 and Ladder 35 includes some of the most diverse and challenging areas in the city from luxury high-rises to brownstones, major subway and power stations, the Time Warner Center, the Metropolitan Opera House, the Julliard School, the New York Philharmonic, and some of the best-known theaters in the world.

Engine Company 40 was established in 1874, and Ladder Company 35 was established in 1907. The two companies have been quartered together since 1918.

The nickname of the firehouse dates to 1988-1993 when both companies were relocated to a temporary firehouse in a garage under Lincoln Center during construction of the new office building. The name also seems fitting for the current office building firehouse as the number of windows is so low the firefighters refer to the locker room window as "the view."

<u>Location:</u> 131 Amsterdam Avenue, Manhattan, New York, NY

<u>Years in Service:</u> 1993-present

<u>Companies Quartered:</u>
Engine 40 (organized 1874, quartered 1993-present)
Ladder 35 (organized 1907, quartered 1993-present)

<u>Apparatus Quartered:</u>
Engine 40 (Seagrave Marauder II, Code 3 #12567, 2011)
Ladder 35 (Seagrave Marauder II, Code 3 with custom graphics)

Shortly before Code 3 abruptly closed its doors in 2011, they released two beautiful tilt-cab Seagrave Marauder II engines representing FDNY E40 & E63. These remain two of Code 3's most sought-after releases.

FDNY Engine 58/Ladder 26 "Fire Factory" First Due Firehouse Replicas #1

Release Date: January 2022

Taken from the booklet included with the firehouse replica:
Code 3 produced three versions of FDNY Engine 58 (two Seagrave models and a lime yellow Mack CF) along with three versions of Ladder 26 (two Seagrave rear mount models and an American LaFrance tiller truck). These companies are part of "The Fire Factory" in East Harlem—the first release from **First Due Firehouse Replicas**. It seems Code 3 had a special appreciation for this world-famous firehouse, so it's fitting to make this our first official release.

The Fire Factory firehouse is located at 1367 5th Avenue, Manhattan, New York City, and was constructed between 1959 and 1960. This historically active firehouse in Harlem saw heavy action during the famous war years of the 1970s making it home to two of the busiest companies in the world. It was so busy a second ladder company (Ladder 26-2) was organized and also responded from this firehouse from 1968 until disbanded in 1974.

Engine Company 58 was established on June 1, 1893 and was first quartered in a new firehouse at 81 West 115th Street. Engine 58 moved in with Ladder 26 (formed in 1902) on November 4, 1948. Both Engine 58 and Ladder 26 relocated to their brand-new firehouse at 1367 Fifth Avenue on March 10, 1960. Engine 58 and Ladder 26 are part of the 12th battalion.

The nickname of the firehouse dates to the 1960s when the company radioed in yet another fire to dispatch and received the on-air reply, "What are you guys running, a fire factory up there?"

FDNY Engine 58/Ladder 26 "Fire Factory" (foam core, mixed media), First Due Firehouse Replicas, USA, 2022, 1:64

Location: 1367 5th Avenue, Manhattan, New York, NY

Years in Service: 1960-present

Companies Quartered:
Engine 58 (organized 1893, quartered 1960-present)
Ladder 26 (organized 1904, quartered 1960-present)
Ladder 26-2 (reorganized 1968, quartered 1968-1974)
Battalion 25 (organized 1968, quartered 1969)

Apparatus Quartered:
Engine 58 (Mack CF, Code 3 #12355, 2001)
Engine 58 (Seagrave, Code 3, #12300, 1998)
Engine 58 (Seagrave 100th Anniversary, Code 3 #12836, 2005)
Ladder 26 (American LaFrance, Code 3 #13049, 2010)
Ladder 26 (Seagrave, Code 3 #12720-0026, 1999)
Ladder 26 (Seagrave 100th Anniversary, Code 3 #12855, 2004)
Battalion 12 (GMC Suburban, Code 3 #12403-12, 1998)
Battalion 12 (Chevrolet Caprice, Golden Wheels #14414, 1993)

FDNY Engine 58/Ladder 26 "Fire Factory"
3D Patch (resin), Code 3 Collectibles, USA, 2004

The 3D patch above was included with Code 3's Ladder 26 special 100th Anniversary release #12855— both were packaged together in a commemorative tin box

FDNY Engine 59/Ladder 30 "Harlem Zoo" (foam core, mixed media),
First Due Firehouse Replicas, USA, 2023, 1:64

FDNY Engine 59/Ladder 30 "Harlem Zoo"
First Due Firehouse Replicas #29

Release Date: February 2023

Taken from the booklet included with the firehouse replica:
Code 3 produced replicas of both New York City Fire Department Engine 59 and Ladder 30 in 2007. These units have been protecting the Harlem district of Manhattan for over 100 years and are collectively referred to as the "Harlem Zoo"—the twenty-ninth release **First Due Firehouse Replicas**.

On November 1, 1962, Engine 59 and Ladder 30 moved in to in their brand-new firehouse on located at 111 West 133rd Street, Manhattan, New York City. Their first due area is made up of old tenements, retail stores and several high-rise projects.

Engine 59 was organized on April 1, 1894, in a new firehouse at 180 West 137th Street, in the then rural area known as Harlem. Their apparatus replicated here is a 2003 Seagrave model JB 1,000 g.p.m. pumper, placed in service on March 5, 2004, and carrying FDNY registration number SP (for Seagrave Pumper) 03039. It is powered by a Detroit Diesel Series 50 engine and has a 500-gallon booster tank.

Engine 59 has been one of the busiest FDNY engines for many years. In 2006, they responded to 4,605 runs, of which 3,278 were workers. Among those, 1,484 were medical emergencies. They were the 8th busiest engine company in Manhattan and 20th for the entire city during 2006.

Ladder 30 was organized as Hook & Ladder 30 in their new quarters at 104 West 135th Street, Harlem on February 1, 1907. Their first apparatus was a new horse-drawn 1907 Seagrave, equipped with a wooden 85-foot aerial, which was pulled by three horses. The 1907 Seagrave was motorized with a Christie tractor in 1916 and remained in service until 1926, when replaced with a new 75-foot Seagrave aerial.

Their apparatus replicated here is a 2002 Seagrave 100-foot rear mount aerial powered by a Detroit Diesel Series 60 engine. It has FDNY registration number SL (for Seagrave Ladder) 02013 and entered service on August 27, 2002. The truck has several distinctive graphics added by the company.

Ladder 30 is considered one of the most decorated and hardest working ladder companies in the city. In 2006, they responded to 3,137 alarms, of which 2,495 were workers.

The members of Ladder 30 were among the emergency responders at the Collyer Mansion following the brothers' death in 1947. The Collyer brothers were hoarders, therefore, it took several hours to dig through the contents of the house to locate them. The incident became so famous that the term "Collyers' Mansion" is now used by firefighters to refer to any house that is made unsafe due to excessive hoarding.

Location: 111 W. 133rd Street, Manhattan, New York, NY

Years in Service: 1962-present

Companies Quartered:
Engine 59 (organized 1894, quartered 1962–present)
Ladder 30 (organized 1907, quartered 1962–present)
Squad 1 (organized 1955, quartered 1962-1972)
Ambulance 1 (quartered 1972-1987), redesignated as:
Mobile Medical Unit 1 (quartered 1987-1988)

Apparatus Quartered:
Engine 59 (Seagrave, Code 3 #12840, 2007)
Ladder 30 (Seagrave, Code 3 #12739, 2007)

FDNY Engine 73/Ladder 42 *"La Casa Caca"/"La Casa Elefante"*
(foam core, mixed media), First Due Firehouse Replicas, USA, 2022, 1:64

FDNY Engine 73/Ladder 42
"La Casa Caca"/"La Casa Elefante"
First Due Firehouse Replicas #15

Release Date: May 2022

Taken from the booklet included with the firehouse replica:

Code 3 produced replicas of FDNY Engine 73 in 1998 and Ladder 42 in 2001. These companies are known as "La Casa Caca" and "La Casa Elefante" in the Bronx—the fifteenth release from **First Due Firehouse Replicas**.

Engine 73's firehouse was erected in 1900 at 659 Prospect Avenue, The Bronx, New York City. For the next 13 years, this single engine company covered the Longwood section of the South Bronx. Ladder 42's firehouse was erected in 1913 directly adjacent to Engine 73's firehouse. The two buildings share a common kitchen area.

Engine 73's two-story Northern European Renaissance Revival building was designed by Horgan & Slattery, and Ladder 42's three-story Neo-Classical house was designed by Hoppin & Koen. Both buildings were landmarked by the City of New York in 2013.

Engine 73 was organized in 1900, and Ladder 42 was organized in 1913. Both companies have remained at their respective firehouses for over 100 years.

Engine 73 and Ladder 42 saw heavy action during the famous war years. In 1969 Engine 73, Ladder 42, Squad 2, and Battalion 55 responded to a mind-boggling 25,000 runs.

Due to the deteriorating conditions, both firehouses were closed from 2000-2001 for renovation. The nickname of the engine company refers to the fragrance of the basement during the pre-renovation period. The ladder company's nickname refers to the large size of many of the firefighters assigned to this company.

Location: 659 Prospect Avenue, The Bronx, New York, NY

Years in Service:
Engine 73: 1900-2000, 2001-present
Ladder 42: 1913-2000, 2001-present

Companies Quartered:
Engine 73 (organized 1900, quartered 1900–2000, 2001-present)
Ladder 42 (organized 1913, quartered 1913–2000, 2001-present)
Squad 2 (organized 1955, quartered 1955–1976)
Battalion 55 (organized 1938, quartered 1969–1988)

Apparatus Quartered:
Engine 73 (Seagrave, Code 3 #12302-0073, 1998)
Ladder 40 (Seagrave, Code 3 #12722, 2001)

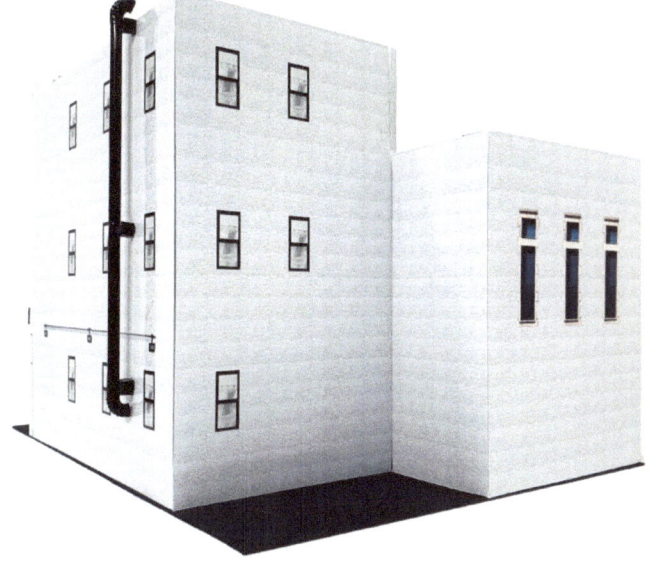

FDNY Engine 75/Ladder 33/Battalion 19
"Animal House" (Old) *Valiant Service* Edition
First Due Firehouse Replicas #6

Release Date: February 2022

Taken from the booklet included with the firehouse replica:
Code 3 produced three versions of FDNY Engine 75 (two Seagrave models and a "Valiant" Mack CF), two versions of Tower Ladder 33 (a Seagrave and a "Valiant" Mack CF), and one version of Battalion 19 (a GMC Suburban). These companies make up the *"Animal House"* in the Bronx—the fifth and sixth releases from **First Due Firehouse Replicas**. For these world-

famous companies we decided to produce replicas of both their current modern firehouse on Walton Avenue (Release #5) as well as their former historical home located under the elevated IRT Jerome Avenue Line (Release #6).

The original *"Animal House"* firehouse is located at 2285 Jerome Avenue, The Bronx, New York City. Engine 75 and Ladder 33 responded to emergencies from this firehouse for nearly 100 years until construction was completed on their new firehouse a few blocks away in 2000.

Code 3 "Valiant Service" Replicas
Code 3 released two "Valiant Service" replicas in 2010—both Mack CF models of FDNY Engine 75 and Tower Ladder 33. These special editions were painted to "depict the hard-working rigs of a bygone era," and were weathered to illustrate the difficult and demanding service these rigs endured. These were the only two "Valiant Service" Code 3 produced in this very short-lived line.

FDNY EMS Station #19

After the *"Animal House"* moved to their new firehouse in 2000, the building was renovated and became the home for FDNY EMS Station #19, "University Heights"/"Da Boogie Down Bronx." For this alternate version of our replica, the basic structure is the same, but the front facade has been updated (changes include signage, additional entry doors, lights, new apparatus bay doors, etc.).

<u>Companies Quartered</u>:
Engine 75 (organized 1901, quartered 1901–2000)
Ladder 33 (organized 1907, quartered 1907–2000)
Battalion 15 (quartered 1902-1903, 1903-1904)
Battalion 18 (quartered 1904–1909)
Battalion 19 (quartered 1930–2000)
Battalion 20 (quartered 1903)

<u>Location</u>: 2285 Jerome Avenue, The Bronx, New York, NY

<u>Years in Service</u>:
as FDNY E75/L33: 1901-2000
as EMS Station #19: 2000-present

FDNY Engine 75/Ladder 33/Battalion 19
"Animal House" (Old) Valiant Service Edition (foam core, mixed media),
First Due Firehouse Replicas, USA, 2022, 1:64

<u>Apparatus Quartered</u>:
Engine 75 (Mack CF, Code 3 Valiant Service #13036, 2010)
Ladder 33 (Mack CF, Code 3 Valiant Service #13037 2010)
Battalion 19 (Chevrolet Suburban, customized Auto World)

Ambulance 122 (Ford F-350, Code 3 #12101, 1999)
Ambulance 304 (Ford F-350, Code 3 #12106, 2000)
Ambulance (International Durastar, Greenlight #29795, 2016)
EMT (Jeep Grand Cherokee, Matchbox Premiers KB Toys Exclusive, 1990s)
EMS Division 1 (Ford Explorer, Greenlight #32100, 2016)

FDNY EMS Station 19
"University Heights"/"Da Boogie Down Bronx" (foam core, mixed media),
First Due Firehouse Replicas, USA, 2022, 1:64

FDNY Engine 75/Ladder 33/Battalion 19
"Animal House" (New)
First Due Firehouse Replicas #5

Release Date: February 2022

Taken from the booklet included with the firehouse replica:
Code 3 produced three versions of FDNY Engine 75 (two Seagrave models and a "Valiant" Mack CF), two versions of Tower Ladder 33 (a Seagrave and a "Valiant" Mack CF), and one version of Battalion 19 (a GMC Suburban). These companies make up the *"Animal House"* in the Bronx—the fifth and sixth releases from **First Due Firehouse Replicas**. For these world-famous companies we decided to produce replicas of both their current modern firehouse on Walton Avenue (Release #5) as well as their former historical home located under the elevated IRT Jerome Avenue Line (Release #6).

The current *"Animal House"* firehouse is located at 2175 Walton Avenue, The Bronx, New York City. Construction was completed in 2000, and the companies officially moved in on July 31st, 2000. This was the first new firehouse built in New York City since Rescue 1 in 1989.

<u>Location:</u> 2175 Walton Avenue, The Bronx, New York, NY

<u>Years in Service:</u> 2000-present

<u>Companies Quartered:</u>
Engine 75 (organized 1901, quartered 2000–present)
Ladder 33 (organized 1907, quartered 2000–present)
Battalion 19 (organized 1930, quartered 2000–present)

<u>Apparatus Quartered:</u>
Engine 75 (Seagrave, Code 3, J.C. Penny special release w/Engine 280 #02449, 1998)
Engine 75 (Seagrave, Code 3 #12571, 2009)
Ladder 33 (Seagrave, Code 3 #12572, 2009)
Battalion 19 (GMC Suburban, Code 3 #12403-0019, 1998)

FDNY Engine 75/Ladder 33/Battalion 19 "Animal House" (New) (foam core, mixed media), First Due Firehouse Replicas, USA, 2022, 1:64

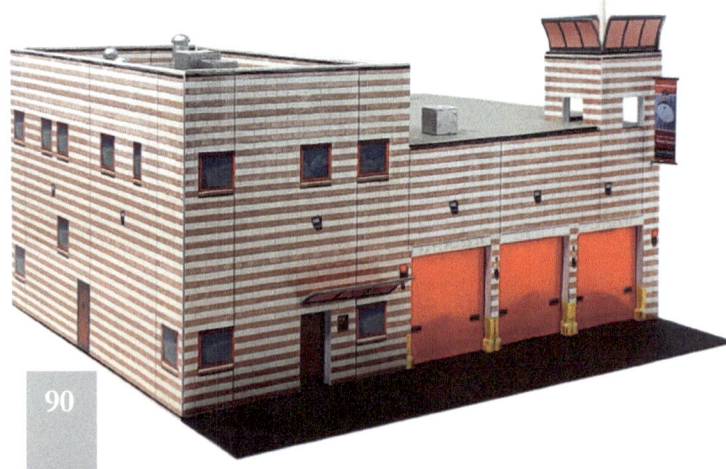

This firehouse features a cinder- and glass-block mural of Tower Ladder 33 on the side wall

Engine 75 and Ladder 33 saw heavy action during the famous war years of the 1970s. Between 1977 and 1978, these companies responded to nearly 40,000 calls making their Jerome Avenue quarters the busiest firehouse in the world. In 2008, Engine 75 led all FDNY engine companies with a total of 5,395 runs.

Engine 75 was first organized in 1901 as combination Engine Company with a horse-drawn steamer, a horse-drawn wagon, and a horse-drawn city service ladder truck. They became a regular engine company on May 15, 1907, when Hook & Ladder Company 33 was organized to take over the operation of the ladder truck.

The nickname of the firehouse refers to the famous frat house movie and seems fitting for such a busy workplace environment.

*FDNY Engine 201/Ladder 114/Battalion 40 "Emerald Isle" (foam core, mixed media),
First Due Firehouse Replicas, USA, 2022, 1:64*

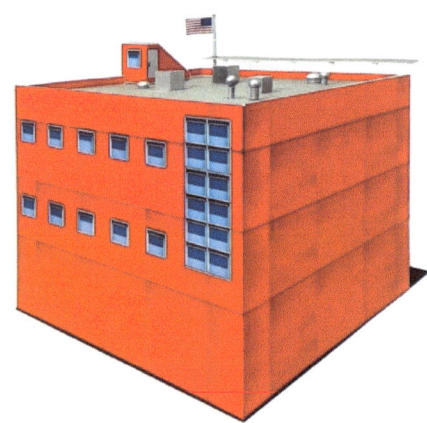

FDNY Engine 201/Ladder 114/Battalion 40
"Emerald Isle"
First Due Firehouse Replicas #10

Release Date: March 2022

Taken from the booklet included with the firehouse replica:
Code 3 produced special holiday replicas of New York City Fire Department Tower Ladder 114 in 2009 and Engine 201 in 2010. These companies are part of "Emerald Isle" in Brooklyn—the tenth release from **First Due Firehouse Replicas**.

In 2007, the New York City Department of Design and Construction worked with the FDNY and RKTB-ERM Architects to build a new firehouse on the lot of Engine 201's existing quarters. The new "Emerald Isle" firehouse was one of the first to be built under the DDC's Design Excellence Program and set the general design standards for all new firehouses.

This project consisted of a complete demolition of the existing two-story firehouse on a 25' x 100' lot and the construction of a new three-story engine, ladder, and battalion chief firehouse on a combined 50' x 100' lot. The new building has a reinforced concrete basement, and the superstructure consists of a steel framed building with concrete floor slabs over metal decking.

The most used areas of the firehouse (lounge, courtyard, kitchen, and dining facilities) are located on the ground floor. The second floor contains offices, bunkrooms, toilets and lockers, and shared storage facilities. The third floor is devoted to the private spaces of the firefighters and includes a dormitory bunk room, study facilities, and separate lockers and showers for men and women.

The importance the firehouse plays in the community is expressed through the use of symbolic elements in the design of the front facade including the use of glazed red brick and the Maltese Cross in a suspended illuminated glass lantern.

Engine Company 201 was first established as Brooklyn Engine 1 on September 15, 1869 and was quartered at 633 4th Avenue. Ladder 114 was first established as Brooklyn Ladder 18 on April 15, 1898 and was reorganized as FDNY Ladder 114 on January 1, 1913. The two companies (along with Battalion Chief 40) moved into their new shared firehouse on January 12, 2009.

Location: 5113 4th Avenue, Brooklyn, New York, NY

Years in Service: 2009-present

Companies Quartered:
Engine 201 (organized 1869, quartered 2009–present)
Ladder 114 (organized 1897, quartered 2009–present)
Battalion 40 (organized 1906, quartered 2009–present)

Apparatus Quartered:
Engine 201 (Seagrave, Code 3 #13031, 2010)
Ladder 114 (Seagrave, Code 3 #12568, 2009)
Battalion 40 (GMC Suburban, Code 3 with custom decals)

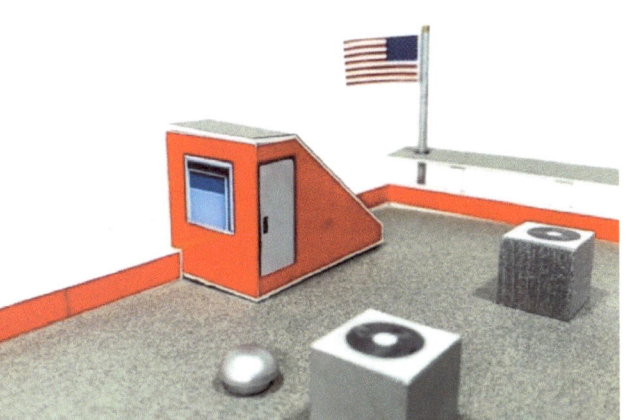

FDNY Engine 207/Ladder 110/Battalion 31/ Super Pumper System "Tillary St. Tigers" First Due Firehouse Replicas #7

Release Date: February 2022

Taken from the booklet included with the firehouse replica:
In 2005, **Code 3** produced a popular high-quality set of models representing FDNY's famous Mack Super Pumper System. The set includes the Super Pumper, Super Tender, and three Satellite units along with a wooden display shelf. For the last ten of their seventeen years in service, the Super Pumper and Super Tender were quartered in Brooklyn with Engine 207, Ladder 110, and Battalion 31, collectively known as the "Tillary Street Tigers"— the seventh release from **First Due Firehouse Replicas**.

The Tillary Street Tigers firehouse is located at 172 Tillary Street, Brooklyn, New York City, and was constructed in the 1970s specifically to house the Super Pumper and Super Tender. These units had previously been quartered with Engine 211 and Ladder 119 at 26 Hooper Street, one exit away on the Brooklyn-Queens Expressway. This area of the city was originally chosen to house the Super Pumper and Tender due to its easy access routes to heavily fire-prone areas of the city with inadequate water supplies such as lower Manhattan, the Williamsburg section of Brooklyn, and Newton Creek, Queens.

Engine Company 207 was first established as a volunteer fire company on September 15, 1869. Ladder 110 was organized on August 1, 1891 and has been quartered with Engine 207 since June 26, 1949. Battalion 31 was organized January 20, 1896, and moved in with Engine 207 on May 1, 1946.

FDNY Engine 207/Ladder 110/Battalion 31/Super Pumper System "Tillary St. Tigers" (foam core, mixed media), First Due Firehouse Replicas, USA, 2022, 1:64

The "Super Pumper" and "Super Tender" names can still be found above the apparatus bays of this firehouse

Location: 172 Tillary Street, Brooklyn, New York, NY

Years in Service: 1971-present

Companies Quartered:
Engine 207 (organized 1869, quartered 1971–present)
Ladder 110 (organized 1891, quartered 1972–present)
Battalion 31 (organized 1896, quartered 1972–present)
Super Pumper Unit (including the Super Pumper & Super Tender) (organized 1965, quartered 1972-1982)
Maxi Water Unit (quartered 1984-1998), redesignated as:
Satellite 6 (quartered 1998–present)
Satellite Officer Car 762 (quartered 1975-1977)
Division 11 (organized 1906, quartered 1990-1995, 1997–present)
Field Communications Unit (quartered 1980–1991, 1998–2003)
Mobile Operations Center (organized 2007, quartered 2007-present)
Brooklyn Borough Command (organized 1973, quartered 1973-present)
Utility Van 4 (organized 1978, quartered 1978)

Apparatus Quartered:
Engine 207 (Mack CF, customized Code 3)
Ladder 110 (Mack CF, customized Code 3)
Battalion 31 (Plymouth Belvedere, customized Greenlight)
Super Pumper (Mack F, Code 3 #16014, 2005)
Super Tender (Mack F, Code 3 #16014, 2005)
Satellite 1, 2, 3 (Mack C, Code 3 #16014, 2005)
Field Communications Unit (GMC Vandura, Greenlight #30277, 2021)

FDNY Engine 242
"The Pride of Bayridge"
First Due Firehouse Replicas Custom Release

Release Date: February 2024

Taken from the booklet included with the firehouse replica:
Engine 242 has been protecting the Bay Ridge section of Brooklyn since 1896. Our 1:50 scale model of this firehouse is a special custom release from **First Due Firehouse Replicas**.

FDNY's Engine 242 Neo-Renaissance firehouse was designed by the architectural firm of C.L. Johnson & Co. and was constructed in 1896. This firehouse originally had two apparatus bay doors with a leaded-glass transom in the center. The first companies quartered at this firehouse were Brooklyn Fire Department Engine 42 and Hook & Ladder 14.

Fire Replicas produced two versions of FDNY Engine 242 in 1:50 scale in 2020 and 2021 *(not included with firehouse)*, only 75 units of each unit were produced. To accompany these releases, four of these special custom-ordered 1:50 scale firehouses were built for current members of this company.

For information about ordering custom models of your firehouse from First Due Firehouse Replicas, please see www.ModelFireEngines.com/custom.html.

*FDNY Engine 242 "The Pride of Bayridge" (foam core, mixed media),
First Due Firehouse Replicas, USA, 2023, 1:50*

Location: 9219 5th Avenue, Brooklyn, New York, NY

Years in Service: 1896-present

Companies Quartered:
Engine 242 (organized 1896, quartered 1896–present)
Combination Engine 42 (organized 1898, quartered 1898–1914)
Ladder 14 (organized 1896, quartered 1896-1898)
Satellite 3 (organized 1965, quartered 1965-1975)
Division 12 (quartered 1975-1991)
Purple K Unit 242 (organized 1995, quartered 1995-1996)
Thawing Unit 4 (organized 1957, quartered 1965)
Recuperation and Care Unit 5 (organized 1996, quartered 1996-2013)

Apparatus Quartered:
Engine 242 (KME Severe Service Pumper,
    Fire Replicas #FR029-242, 2020, 1:50)
Engine 242 (Mack R Pumper,
    Fire Replicas #FR074-242, 2021, 1:50)

Providing station coverage for Engine 242:
Demo Fire Engine (Emergency-One Hush, Conrad #5510, 1993, 1:50)

Engineer checking the oil levels before duty in this rear-engine "Hush" pumper

Code 3 Collectibles Collectors Club Newsletter,
Vol. 8, No. 2, Second Quarter 2004

*FDNY Engine 273/Ladder 129 "The Mouse House" (foam core, mixed media),
First Due Firehouse Replicas, USA, 2023, 1:64*

FDNY Engine 273/Ladder 129 "The Mouse House"
First Due Firehouse Replicas #34

Release Date: September 2023

Taken from the booklet included with the firehouse replica:
Code 3 Collectibles produced replicas of New York City Fire Department Engine 273 in May 2004 and Ladder 129 in June 2004. These two companies are part of "The Mouse House"—the thirty-fourth release from **First Due Firehouse Replicas**.

This two-bay, two-story firehouse located at 40-18 Union Street near Roosevelt Avenue in Flushing, Queens is quarters to Engine 273 and Ladder 129, both part of the 52nd Battalion. Known as "The Mouse House," this building is similar to the firehouses of both Engine 155 and Engine 158 on Staten Island.

Engine Company 273 was originally organized as Engine Company 173 on December 1, 1908, in the former quarters of volunteer Mutual Engine 1 at 40-16 Union Street in the Flushing section of the Borough of Queens. They were re-numbered as Engine 273 on January 1, 1913.

On April 27, 1931, Engine 273 was temporarily relocated to a nearby firehouse while their former volunteer fire station was replaced with a new firehouse at the same location. The address was changed to 40-18 Union Street—they occupied the new house on February 3, 1932.

On that same date, Hook and Ladder Company 129, formerly located at nearby Engine 272, was moved to the new quarters of Engine 273 which they still share. Their first-alarm area presently consists of many large apartment houses, along with single family homes, retail stores, and shopping centers.

Engine 273 and Ladder 129 are the first due companies to Citi Field (ex-Shea Stadium)—the home of the New York Mets National League baseball team. Their apparatus both display various Mets logos.

Location: 40-18 Union Street, Flushing, Queens, New York, NY

Years in Service: 1932-present

Companies Quartered:
Engine 273 (organized 1908, quartered 1932–present)
Engine 274 (quartered 1938-1940)
Ladder 129 (organized 1908, quartered 1932–present)
Battalion 52 (quartered 1974-1976)

Apparatus Quartered:
Engine 273 (Seagrave, Code 3 #12832, 2004)
Ladder 129 (Seagrave, Code 3 #12852, 2004)

FDNY Ladder 8 *"Ghostbusters"*
First Due Firehouse Replicas #18

Release Date: June 2022

Taken from the booklet included with the firehouse replica:
Code 3 never released a model of New York City Fire Department's Ladder 8, however—this unit can be easily replicated from an existing Seagrave rear mount model. A printed sheet of unit numbers is included with the firehouse to assist in converting an existing model. Due to numerous special requests—we are happy to present our model of this beautiful world-famous firehouse made popular by its appearance in *"Ghostbusters"*—the eighteenth release from **First Due Firehouse Replicas**.

FDNY Ladder 8's firehouse is located at 14 North Moore Street at its intersection with Varick Street in the Tribeca neighborhood of Manhattan, New York City. The firehouse was built in 1903 (after the establishment of the FDNY) at the site of the formerly independent Hook and Ladder Fire Company 8. The building was designed as the first of a series of Beaux-Arts style firehouses by the city superintendent of buildings, Alexander H. Stevens. The original building (which had an identical duplicate next door) was halved in size in when Varick Street was widened in 1913.

The firehouse was selected as the base of the *Ghostbusters* for the 1984 film after an early draft of the script envisaged the ghostbusters as a public service much like the fire department. Reportedly the firehouse was chosen because writer Dan Aykroyd knew the area and liked the building. While the firehouse served as the set for exterior scenes, the interior of the *Ghostbusters* base was shot in a Los Angeles studio and in Fire Station No. 23, a decommissioned Los Angeles firehouse.

The firehouse has also appeared in the 2005 film *Hitch* and in episodes of the television series *Seinfeld* and *How I Met Your Mother*. In 2015, LEGO announced a 4,634-piece "*Ghostbusters* Firehouse Headquarters" set based on the building. Released in January 2016, it is the ninth-largest set ever made by LEGO (see page 19).

In 2011, the firehouse was threatened with closure as the city planned to close 20 fire companies. After a public campaign to save it supported by future Mayor Bill de Blasio and actor Steve Buscemi (a FDNY firefighter from 1980-1984), the firehouse remained in service. The building underwent a complete renovation between 2016 and 2018 at a cost of $6 million.

Ladder Company 8 was first established as a volunteer company on October 16, 1865 and was quartered at 153 Franklin Street. They moved to their new quarters at 14 North Moore Street on June 18th, 1905.

Location: 14 North Moore Street, Manhattan, New York, NY

Years in Service: 1905-present

Companies Quartered:
Ladder 8 (organized 1865, quartered 1905–present)
Ladder 8-2 (organized 1905, quartered 1905, 1906-1914, 1917-1918)

Apparatus Quartered:
Ladder 8 (Seagrave, customized Code 3)
Ecto-1 (Cadillac, Hot Wheels #DJF42, 2009)
Ecto-1A (Cadillac, Johnny Lightning #JLSS004-SP, 1996)

FDNY Ladder 8 "Ghostbusters" (foam core, mixed media), First Due Firehouse Replicas, USA, 2022, 1:64

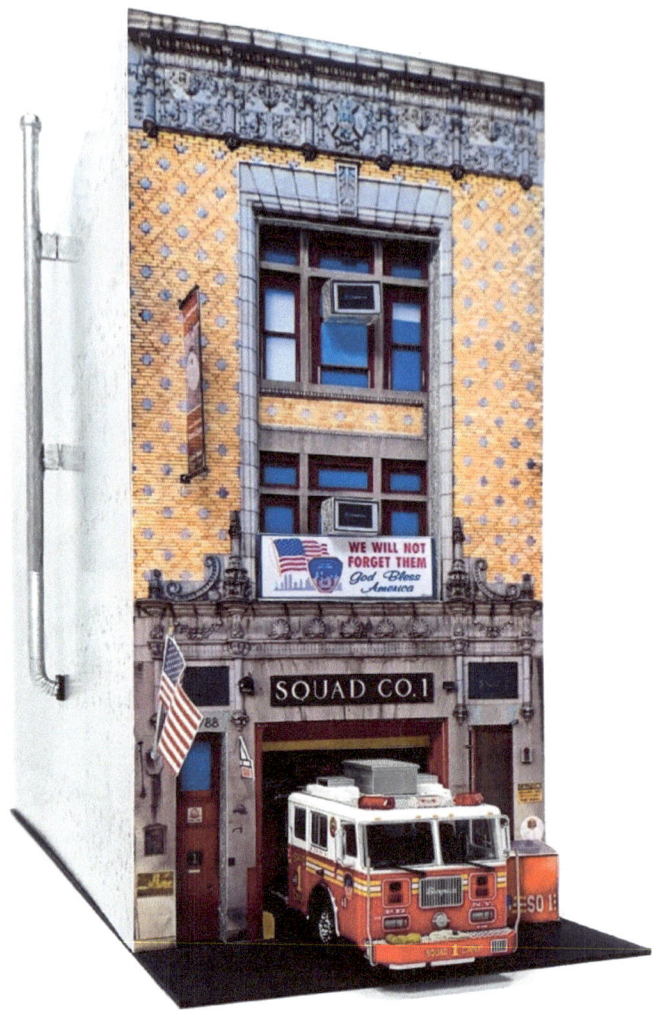

FDNY Squad 1 "The One and Only"
First Due Firehouse Replicas #3

Release Date: January 2022

Taken from the booklet included with the firehouse replica:
New York City Fire Department Squad Company 1 is one of only eight squads in the FDNY Special Operations Command (SOC), which includes rescue, hazmat, and marine units. Squad 1 responds to fires and other emergencies throughout New York City, operating primarily in Brooklyn from their firehouse in the Park Slope neighborhood. Squad 1 is the third release from **First Due Firehouse Replicas**.

Squad 1's ornate firehouse is located at 788 Union Street in Brooklyn, New York. The building was designed by the Parfitt Brothers Architects, one of Brooklyn's best and busiest architectural firms of the late 19th and early 20th centuries.

Squad 1 was reestablished in 1977 in Brooklyn at 788 Union, Street, the former quarters of Engine Company 269 which had been closed in 1975 during a budget crisis. The community placed great pressure on the city to reopen the former house and the city responded by making it the new quarters for Squad 1.

Squad 1 responds as an engine in its first, second and third due assignments, and as a Squad Company to working fires, high-angle, collapse, confined space, subway emergencies and hazardous material emergencies in Brooklyn and throughout the city as needed.

The company's "One and Only" slogan refers back to the period when Squad 1 was the only active squad in the FDNY.

Location: 788 Union Street, Brooklyn, New York, NY

Years in Service:
as Engine 269: 1908-1975
as Squad 1: 1977-present

Companies Quartered:
Engine 269 (organized 1908, quartered 1908–1975)
Squad 1 (reorganized 1977, quartered 1977–present)
Technical Response Vehicle (organized 1993, quartered 1993-1998)

Apparatus Quartered:
Squad 1 (Seagrave, Code 3 #02453, 1997)
Squad 1 (Seagrave, Code 3 #12657 from FDNY Squad Seven Piece Set, 2003)
Squad 1 Technical Response Vehicle (International/Saulsbury, customized Road Champs)
Squad 1 Second Piece (Freightliner M2, customized SpecCast)

FDNY Squad 1 "The One and Only" (foam core, mixed media), First Due Firehouse Replicas, USA, 2022, 1:64

FDNY Squad 288/HazMat 1 "Fortuna Favet Fortibus" (foam core, mixed media), First Due Firehouse Replicas, USA, 2022, 1:64

FDNY Squad 288/HazMat 1
"Fortuna Favet Fortibus"
First Due Firehouse Replicas #23

Release Date: August 2022

Taken from the booklet included with the firehouse replica:
In the early 2000s, **Code 3** produced replicas of FDNY Squad 288 (as part of a seven-piece set) along with three different units belonging to FDNY's largest company—HazMat 1. These two highly-specialized companies have been quartered together in the Maspeth neighborhood of Queens since 1984—the twenty-third release from **First Due Firehouse Replicas.**

Squad 288/HazMat 1's firehouse is located at 56-29 68th Street, Queens, New York City. The building was designed by architects Morgan & Trainer and was constructed between 1912 and 1914. Firehouse design began to change toward mechanized apparatus around 1912—this firehouse was one of the new designs. This structure is nearly identical to E287/L136 (also in Queens) and E153/L77 (on Staten Island).

Engine Company 288 was established on September 1, 1913 and was quartered in their new firehouse October 1, 1914. Engine 288 was disbanded to form Squad 288 on July 1, 1998. Squad 288 can respond as an engine, truck, or manpower unit depending on the needs of the incident commander. Squad 288's members are trained in high-angle rescue, building collapse, auto extrication, and swift-water rescue.

FDNY HazMat 1 responds to all major citywide hazardous materials incidents, building collapses, contamination-related incidents, terrorism-related disasters, and a variety of other incidents in which their services may be needed.

Like the rescue and squad companies of the FDNY, members of HazMat Company 1 are experienced and specially trained to deal with numerous hazardous situations. The HazMat company operates as a two-piece unit and is assigned two large trucks similar to the vehicles used by the rescue companies.

<u>Location:</u> 56-29 68th Street, Queens, New York, NY

<u>Years in Service:</u> 1914-present

<u>Companies Quartered:</u>
Engine 288 (organized 1913, quartered 1914–1998)
Squad 288 (organized 1998, quartered 1998–present)
HazMat 1 (organized 1984, quartered 1984-present)
Thawing Unit 5 (quartered 1973-1974)
Emergency Utility Unit 1 (quartered 1959-1960)
Foam Power Supply Unit (quartered 1959-1960)
Searchlight 4 (quartered 1966-1968)

<u>Apparatus Quartered:</u>
Squad 288 (Seagrave, Code 3 #12651 from FDNY Squad Seven Piece Set, 2003)
HazMat 1 (Mack CF, Code 3 #12370, 2002)
HazMat 1 (Saulsbury, Code 3 #12705, 2003)
HazMat 1 (Mack MR/Saulsbury, Code 3 #12555, 2007)
HazMat 1 (Dodge B-100, Greenlight #29504, 2014)
HazMat 1 (Chevrolet M1008 with Cargo Trailer, Greenlight Hitch & Tow #32190, 2020)

*FDNY Rescue 2 "The Bulldog" (New)
(foam core, mixed media), First Due Firehouse Replicas, USA, 2022, 1:64*

FDNY Rescue 2 "The Bulldog" (New)
First Due Firehouse Replicas #2

Release Date: January 2022

Taken from the booklet included with the firehouse replica:
FDNY's highly-specialized Rescue Company 2 is one of the most famous fire companies in the world. They were first organized on March 1, 1925 in the quarters of Engine Company 210 at 160 Carlton Avenue, Brooklyn, New York. On July 26, 1985, they moved to 1472 Bergen Street, formerly the quarters of Engine Company 234 and later Fire Salvage 1. Rescue 2 is the second release from **First Due Firehouse Replicas**.

After spending 34 years at the 126-year-old building on Bergen Street (see page 154), Rescue 2 moved into their brand-new firehouse on November 14, 2019. The new building is a stunning $32 million, 21,414-square-foot* state-of-the-art station which was designed chiefly with training in mind, as well as housing the apparatus and firefighters assigned to the company. The new rescue station at 1815 Sterling Place is located in the Crown Heights/Weeksville/Brownsville area of Brooklyn, about a mile from their previous quarters.

Studio Gang Architects cleverly integrated red terracotta used on the city's historic firehouses into the new station. Michaela Metcalf (director of the New York City Department of Design and Construction's Project Excellence Program) states, "They brought that forward into a contemporary rendition on the facade, with simple, understated pre-cast concrete panels, along with the elegance of terracotta in the openings on the building."

The firehouse is organized around a large interior void—a space that extends from the ground to roof level. This void enables the company to practice rescue scenarios common to the city. The structure contains a trench rescue training area, a manhole for confined space rescue, a simulation room that can simulate smoky conditions, a forty-six-foot-high training wall, a training catwalk, and a tie-back on the roof for rappelling.

The building includes a number of environmentally conscious design elements, including geothermal heating and cooling from nine wells on site, solar-heated domestic water with panels for energy to power the pumps, a dimmable LED lighting system with occupancy sensors, a centrally located 20' by 40' skylight to maximize daylight, a green roof to reduce the urban heat island effect and help mitigate storm water runoff, and an underground storm water detention tank to control runoff.

*Note: In order to keep our model of FDNY Rescue 2 at a reasonable display size, the replica includes the front half of the building, with enough room to house two 1:64 scale Code 3 heavy rescues in the apparatus bays.

<u>Location:</u> 1815 Sterling Place, Brooklyn, New York, NY

<u>Years in Service:</u> 2019-present

<u>Companies Quartered:</u>
Rescue 2 (organized 1925, quartered 2019–present)
Collapse Rescue 2 (quartered 2019–present)

<u>Apparatus Quartered:</u>
Rescue 2 (HME/Saulsbury, Code 3 #12821-0002 from Battalion 44 Box Set, 1999)
Rescue 2 (Emergency-One, Code 3 #12694, 2002)
Rescue 2 (Mack MR, Code 3 #12554, 2006)
Rescue 2 (Mack R600, Solido Toner Cam II with custom decals, 1:60)

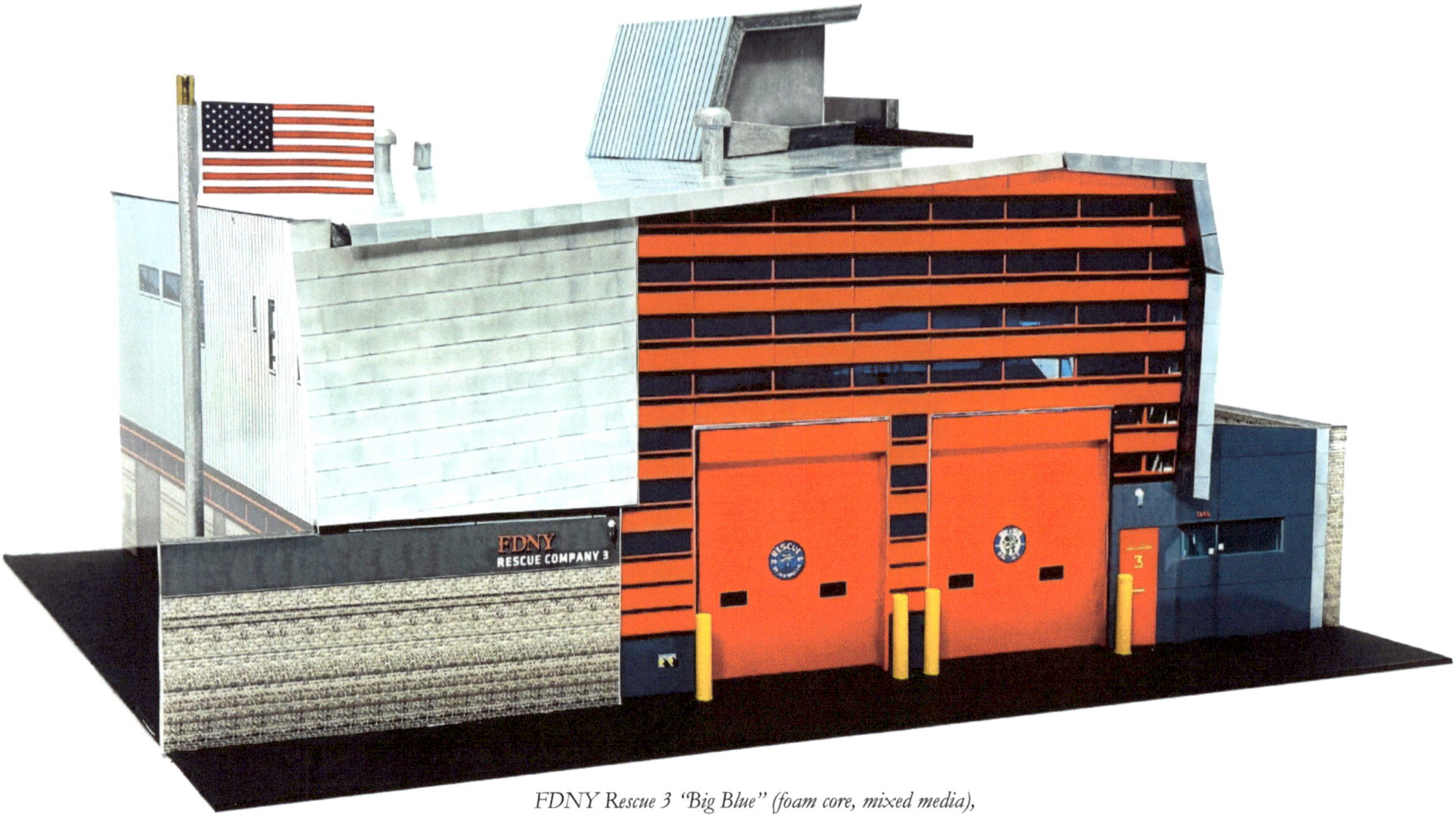

FDNY Rescue 3 "Big Blue" (foam core, mixed media),
First Due Firehouse Replicas, USA, 2023, 1:64

FDNY Rescue 3 "Big Blue"
First Due Firehouse Replicas #36

Release Date: November 2023

Taken from the booklet included with the firehouse replica:
FDNY's highly-specialized Rescue Company 3 protects the borough of the Bronx and northern Harlem. Their former quarters on 176th Street in the Bathgate section of the Bronx was located three blocks north of their current stunning Washington Avenue firehouse—the thirty-sixth release from **First Due Firehouse Replicas.**

Rescue 3's firehouse was designed by Polshek Partnership Architects and was the first FDNY firehouse designed specifically to accommodate a rescue company. The building was also one of the first firehouses to be constructed under the design excellence program of the New York City Department of Design and Construction.

The building's aluminum facade and zinc-clad roof distinguish it as a commanding and secure civic structure, while its oversized FDNY-red apparatus doors reinforce the FDNY's identity and welcoming presence in the community. The firehouse exterior consists of colorful Alpolic panels, Mapes panels, flat-lock zinc panels, a standing-seam roof, skylights, and clearstory windows.

The space is organized into "dirty" and "clean" functional spaces—the ground and basement levels contain tool storage, work areas, and the apparatus bays, the second level consists of rest and dining areas, and the mezzanine features a training and

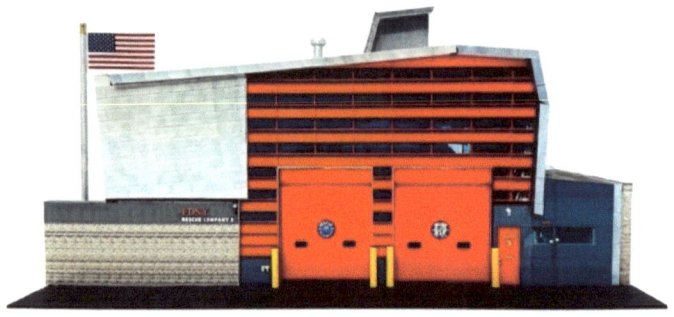

fitness space. The design for this facility captures the essence of the FDNY—toughness, strength, stalwartness, discipline, and generosity.

In its organization, the building is analogous of the company's apparatus rig—the most important piece of equipment in the house. All spaces in the building are strategically located in relation to the centrally-placed rig but are stacked to accommodate the restricted site.

Location: 1655 Washington Avenue, Bronx, New York, NY

Building Awards:
- Award for Excellence in Design, The Art Commission of the City of New York (2007)
- New York Construction, Best of the Year, Merit Award, Government/Public Buildings (2010)

Years in Service: 2009-present

Companies Quartered:
Rescue 3 (organized 1931, quartered 2009–present)
Collapse Rescue 3 (quartered 2009–present)
Recuperation and Care Unit 3 (quartered 2009–present)

Apparatus Quartered:
Rescue 3 (HME/Saulsbury, Code 3 #12701, 1998)
Rescue 3 (Emergency-One, Code 3 #12693, 2004)
Collapse Rescue 3 (Ford Cargo, Corgi Juniors cab with custom trailer)
RAC 3 (Ford E-350, Code 3 with custom decals)
RAC 3 (Ford Transit, Greenlight with custom decals)

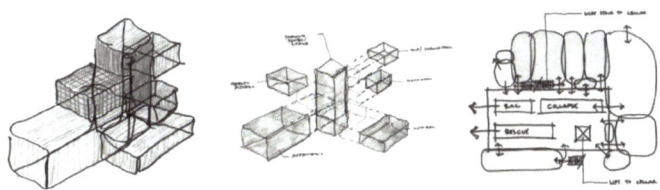

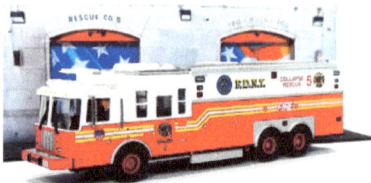

FDNY Rescue 5/Engine 160 "Blue Thunder"/"The Hillbillies"
(foam core, mixed media), First Due Firehouse Replicas, USA, 2023, 1:64

With its classical-column facade and Quonset hut garage, this firehouse proved to be one of our most challenging replicas to design and construct

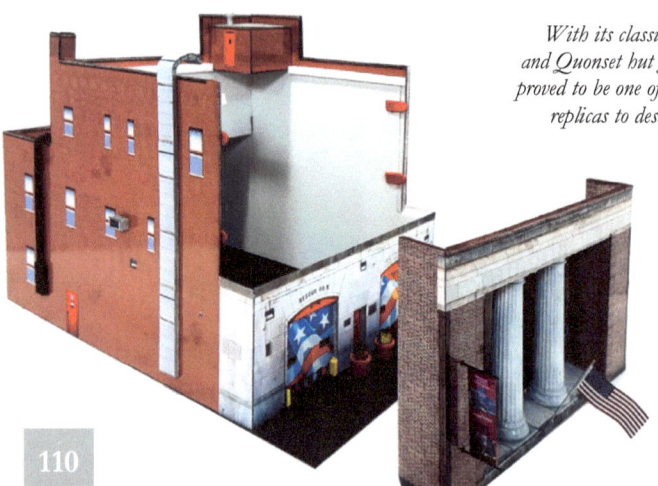
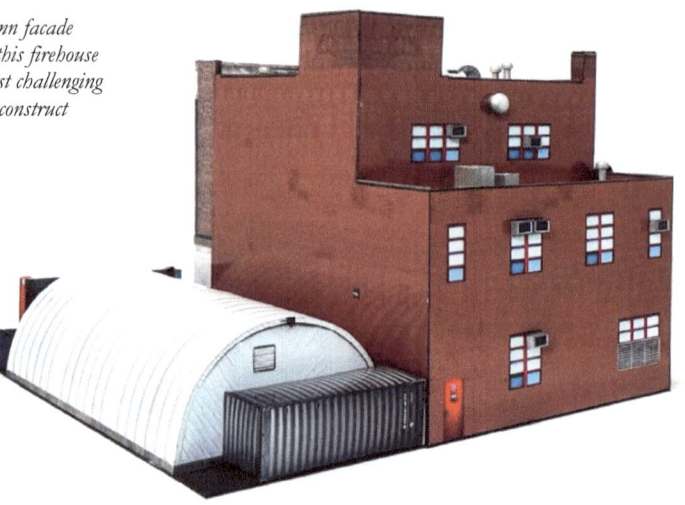

FDNY Rescue 5/Engine 160
"Blue Thunder"/"The Hillbillies"
First Due Firehouse Replicas #37

Release Date: December 2023

Taken from the booklet included with the firehouse replica:
FDNY Rescue 5 was originally organized on May 16th, 1948. They were disbanded on June 1st, 1962 and reorganized on August 20th, 1984. The firehouse they share with Engine 160, Division 8, and Tactical Support Unit 2 in the Concord section of Staten Island was designed by Macdonald & Reddy in 1915—the thirty-seventh release by **First Due Firehouse Replicas**.

This firehouse replica includes the Quonset hut garage to house auxiliary apparatus

Rescue 5, known as "Blue Thunder," responds on all 10-75's (working fires) in Staten Island and southwestern Brooklyn from their classically-designed three-story firehouse. Rescue 5 is a scuba-trained unit, several rescue boats are stored outside the firehouse.

Engine 160 was given the nickname "The Hillbillies" as they cover areas on Staten Island known as Park Hill, Grymes Hill, Emerson Hill, Todt Hill, Fox Hill, and Dongan Hills. In 2015 Engine 160 celebrated their 100th anniversary.

Tactical Support Unit 2, Collapse Rescue 5, and other units assigned to this firehouse are stored across the street in a Quonset hut garage to keep the vehicles out of the snow and elements. In 2009 designs were drawn up by the Marble Fairbanks firm for a large five double-bay garage structure to house these auxiliary units, but unfortunately the project was shelved. You can see images of their proposed designs at www.marblefairbanks.com/portfolio/engine-160/

Unrealized 2009 design for an auxiliary apparatus garage

<u>Location:</u> 1850 Clove Road, Staten Island, New York, NY

<u>Years in Service:</u> 1915-present

<u>Companies Quartered:</u>
Rescue 5 (reorganized 1984, quartered 1984-present)
Collapse Rescue 5 (quartered 2005-present)
Engine 160 (organized 1915, quartered 1915-present)
Tactical Support Unit 2 (organized 1998, quartered 1998-2000, 2001-present)
Division 8 (quartered 1930-1932, 1940-1941, 1951-1974, 1990–present)
Decontamination Unit 160 (organized 2008, quartered 2008-present)
Thawing Unit 3 (quartered 1963-1974)
Brush Fire Patrol 3 (organized 1955, quartered 1955-1956)
Foam Squirt (organized 1980, quartered 1980-1984)
Gas & Oil Unit 5/15 (organized 1955, quartered 1955-1956/1956-1962)
ATV 160 and Transport Vehicle (organized 2004, quartered 2004)
Staten Island Borough Command (quartered 1973-2005)

<u>Apparatus Quartered:</u>
Rescue 5 (HME/Saulsbury, Code 3 #12702, 1998)
Rescue 5 (Emergency-One, Code 3 #12691, 2004)
Rescue 5 (Mack R/Hammerly, Don Mills/Solido, 1980s, 1:60)
Collapse Rescue 5 (HME/Saulsbury, Code 3 with custom decals)
Engine 160 (Seagrave, Code 3 with custom decals)
Tactical Support Unit 2 w/Special Operations Trailer (International 7500, customized Greenlight)
Division 8 (GMC Suburban, Code 3 with custom decals)
Division 8 Messenger (Ford Transit, Greenlight with custom decals)
Car 160 (Mercedes-Benz 450SEL (red), Matchbox, 1979)
Car 160 (Mercedes-Benz 450SEL (white), Matchbox, 1979)
Brushfire Unit Transport 160 (Dodge Ram 3500 Ramp Truck, customized Greenlight)
Brushfire Unit Transport 160 (Chevrolet Silverado 3500HD w/gooseneck trailer, customized Greenlight)
ATV Unit 160 (customized Matchbox)
ATV Unit 160 (customized Matchbox)

Oceanic VFDNY H&L Co. No.1
Engine 1/Brush Fire Unit 1
First Due Firehouse Replicas #13

Release Date: April 2022

Location:
29 Chelsea Avenue (1881-1902)
4010 Victory Boulevard (1902-present)
Travis, Staten Island, NY

Years in Service: 1881-present

Companies Quartered:
Engine 1 (organized 1881, quartered 1881-present)
Brush Fire Unit 1

Apparatus Quartered:
Engine 1 (Mack CF, Code 3 #12373, 2002)
Engine 1 (Seagrave, customized ex-FDNY Code 3)
Brushfire Unit 1 (Dodge M37, customized Solido)

Taken from the booklet included with the firehouse replica:
For the last 140 years, whenever there has been a call for help the volunteers of Oceanic Hook & Ladder Company Number 1 have responded with speed and professionalism. To commemorate this time-honored company, **Code 3** replicated Oceanic's Mack CF pumper in 2002. Our model of this historical firehouse is the thirteenth release from **First Due Firehouse Replicas**.

Oceanic Hook and Ladder Company Number 1 is New York City's oldest active volunteer fire company. Established in 1881, Oceanic is located on the west shore of Staten Island in the community of Travis. While once the only regional fire department in the area, today Oceanic supports and augments the paid New York City Fire Department.

The firehouse was originally located on Chelsea Avenue but was moved in October of 1902 to its present location at the corner of Victory Boulevard and Burke Avenue. At the time the building only consisted of the front part of the structure that now encompasses the main apparatus bay and the second floor. The task of moving the building was accomplished by rolling it on logs using four horses with the assistance of a dozen men from the fire company. The long, low rear section and the second bay (brush truck room) were added some years later.

In the early years, the main piece of apparatus was a horse-drawn wooden ladder truck. When the alarm was sounded, local delivery men were required to report to the firehouse with their horses which were rented for a flat rate of $3 a run, whether the alarm lasted for ten minutes or ten hours.

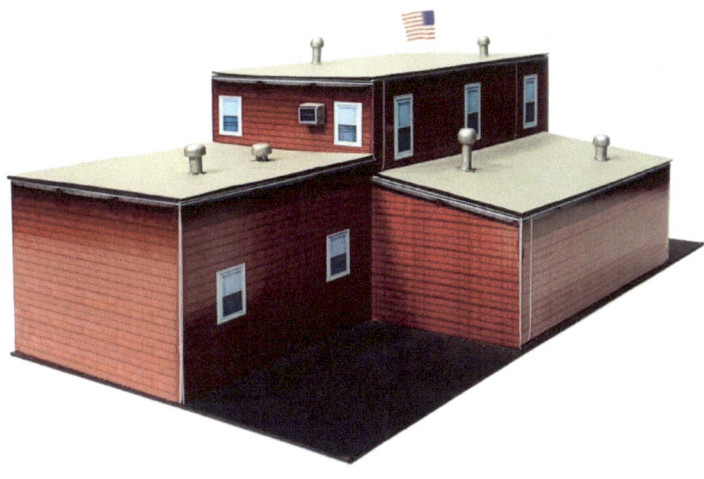

Oceanic VFDNY H&L Co. No.1 Engine 1/Brush Fire Unit 1 (foam core, mixed media), First Due Firehouse Replicas, USA, 2022, 1:64

Our replica of Oceanic's 1959 Brush Fire Unit 1 unit was created from a 1980s Solido model—yes, that's an anchor hanging on the front grill

Yonkers Engine 313/Truck 73 "Far East"
First Due Firehouse Replicas #19

Release Date: June 2022

Taken from the booklet included with the firehouse replica:
Code 3 produced a special Christmas edition of Yonkers Fire Department Engine 313 in 2008. This model is ready to parade down the streets of Yonkers as it replicates the actual Engine 313 all decked out for the holidays.

Engine 313 was designated the Santa Engine for 2008 in this inner suburb of New York City (Yonkers shares a border with The Bronx) and was used in Christmas parades and to thrill kids as it arrived to deliver special packages at a magical time of year. Carefully decorated by the members of Station 13 on Kimball Avenue in Yonkers, it faithfully conveys the goodwill of this stellar fire department.

Engine 313 and Truck 73 are part of the "Far East" in Yonkers—the nineteenth release from **First Due Firehouse Replicas**.

The Far East firehouse is located at 340 Kimball Avenue, Yonkers, New York, and was constructed in 1956. Each year, the Yonkers Fire Department responds to over 15,000 alarms. The department is an all-hazards fire department—while fighting fires remains their primary duty, the department's missions also include providing emergency medical care, controlling hazardous materials incidents, vehicle accident extrication, technical rescue, disaster preparedness and response, fire prevention, plans review, fire safety education, fire investigation, and more.

Engine 313 is a model CMU 1000, Series 60 Detroit sporting a Waterous 1,000 g.p.m. pump. This apparatus was put into service in 2002 and has a Freightliner chassis with an American LaFrance cab and body. The apparatus carries one officer and three firefighters and has four regular and two jump seats.

The Yonkers Fire Department has six ladder companies—four are Smeal 100-foot rear mount aerial ladders and two are American LaFrance/Ladder Towers Incorporated 75-foot tower ladders. In addition to typical equipment such as portable ground ladders, saws, forcible entry tools, and salvage equipment, the YFD's ladder companies are also supplied with special purpose equipment such as power extrication tools, lifting air bags, carbon monoxide detectors and high-angle rescue equipment.

Location: 340 Kimball Avenue, Yonkers, NY

Years in Service: 1956-present

Companies Quartered:
Engine 313 (organized 1956 as Engine 13,
   changed to Engine 313 in 1978, quartered 1956–present)
Truck 73 (organized 1956 as Truck 6, changed to Truck 13 in 1975,
   changed to Truck 73 in 1978, quartered 1956–present)
Foam Unit

Apparatus Quartered:
Engine 313 (American LaFrance, Code 3 #12806, 2008)

Providing station coverage for Truck 73:
Tower Ladder 71 (American LaFrance, Code 3 #12720-0026, 2002)

*Yonkers Engine 313/Truck 73 "Far East" (foam core, mixed media),
First Due Firehouse Replicas, USA, 2022, 1:64*

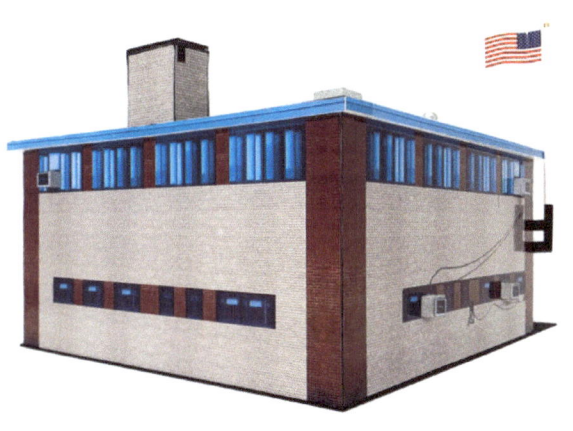

Buffalo Engine 2/Ladder 9/Battalion 56
(foam core, mixed media), First Due Firehouse Replicas, USA, 2023, 1:64

Buffalo Engine 2/Ladder 9/Battalion 56
First Due Firehouse Replicas #35

Release Date: October 2023

Taken from the booklet included with the firehouse replica:
Code 3 Collectibles produced a replica of Buffalo Fire Department Engine 38 in August 2007 (which can be converted to Engine 2), and **ERTL** released replicas of Buffalo Engine 2, Ladder 2, and Tanker 2 in 1992. Buffalo Fire Station 2 is the thirty-fifth release from **First Due Firehouse Replicas**.

Buffalo Fire Department Fire Station 2 is located at 376 Virginia Street at Elmwood Avenue in Buffalo, New York. Formerly the Painters Union Hall (c. 1972), it underwent a two-million-dollar conversion and opened as a firehouse in 1997. The Buffalo architectural firm of Stieglitz, Stieglitz & Mach added a three-truck equipment bay with brick arches, limestone collars and the hose tower to tie together the two existing brick structures and give it all the feel of an old-fashioned fire hall.

The intent of the design of the fire station was to create a new landmark for the neighborhood with a symbolic brick tower as a primary element, paying architectural tribute to the past history of firehouses. Due to its location within the historic Allentown district, the facade incorporates arched brick and limestone detailing to blend the structure with the dominantly Victorian styles of the surrounding streets.

The interior features a sky-lit lobby with custom-designed metal panels depicting silhouetted images of firefighting scenes. This station is one of Buffalo's most active firehouses, and also serves as the preferred venue for public tours.

Their previous quarters, Engine House No. 2 and Hook and Ladder No. 9 (built in 1875 and known as the "Jersey Street Firehouse"), was listed on the National Register of Historic Places in 2011. Ladder 9 was disbanded in 2004 due to budget cuts.

Buffalo Fire Department's "Ut Vivant Alii" slogan is a Latin phrase which translates to "so others may live."

Dedicated to firefighter Jason Arno who made the ultimate sacrifice battling a 3-alarm fire in downtown Buffalo in March of 2023.

In the early 1990s **Winross** (Rochester, NY) produced three Ford CL 9000/LTL tractor/trailers representing Guardian Fire Equipment, Inc. These replicas displayed the trailering of damaged fire trucks back to Emergency-One's refurbishing plant in Florida to be repaired. Each of the ERTL Buffalo Fire Department Engine 2, Ladder 2, and Tanker 2 loads were individually "altered by hand" at Guardian before being mounted by Winross.

Guardian Fire Equipment Winross Truck

Guardian Fire Equipment is a dealer for Emergency-One (E-One) Fire Apparatus and is issuing this model to acknowledge the success of E-One's Refurbishing/Recycling Center in Ocala, Florida. E-One is the world's largest manufacturer of a complete line of emergency vehicles, from ambulances all the way up to crash trucks.

The newly introduced, already expanding refurb center can handle anything from minor body work to a complete glider kit with a turn-around time unmatched in the industry.

This model is displaying the trailering of a damaged fire truck back to Florida to be redone and returned as good as new.

There are three separate "loads"; a pumper, tanker and aerial. All have been individually altered by hand at Guardian before being mounted by Winross.

The above printed information card is included in the box with each Guardian Fire Equipment Winross/ERTL release

<u>Location:</u> 376 Virginia Street, Buffalo, NY

<u>Years in Service:</u> 1997-present

<u>Companies Quartered:</u>
Engine 2 (organized 1875, quartered 1997–present)
Ladder 9 (organized 1897, quartered 1997–2004)
Battalion 56/Division Chief
Fire Marshal 10/11/12
Mobile Command Post

<u>Apparatus Quartered:</u>
Engine 2 (American LaFrance Eagle Pumper, Code 3 with custom graphics)
Engine 2 (Pierce Lance Pumper Fire Truck, ERTL #2403, 1992)
Ladder 2 (Pierce Arrow 55' Aerial Ladder Fire Truck, ERTL #2401, 1992)
Tanker 2 (Pierce Arrow Tanker Fire Truck, ERTL #2402, 1992)
Battalion 56/Division Chief (GMC Suburban, Code 3 with custom graphics)

<u>Guardian Fire Equipment:</u>
Flatbed Trailer Towing Damaged Buffalo Fire Department Engine 2 (Ford CL 9000/LTL, Winross, 1993)
Flatbed Trailer Towing Damaged Buffalo Fire Department Ladder 2 (Ford CL 9000/LTL, Winross, 1993)
Flatbed Trailer Towing Damaged Buffalo Fire Department Tanker 2 (Ford CL 9000/LTL, Winross, 1993)
Utility Truck (Kenworth T800, Winross, 1994)

Syracuse Fire Department Truck 1, Sutphen, Code 3 Collectibles #12931, 2001, 1:64

Syracuse Fire Station 1
First Due Firehouse Replicas #20

Release Date: July 2022

Taken from the booklet included with the firehouse replica:
The Syracuse Fire Department protects a 25-square-mile area with a population of 144,000 that grows significantly during daytime hours. The department provides fire protection and prevention services for four major hospitals, many downtown office buildings, Hancock International Airport, Interstates 81 and 690, as well as Syracuse University and the Carrier Dome. Currently over 350 firefighters staff the department and answer over 21,000 alarms a year of which over 1,000 are fires.

The Syracuse Fire Department holds an ISO class 1 rating. Nationally there are 241 ISO Class 1 Departments—Syracuse is one of only five in New York State with this rating. This firehouse is the twentieth release from **First Due Firehouse Replicas**.

The Syracuse Fire Department has eleven fire stations which house nine engine companies and five truck companies along with a rescue company and haz-mat unit. All addresses in the city of Syracuse are less than 2 miles away from a firehouse, this ensures an average response time of less than 4 minutes anywhere in the city.

Fire Station 1, which covers an area north to James Street, south to Dr. Martin Luther King, west to West Street, and east to Syracuse University, is part of the 3rd District and is the city's busiest fire station.

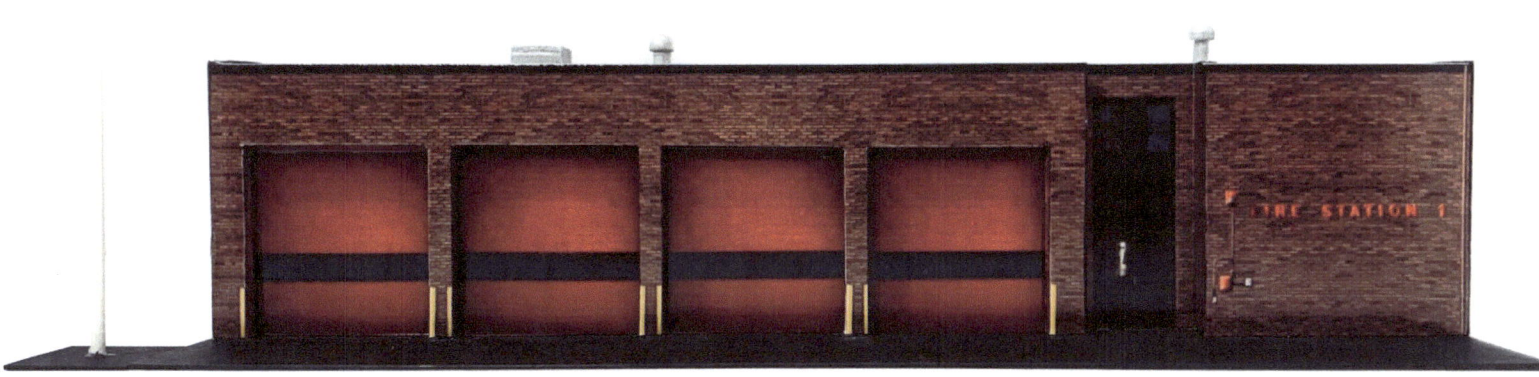

Syracuse Fire Station 1 (foam core, mixed media), First Due Firehouse Replicas, USA, 2022, 1:64

<u>Location:</u> 900 S. State Street, Syracuse, NY

<u>Years in Service:</u> 1974-present

<u>Companies Quartered:</u>
Truck 1 (organized 1874, disbanded 2011)
Squad 1 (reorganized 2011)
Engine 1
Mini 1
Ladder 1
Community Service Van

<u>Apparatus Quartered:</u>
Truck 1 (Sutphen, Code 3 #12931, 2001)
Engine 1 (Mack R600, Solido Toner Cam II #3106, 1980s, 1:60)
Engine 1 (Maxim, Don Mills/Hobbytown, 1980s, 1:60)
Mini Pumper 1 (Ford F-550, Matchbox #MB817, 2011, 1:72)
Community Service Van 1 (Volkswagen T2 Bus, Siku #1315, 1975-88, 1:60)
Scuba Rescue 1 (Hummer H1, Johnny Lighting #333-02, 2002)
Chief 1 (International Scout II, customized Johnny Lighting)
Utility 1 (Jeep Gladiator, customized Greenlight)

*West Haverstraw's three-way diaphone
replicated in 1:64 scale*

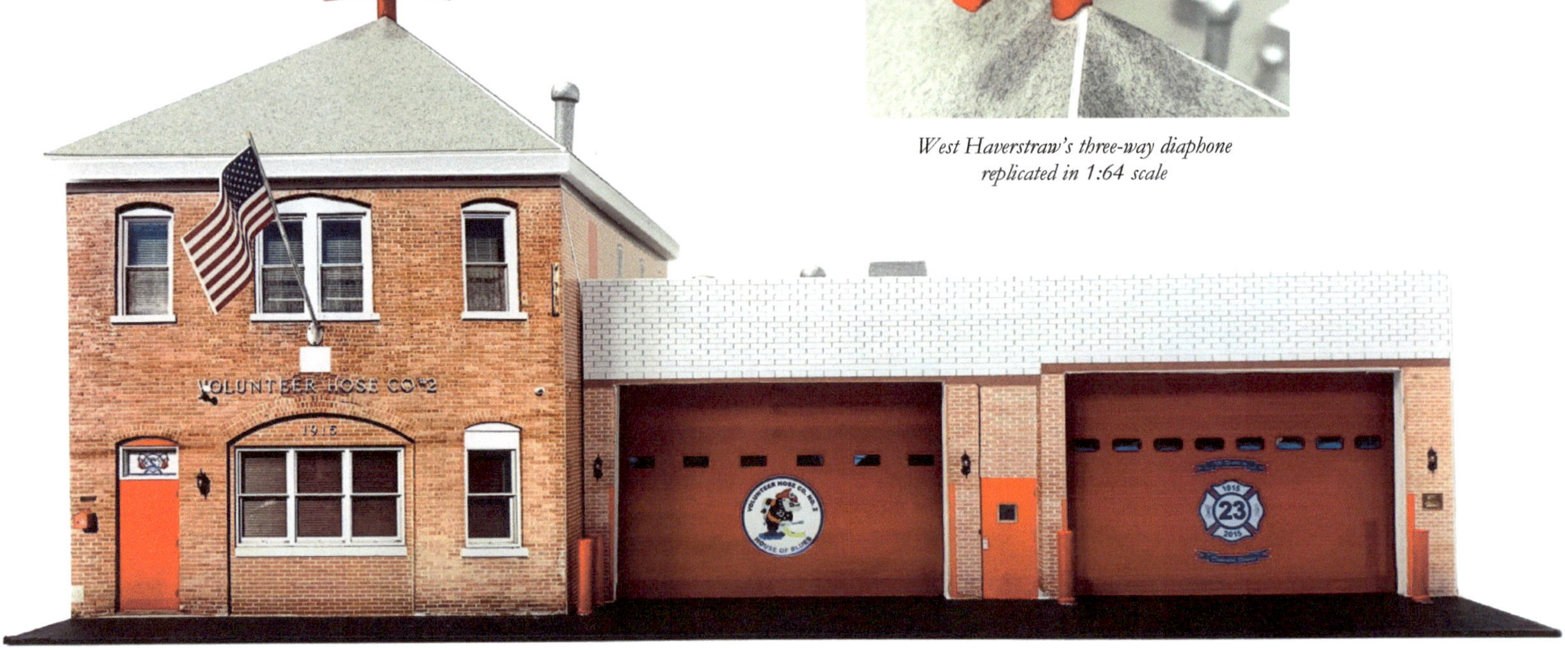

*West Haverstraw Hose Co#2 Engine 23/Rescue 23 "House of Blues"
(foam core, mixed media), First Due Firehouse Replicas, USA, 2022, 1:64*

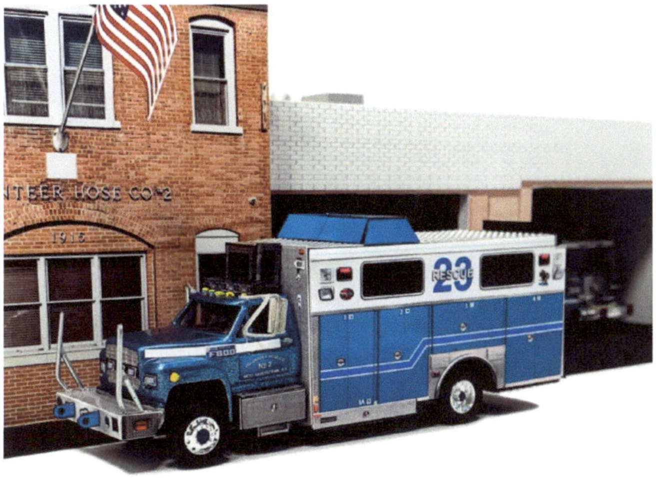

West Haverstraw Hose Co#2
Engine 23/Rescue 23 "House of Blues"
First Due Firehouse Replicas #17

Release Date: June 2022

Taken from the booklet included with the firehouse replica:
In early 1915 the Village Board of West Haverstraw, New York approved the formation of Volunteer Hose Company No. 2. Eighty-five years later, **Code 3** replicated the company's brand-new 2000 Sutphen pumper in 1:64 scale. Our replica of this historical firehouse is the seventeenth release from **First Due Firehouse Replicas**.

The newly-formed Volunteer Hose Company No. 2 purchased the former site of the Manhattan Theater on Railroad Avenue for $500, and construction of the original one-bay firehouse began in 1919. Bricks were donated for the new firehouse as a gesture of gratitude after the company extinguished a fire at a local brickyard. The members of the company performed most of the labor themselves.

Financial help was received from the Village Board with the appropriation of $8,000 toward the cost of materials and any additional hired labor. When completed, the building was turned over to the Village of West Haverstraw.

The two double-apparatus bays were added at later dates. The original building (with the bay door replaced by a window) now serves as the company's lounge which was renovated by the members for their 100th anniversary. Company No. 2 is proud of their rich history and of the job well done by the members and village officials through the years.

<u>Location:</u> 30 Railroad Avenue, West Haverstraw, NY

<u>Years in Service:</u> 1919-present

<u>Companies Quartered:</u>
Engine 23 (organized 1915, quartered 1919–present)
Engine 23-1000 (retired Mack B parade unit)
Rescue 23
Patrol 23

<u>Apparatus Quartered:</u>
Engine 23-1501 (Sutphen, Code 3 #12291, 2001)
Rescue 23 (Ford F-800/Saulsbury, custom-built by Andrew Benzie)
Rescue 23 (KME Severe Service, custom-built by Nghia Takeshi)
Patrol 23 (Ford F350, ERTL with custom decals)
Ambulance 23 (Cadillac/Miller-Meteor Ambulance, Johnny Lightning with custom decals)

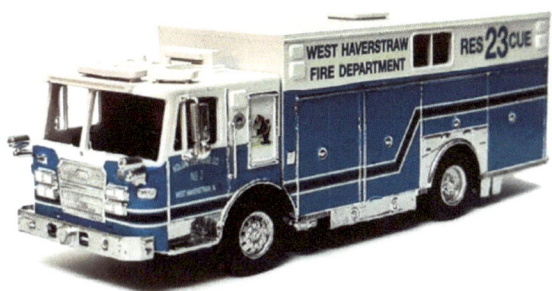

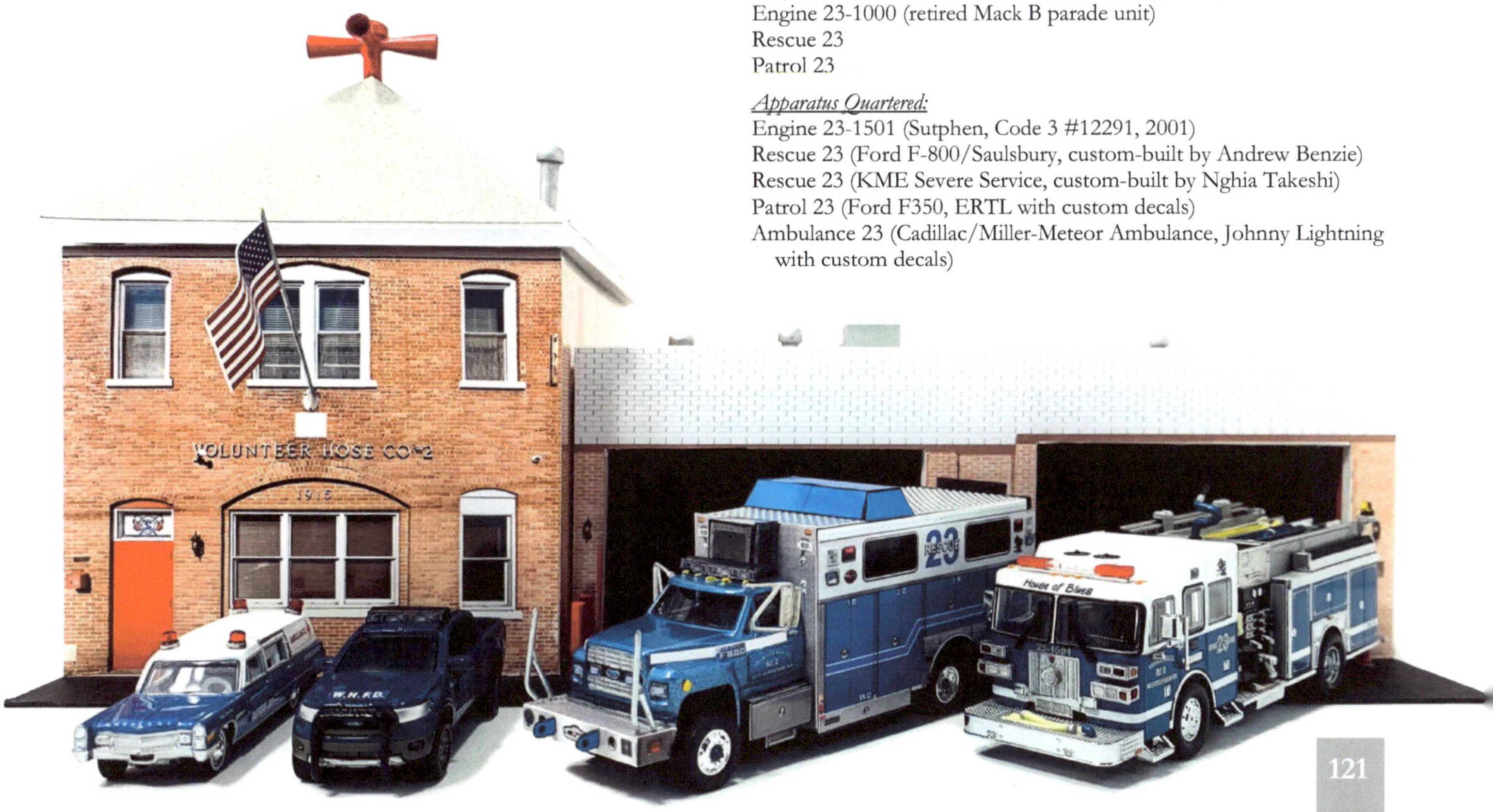

West Haverstraw's previous 1990 Ford-F800 Rescue 23 custom-built by Andrew Benzie, 2022, 1:64

West Haverstraw's current 2021 KME Severe Service Rescue 23 in the process of being custom-built by Nghia Takeshi, 2024, 1:64— final step: installation of windows

Philadelphia Engine 50/Ladder 12 "Northern Knights"
(foam core, mixed media), First Due Firehouse Replicas, USA, 2023, 1:64

Philadelphia Engine 50/Ladder 12 "Northern Knights"
First Due Firehouse Replicas #33

Release Date: June 2023

Taken from the booklet included with the firehouse replica:
During their 14 years of existence, **Code 3** produced a number of replicas representing the Philadelphia Fire Department including a series of Seagrave engines in 1997. P.F.D.'s Engine 50/Ladder 12 "Northern Knights" firehouse is one of the city's oldest and busiest—the thirty-third release from **First Due Firehouse Replicas**.

Engine 50 and Truck 12 "Northern Knights" were organized on May 6, 1901 at their new firehouse at 1325 West Cambria Street in the Glenwood district of north Philadelphia. Both companies continue to respond from their classical-style firehouse—the second-oldest firehouse in operation in the city.

On April 24, 1984, Rescue 22 moved to this firehouse from Engine 45. Battalion 8 was quartered at this firehouse from July 6, 1988 through November 23, 2019 when they relocated to Engine 59's station at 22nd & Hunting Park Avenue.

The building has been renovated several times over the years, including the removal of the third floor and mansard roof in 1950 (our replica includes a removable plastic black & white third floor facade). This structure also has a unique bonus for the firefighters—a swimming pool located in the basement.

The companies here have long been known for the heavy fire duty encountered in their first due area and have consistently been ranked as two of the busiest across the city.

This firehouse replica comes with a removable plastic black & white third floor façade

Early photo of Philadelphia Fire Department Engine 50 firehouse showing original mansard roof

In 2019 a mural was painted on the east side of the building by the Mural Arts Program to memorialize firefighter Gabriel Lee, a 17-year veteran of the P.F.D. who died in the line of duty in 2016.

A colorful mural promoting empathy and peace covers the entire west wall of this firehouse

<u>Location:</u> 1325 West Cambria Street, Philadelphia, PA

<u>Years in Service:</u> 1901-present

<u>Companies Quartered:</u>
Engine 50 (organized 1901, quartered 1901–present)
Ladder 12 (organized 1901, quartered 1901–present)
Medic 22 (quartered 1984–present)
Medic 57B
Rescue 22
Battalion 8 (quartered 1988–2019)
Safety Officer–Division 1

<u>Apparatus Quartered:</u>
Engine 50 (Seagrave, Code 3 with custom decals)
Engine 50 (International, Road Champs with custom decals)
Ladder 12 (Ladder Towers Incorporated, Code 3 with custom decals)
Telesquirt 12 (Boardman/HME, Road Champs with custom decals)
Medic 22 (Ford E-350, Code 3 with custom decals)
Medic 57B (Ford E-350, Corgi Fire Heroes with custom decals)
Rescue 1 (International, Road Champs with custom decals)
Battalion 8 (GMC Suburban, Code 3 with custom decals)
Safety Officer, Division 1 (Chevy Silverado, Greenlight with custom decals)

Boston Engine 30/Ladder 25 (foam core, mixed media),
First Due Firehouse Replicas, USA, 2023, 1:64

Boston Engine 30/Ladder 25
First Due Firehouse Replicas #28

Release Date: January 2023

Taken from the booklet included with the firehouse replica:

Code 3 produced replicas of both Boston Fire Department Engine 30 and Ladder 25 in 2007. These companies have been quartered together in the West Roxbury section of Boston for over 100 years. Their firehouse located at 1940 Centre Street (near Park Street) was built in 1898—the twenty-eighth release from **First Due Firehouse Replicas**.

Boston Fire Department Engine 30 and Ladder 25 respond to the West Roxbury, Roslindale, Jamaica Plain and Hyde Park sections of the city located about five miles southwest of downtown Boston. The neighborhoods served have a mostly suburban feel to them with tree-lined streets of single and multi-family homes. The firehouse opened on June 1, 1898 when Engine 30 relocated from a nearby firehouse on Mt. Vernon St.

Engine 30 was first put into service on July 10, 1883. Up until 1921, Engine 30's apparatus was a horse-drawn pumper. Code 3's replica of Engine 30 is a 1996 Emergency-One Cyclone II pumper with 1,250 g.p.m. pump and a 750-gallon tank.

Ladder 25 took up residence with Engine 30 in this firehouse on April 21, 1905. Ladder 25 was horse-drawn until April 24, 1917. Code 3's reproduction of Ladder 25 is a 1990 Emergency-One rear-mount 110' aerial ladder. Both units report to the District 10 chief.

Plaques are mounted on the exterior of the firehouse to commemorate firefighters who have died in the line of duty. A memorial stone and plaque are located near the front corner of the firehouse in memory of a West Roxbury native who died at the World Trade Center in New York City on 9/11/01.

Location: 1940 Centre Street, Boston, MA

Years in Service: 1898-present

Companies Quartered:
Engine 30 (organized 1883, quartered 1898–present)
Ladder 25 (organized 1905, quartered 1905–present)

Apparatus Quartered:
Engine 30 (Emergency-One Cyclone, Code 3 #12337, 2007)
Ladder 25 (Emergency-One, Code 3 #12847, 2007)
Fuel Tanker (GMC, Corgi Fire Heroes #90099, 2003)
Tow Truck (Ford F-150, Racing Champions Fire & Rescue #4, 1999)

Chicago Engine 18 "Devil Dogs"
First Due Firehouse Replicas #31

Release Date: April 2023

Taken from the booklet included with the firehouse replica:
Code 3 produced a replica of Chicago Fire Department Engine 18 in August of 2001. Several other versions of this famous engine company have also been replicated over the years. Chicago's original Engine 18 firehouse protected the residents of the Near West Side for 135 years—the thirty-first release from **First Due Firehouse Replicas**.

Chicago Fire Department Engine 18 was the first firehouse built after the Great Chicago Fire of 1871. It was constructed in 1872 and opened in 1873. Engine 18 moved into the building in 1873 and remained there until 2008.

Chicago Fire Department Engine 18

The rear area of the building housed the horses and the front was used to store the wagons. The second floor included offices and living quarters for the men—each room was equipped with a fire pole for quick access to the lower level.

In 1916 the front facade was redesigned and recessed making room for the widening of Roosevelt Road. At this time the rear of the building was also expanded, the floors were reinforced, and the overhead doors were enlarged to make room for a new era of fire trucks which would soon replace the horses and wagons. This was the only major alteration in the building's lengthy history—most of the original features remain intact.

In the 1950s, the entire surrounding city block was leveled and replaced with public housing high-rise apartments. Due to its central location, the firehouse became a community gathering place for the entire neighborhood. The building became even more popular with the city's addition of a public swimming pool behind the firehouse.

On August 2, 2008, Mayor Richard M. Daley cut the ribbon for a new Engine Company 18 firehouse located two blocks away from the old firehouse. Engine 18's new quarters is a fan favorite as it is the firehouse used to film the exterior shots of the *Chicago Fire* television series. Along with Engine 18, the units currently quartered at this new 1.5-acre, 16,000 square foot facility include Ambulance 65, District Chief 2-1-21, Deputy District Chief 2-2-1, and High-Rise Unit 6-4-16.

The old firehouse is now home to the **Firehouse Community Art Studio** (www.firehouseartstudio.com)—a gathering place to celebrate life, community, and art in Chicago's oldest firehouse. This organization provides a diverse range of art classes with a focus on pottery and ceramics for all ages and skill levels. During the renovation process great care was taken to preserve the central staircase, tin ceiling, hose-drying tower, kitchen, horse corridor, and the original telegraph stand. Throughout the building, nothing historical was removed or altered, including the same fire poles that firefighters slid down for over 135 years.

Chicago Engine 18 "Devil Dogs" (foam core, mixed media), First Due Firehouse Replicas, USA, 2023, 1:64

Location: 1123 West Roosevelt Road, Chicago, IL

Years in Service: 1873–2008

Companies Quartered:
Engine 18 (organized 1872, quartered 1873–2008)

Apparatus Quartered:
Engine 18 (Mack C, Code 3 Past Time Hobbies special release #12348, 2001)
Engine 18 (Mack CF, Corgi Classics #98484, 1994, 1:50)
Engine 18 (GMC, Corgi Fire Heroes #CS90009, 2002)
Fire Marshal, 3rd Division (Buick Riviera, Racing Champions Fire & Rescue Series #2T, 1998)

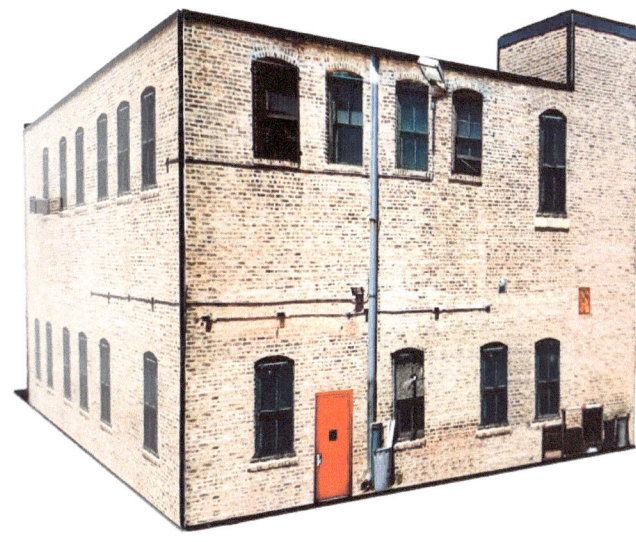
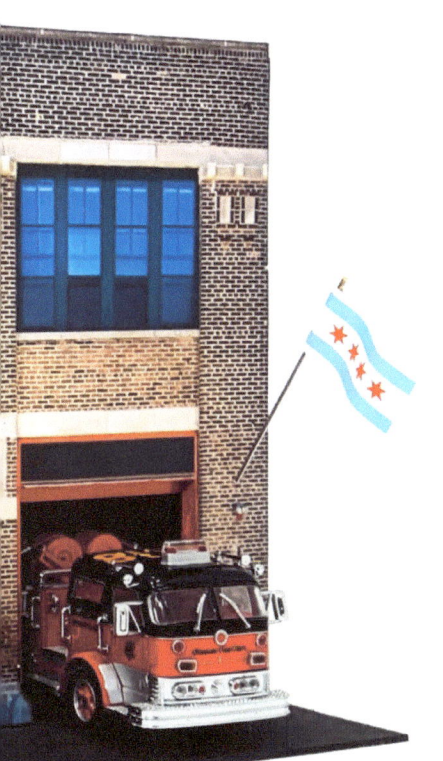

Chicago Engine 18 Mack CF (metal),
Corgi Classics #98484, England, 1994, 1:50
with
Chicago 7th Battalion Engine Co. No. 18 Figures (metal),
Corgi Heroes Under Fire #59002, England, 2006, 1:50

Chicago Fire Department Engine 42/Truck 3/Squad 1 "The Iron Ring" (foam core, mixed media), First Due Firehouse Replicas, USA, 2022, 1:64

Chicago Engine 42/Truck 3/Squad 1 "Iron Ring"
First Due Firehouse Replicas #4

Release Date: January 2022

Taken from the booklet included with the firehouse replica:
Code 3 produced an assortment of Chicago Fire Department replicas between 1997 and 2011 including a series of Luverne pumpers, HME squads, Pierce rear mount ladders, Ford ambulances, and LDV command vehicles. Engine 42, Truck 3, Squad 1 & 1A are part of "The Iron Ring"—the fourth release from **First Due Firehouse Replicas**.

Chicago Fire Department Engine 42's firehouse is located downtown at the southwest corner of Illinois and Dearborn streets in River North and has been in service since 1968. This busy firehouse is home to Engine 42, Truck 3, Ambulance 42, Squad 1 & 1A, Mobile Command Post 2-7-1, and Paramedic Field Chief 4-5-1 making for a very crowded dinner table each night. This large building has six apparatus bay doors in front and two in back and is also home to the Fire Prevention Bureau.

Engine Company 42 was established in 1887 and was first quartered at 228 West Illinois Street. This original building (along with twelve other historic Chicago firehouses) was designated as a Chicago Landmark in 2003.

In 2018, the City of Chicago approved plans for a new $20.2 million state-of-the-art replacement fire station topped by a 30-story mixed-use office building. The plan involves completing a new three-story station just west of the existing Engine Co. 42 firehouse, and then demolishing the old facility to construct the new office tower in its place. The new building will be known as *Rivere* which is a reference to a hotel that once operated nearby and is expected to open in 2024.

Artist's interpretation of the new Chicago Fire Department Engine 42 firehouse

Engine Company 42's original firehouse at 228 W. Illinois Street

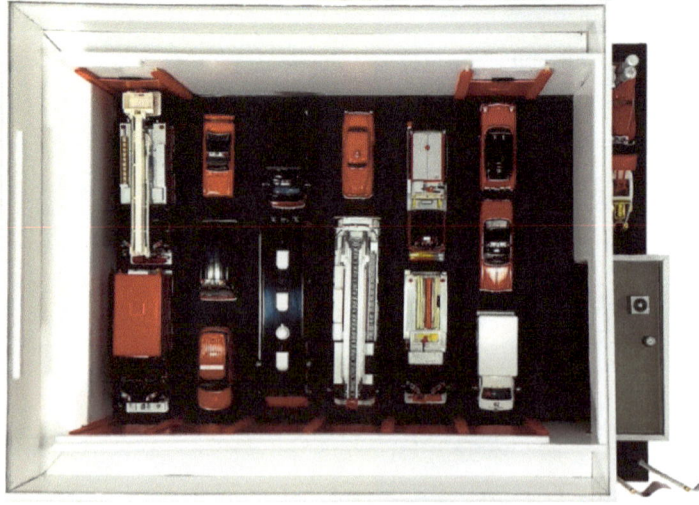

Location: 55 W Illinois Street, Chicago, IL

Years in Service: 1968–present

Companies Quartered:
Engine 42 (organized 1887, quartered 1968–present)
Truck 3 (organized 1871, quartered 1968–present)
Squad 1 & 1A (organized 1913, quartered 1982-1983, 2004–present)
Ambulance 42 (organized 1974, quartered 1974–present)
Mobile Command Post 2-7-1
Paramedic Field Chief 4-5-1

Apparatus Quartered:
Engine 42 (Luverne, Code 3 Past Time Hobbies special release #12844, 2007)
Engine 42 (Ford C8000, Hallmark with custom decals)
Truck 3 (Pierce, Code 3 #12919, 2005)
Squad 1 (HME/Central States, Code 3 #16021, 2005)
Squad 1A (HME/Central States, Code 3 #16021, 2005)
Ambulance 42 (Ford E-350, Code 3 with custom decals)
Mobile Command Post (LDV Command Vehicle, Code 3 #12532, 2005)
Paramedic Field Chief 4-5-1 (Ford Interceptor, Greenlight with custom decals)

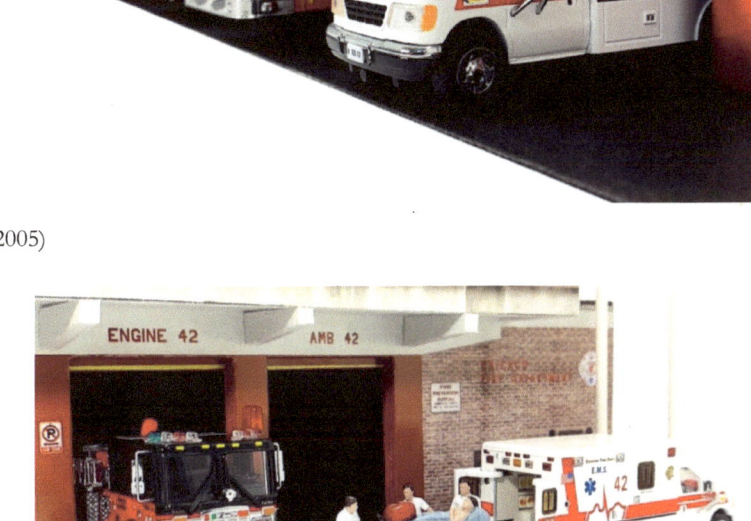

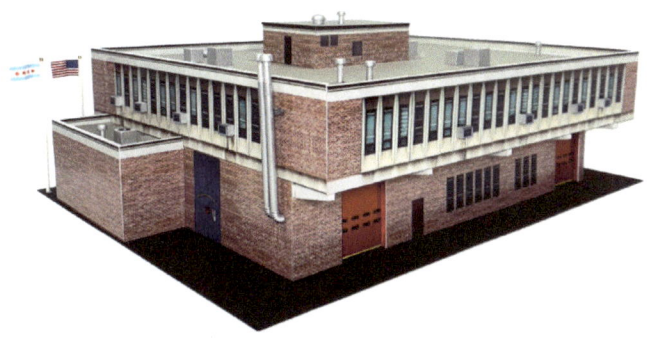

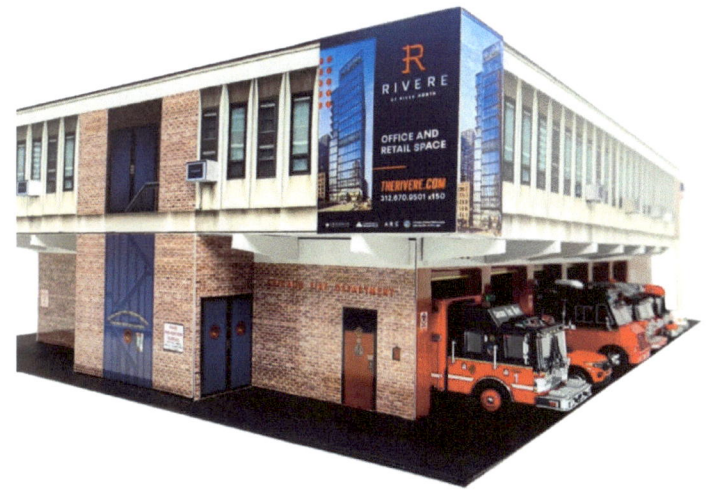

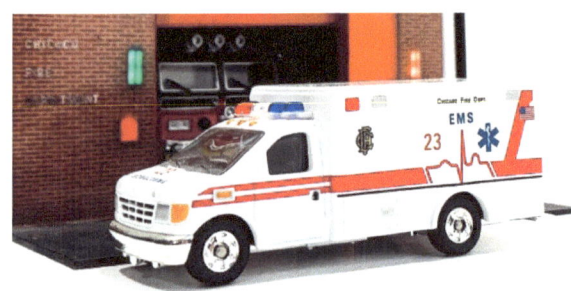

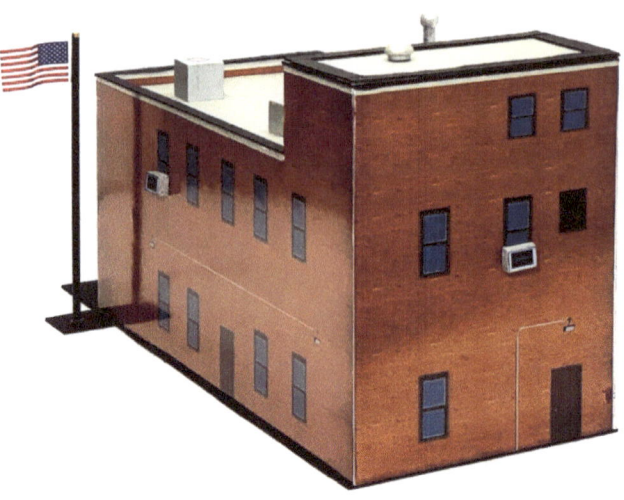

Chicago Engine 113
First Due Firehouse Replicas #14

Release Date: April 2022

Taken from the booklet included with the firehouse replica:

Code 3 produced a replica of Chicago Fire Department Engine 113 in June of 2005. This model is a twin of Engine 17 which appeared in the movie *Backdraft*. This 1970 Ward LaFrance pumper was refurbed in 1990 with a Ranger cab and Emergency-One body.

Chicago's Firehouse 113 protects the Oak Park district of Chicago located about five miles west of downtown—the fourteenth release from **First Due Firehouse Replicas**.

James Horan was appointed Fire Marshal of the Chicago Fire Department in 1906, and he immediately began to renovate. Between 1906 and 1910, Chicago constructed a large number of new firehouses, and during this period Engine 101 through 117 and truck 30 through 34 were organized.

Chicago's Engine 113 moved to their new firehouse located at 5212 West Harrison Street in 1955. This structure is the last single-engine company firehouse built in the city of Chicago. The three-story brick building has traditional C.F.D. red and green lights either side of the apparatus door.

About the Red and Green

In 1927 Albert Goodrich was appointed as Fire Commissioner. Goodrich's family owned a steamship line, so he was well aware of the required red and green lights on ships identifying their port and starboard sides, allowing for safe passing during inclement weather. At his request, red and green lights were installed on fire apparatus and stations based upon this nautical theme.

About the Black Over Red

In the late 1920s, the City of Chicago purchased 28 Model A Fords for their battalion chiefs. The roofs of the cars were composed of a tar composition that could not be painted and were left black. This color scheme has remained intact with the Chicago Fire Department for the last one hundred years.

<u>Location:</u> 5212 West Harrison Street, Chicago, IL

<u>Years in Service:</u> 1955-present

<u>Companies Quartered:</u>
Engine 113 (organized c.1906–1910, quartered 1955–present)
Rescue Ambulance 23 (organized 1963, quartered 1991–present)

<u>Apparatus Quartered:</u>
Engine 113 (Ward LaFrance, Code 3 Past Time Hobbies special release #12396, 2005)
Ambulance 23 (Ford E350, Corgi Fire Heroes with custom decals)
Fire Chief (Chevrolet Caprice, Johnny Lightning Search & Rescue Series, 2005)

Chicago Engine 113 (foam core, mixed media),
First Due Firehouse Replicas, USA, 2022, 1:64

Chicago Engine 124/Truck 38
"Hole In the Wall Gang"
First Due Firehouse Replicas #27

Release Date: December 2022

Taken from the booklet included with the firehouse replica:

Code 3 Collectibles produced a highly-detailed replica of Chicago Fire Department Engine 124 in April of 2006, and **Corgi Classics** produced a replica of its stablemate Truck 38 in 1995. To complete the 1950s-1970s era lineup for this popular firehouse among die-cast manufacturers, **Racing Champions** produced a replica of Battalion 10 in 1999. **Greenlight** produced a model of a generic Ford Club Wagon Ambulance in 2021 which can be easily numbered for Ambulance 32. A printed sheet of unit numbers is included with the firehouse to assist in converting this existing model.

Chicago Fire Department's busy Engine 124/Truck 38/Ambulance 32/Battalion 10 firehouse is located five miles north of downtown Chicago—this museum-quality replica is the twenty-seventh release from **First Due Firehouse Replicas**.

Engine 124/Truck 38's firehouse is located in the Albany Park district of Chicago—this area experienced extensive growth following the extension of the Ravenswood branch of the Elevated Line in 1907. By the 1920s the area had grown to include numerous commercial areas and apartment buildings.

The lot at 4426 North Kedzie Avenue was purchased by the City of Chicago on July 13, 1915. The first firehouse built on the property was a one-bay, two-story brick building constructed in 1916. This building was razed in 1964 to make room for a new firehouse which was built on the same site in 1965.

The new three-bay firehouse included separate apparatus bays for the engine and truck company, and a shared bay for the ambulance and battalion chief. The firehouse has a traditional red bench located in front between apparatus bays, typical of many Chicago firehouses. What appear to be two militia-era toy soldiers bravely stand guard on either side of the firehouse.

The "Hole in the Wall Gang" slogan is in reference to a hole in the wall in the basement where the foundation of the original firehouse can still be seen.

Chicago Engine 124/Truck 38 "Hole in the Wall Gang"
(foam core, mixed media), First Due Firehouse Replicas, USA, 2022, 1:64

Location: 4426 North Kedzie Avenue, Chicago, IL

Years in Service: 1965–present

Companies Quartered:
Engine 124 (organized 1916, quartered 1965–present)
Truck 38 (organized 1925, quartered 1965–present)
Ambulance 32 (organized 1970, quartered 1972–present)
Battalion 10 (organized 1885, quartered 1985–present)
Battalion 30 (quartered 1965–1982)

Apparatus Quartered:
Engine 124 (American LaFrance Century Series, Code 3 #12863, 2006)
Truck 38 (Mack B Series Tractor-Drawn Aerial Ladder Truck, Corgi Classics #52701, 1995, 1:50)
Ambulance 32 (Ford Club Wagon Ambulance, Greenlight with custom decals)
Battalion 10 (1956 Chevrolet Nomad, Racing Champions Fire Rescue USA Series #11 #94720, 1999)

Denver Engine 3
"Pride of the Points"/"Eye of the Storm"
First Due Firehouse Replicas #30

Release Date: March 2023

Taken from the booklet included with the firehouse replica:
Code 3 produced die-cast models of fire apparatus from 1997 to 2011. The first series consisted of Seagrave pumpers representing five different engine company numbers, each from various large cities including the Denver Fire Department. D.F.D.'s unique, white-painted engines also included the only "unnumbered" or "blank" release from Code 3, which can be easily numbered for Engine 3—a printed sheet of unit numbers is included with the firehouse to assist in converting this existing model.

Denver Fire Station 3 has unprecedented historical and cultural significance, and some believe this "Pride of the Points" firehouse is haunted by ghosts from the past—the thirtieth release from **First Due Firehouse Replicas**.

way intersection that gives the Five Points neighborhood its name. Thus, the house became known as the "Pride of the Points," as well as the "Eye of the Storm" due to its unwavering commitment to providing a safe and secure place in the community.

In 1893, the city allowed an all-African American company (a first for Denver), under the command of a white captain, to serve at this company. Four years later, Engine 3 became the first and only all African American company in the Denver Fire Dept. Engine 3 remained the only African American company for over 60 years until the D.F.D. was desegregated in 1958.

Due to its location, rich history, and diversity, this station is considered a favorite among the firefighters. Some house members claim the station is haunted tracing back to an entire crew that perished in a hotel fire in 1895. They describe footsteps, flickering lights, and cabinet doors that swing open and close on their own.

Denver Engine 3 "Pride of the Points"/
"Eye of the Storm" (foam core, mixed media),
First Due Firehouse Replicas, USA, 2023, 1:64

Denver Fire Department Fire Station 3 (designated an historical landmark) located at 2500 N. Washington Street has been in service since 1931, making it the oldest active house in the department. It is also the department's smallest firehouse—the fit for the apparatus is also the tightest in the city with about three inches of clearance on each mirror.

The building's design was influenced by two notable changes in firehouse architecture—smaller motorized fire engines that replaced horse-drawn equipment, and a growing desire by city planners to see public buildings that were more responsive to their architectural context. The result was this small, one-story firehouse designed by C. Francis Pillsbury in a Spanish-Bungalow style which fits seamlessly into the neighborhood. The building is D.F.D.'s only single-engine and single-bay firehouse and operates with a 4-person crew which answers nearly 4,500 calls a year.

This firehouse stands across the street from its predecessor (still in existence), the former Fire Station No. 3 at 2563 Glenarm Place. Both firehouses are located one block south from the 5-

Denver Fire Department Engine 3

<u>Location:</u> 2500 N. Washington Street, Denver, CO

<u>Years in Service:</u> 1931–present

<u>Companies Quartered:</u>
Engine 3 (organized 1882, quartered 1931–present)

<u>Apparatus Quartered:</u>
Engine 3 (Seagrave, Code 3 with custom decals)
Engine 3 (Seagrave 70th Anniversary, Corgi Fire Heroes with custom decals)
Engine (Maxim "Denver" Pumper, Matchbox #29-C, 1966-1970)
Engine (Maxim "Denver" Pumper, Hallmark Keepsake #8846, 2002)

Orlando Engine 2/Ladder 2 "The Pride of Parramore"
(foam core, mixed media), First Due Firehouse Replicas, USA, 2022, 1:64

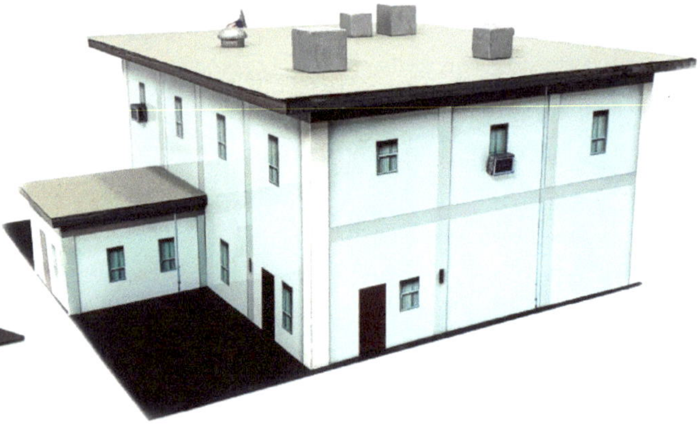

*Code 3 Collectibles Collectors Club Newsletter
Volume 4, Number 2, Second Quarter 2001*

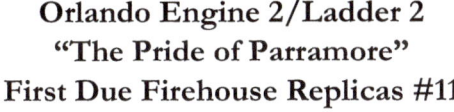

Orlando Engine 2/Ladder 2
"The Pride of Parramore"
First Due Firehouse Replicas #11

Release Date: April 2022

Taken from the booklet included with the firehouse replica:
Code 3 produced replicas of Orlando Fire Department Engine 2 and Tower Ladder 2 in July of 2001. Labeled "When Seconds Count," these units were the first models Code 3 created of Sutphen apparatus and were welcomed by collectors at the time of release.

The original Orlando Fire Station #2 (built in 1925) was replaced in 1966 by this new three bay firehouse in the Parramore district of Orlando on the corner of South Parramore Avenue and West Central Boulevard—the eleventh release from **First Due Firehouse Replicas**.

Orlando Fire Department Fire Station 2 is one of the busiest of the seventeen stations in the department. Station 2 is part of the department's 3rd district and serves several neighborhoods along Interstate 4 including Holden Heights, Spring Lake, and Lake Dot.

This fire station proudly served the city of Orlando for over 50 years. The station was a fixture to the neighborhood—local kids used to love playing basketball at the station's court.

A new state-of-the-art "Pride of Parramore" fire station opened in 2017 at 1215 West Robinson Street (about a half-mile from the previous location). Unfortunately, the old firehouse was razed to make room for the new Orlando City Stadium (now Exploria Stadium). This 25,000-seat soccer-specific stadium is home of the Orlando City Soccer Club and the National Women's Soccer League affiliate club the Orlando Pride.

<u>Location Site:</u> Corner of North Parramore Avenue and West Central Boulevard, Orlando, FL

<u>Years in Service:</u> 1966–2017

<u>Companies Quartered:</u>
Engine 2 (organized 1925, quartered 1966–2017)
Ladder 2 (organized 1925, quartered 1966–2017)
Rescue 2

<u>Apparatus Quartered:</u>
Engine 2 (Sutphen Monarch, Code 3 #12290, 2001)
Tower Ladder 2 (Sutphen, Code 3 #12930, 2001)
Rescue 2 (Ford E350, Corgi Fire Heroes with custom decals)
Fire Chief 121 (Dodge Monaco, Johnny Lightning #50258, 2006)

LAFD Engine 18 "Knollwood"
First Due Firehouse Replicas #16

Release Date: May 2022

LAFD Engine 18 "Knollwood" (foam core, mixed media), First Due Firehouse Replicas, USA, 2022, 1:64

Taken from the booklet included with the firehouse replica:
Code 3 produced their first die-cast models in April of 1997. This series consisted of five Seagrave pumpers representing Los Angeles Fire Department (LAFD) Engine Companies 18, 39, 51, 88, and 90. Code 3 also released a model of Engine 18's previous 1960s Crown Firecoach in 2000.

LAFD's historic Fire Station 18 is located less than a mile west of downtown Los Angeles—the sixteenth release from **First Due Firehouse Replicas**.

Built in 1904, this fire station was designed in the Mission-Revival style by architect John Parkinson, whose later works included Los Angeles City Hall, Union Station, and Bullocks Wilshire. In 1915, Engine House No. 18 was one of a dozen stations closed because of budget cutbacks resulting from the "two-platoon ordinance" passed by the Los Angeles City Council. The station reopened in 1920 and remained an operating fire station until 1968.

Engine Company 18 was organized on April 1, 1906 and responded from their quarters on South Hobart Street for 62 years. The company moved to their new quarters at 2050 Balboa Boulevard in Granada Hills in 1968.

Engine Company 18 under construction in 1904

LAFD Station 18 is one of the few remaining firehouses dating from the days of the horse and carriage. The building was declared an Historic-Cultural Monument by the City of Los Angeles in March 1988.

In 2011, the **Exceptional Children's Foundation** purchased Engine House No. 18 and converted the cultural landmark into a fine arts training center for adults with special needs and a community creative space for the residents of South Los Angeles.

Annually, approximately 50 participants with developmental disabilities are provided with daily fine art instruction, life skills training, and case management services at this location. The center also hosts exhibits of the participant's artwork along with creations by other community artists.

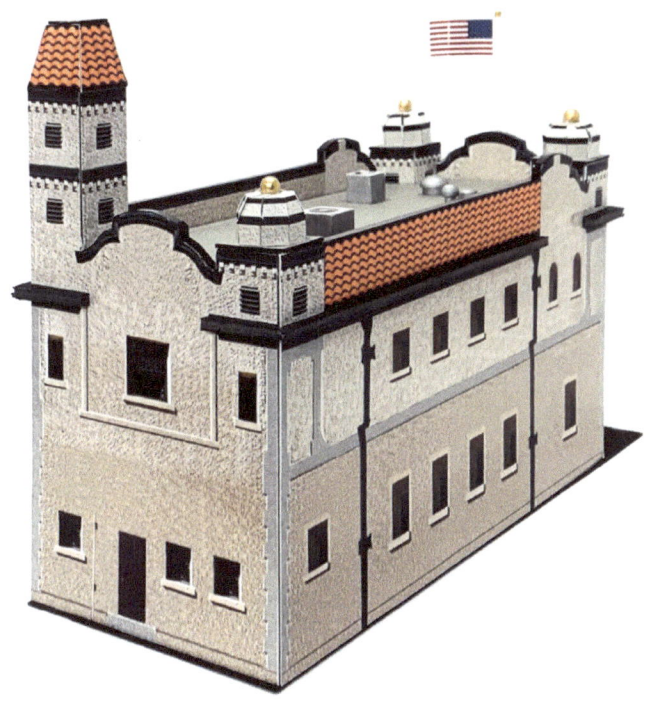

Location: 2616 South Hobart Street, Los Angeles, CA

Years in Service: 1906-1915, 1920-1968

Companies Quartered:
Engine 18 (organized 1906, quartered 1906–1915, 1920–1968)
Rescue Ambulance 18

Apparatus Quartered:
Engine 18 (Seagrave, Code 3 #02450-0018, 1997)
Engine 18 (Crown, Code 3 #12952 sold as set with Pumper 80, 2000)
Ambulance 18 (Chevrolet G20, Greenlight with custom decals)

LAFD Engine 39/Truck 39
"The Big House"/"Hub of the Valley"
First Due Firehouse Replicas #8

Release Date: February 2022

LAFD Fire Station 39, 1930s

Taken from the booklet included with the firehouse replica:

Between April 1997 and October 2000, **Code 3** released five models of units quartered at Los Angeles City Fire Department (LAFD) Fire Station 39. These included two versions of Engine 39 (Seagrave and Pierce models), Truck 39 (Ladder Towers Incorporated), Ambulance 39 (Ford), and Battalion 10 (GMC).

These units are all part of LAFD's "The Big House, Hub of the Valley"—the eighth release from **First Due Firehouse Replicas**. As this firehouse was located less than three miles from Code 3's office, it's understandable why they replicated so many units from this fire station.

Up until November of 2019, LAFD Fire Station 39, located on Sylvan Street in the city of Van Nuys, was the oldest active fire station in the department. The Neo-Classic building (originally built in 1919 and rebuilt in 1939) is located on a narrow street across from Van Nuys Civic Center which has very little room to maneuver the vehicles in and out of the station.

Unfortunately, the station could not adequately accommodate modern-sized fire apparatus and the current infrastructure needs of firefighters, so after a decade of planning, a new $19.2 million Fire Station 39 was opened in November 2019 at 14615 Oxnard Street. The beloved and missed old Sylvan Street fire station proudly served the community for 100 years. It will be used by the city for a yet undetermined purpose.

Engine Company 39 was organized in 1919 and responded from their quarters on Sylvan Street for 100 years. Truck 39 was organized in 1939 and responded from their quarters on Sylvan Street for 80 years.

Location: 14415 Sylvan Street, Van Nuys, Los Angeles, CA

Years in Service: 1919–2019

Companies Quartered:
Engine 39 (organized 1919, quartered 1919–2019)
Truck 39 (organized 1939, quartered 1939–2019)
Engine 239 (responds with Truck 39 as Lightforce 39)
Paramedic Rescue Ambulance 39
BLS Rescue Ambulance 839
Battalion 10
HazMat Squad 39 (organized 1978, quartered 1978–2001)

Apparatus Quartered:
Engine 39 (Seagrave, Code 3 #02450-0039, 1997)
Engine 39 (Pierce, Code 3 #12888, 2000)
Truck 39 (Ladder Towers Incorporated, Code 3 #12664-0039, 1999)
Ambulance 39 (Ford E350, Code 3 #12053-0039, 1999)
Battalion 10 (GMC Suburban, Code 3 #12400-0010, 1998)
Division 3 (GMC Suburban, Code 3 #12400-0003, 1998)
Fire Chief 1 (Mercury, Matchbox #59b, 1981)
Brush Patrol 109 (Hummer H1, Corgi Fire Heroes, #90236, 2003)

LAFD Engine 39/Truck 39 "The Big House"/"Hub of the Valley" (foam core, mixed media), First Due Firehouse Replicas, USA, 2022, 1:64

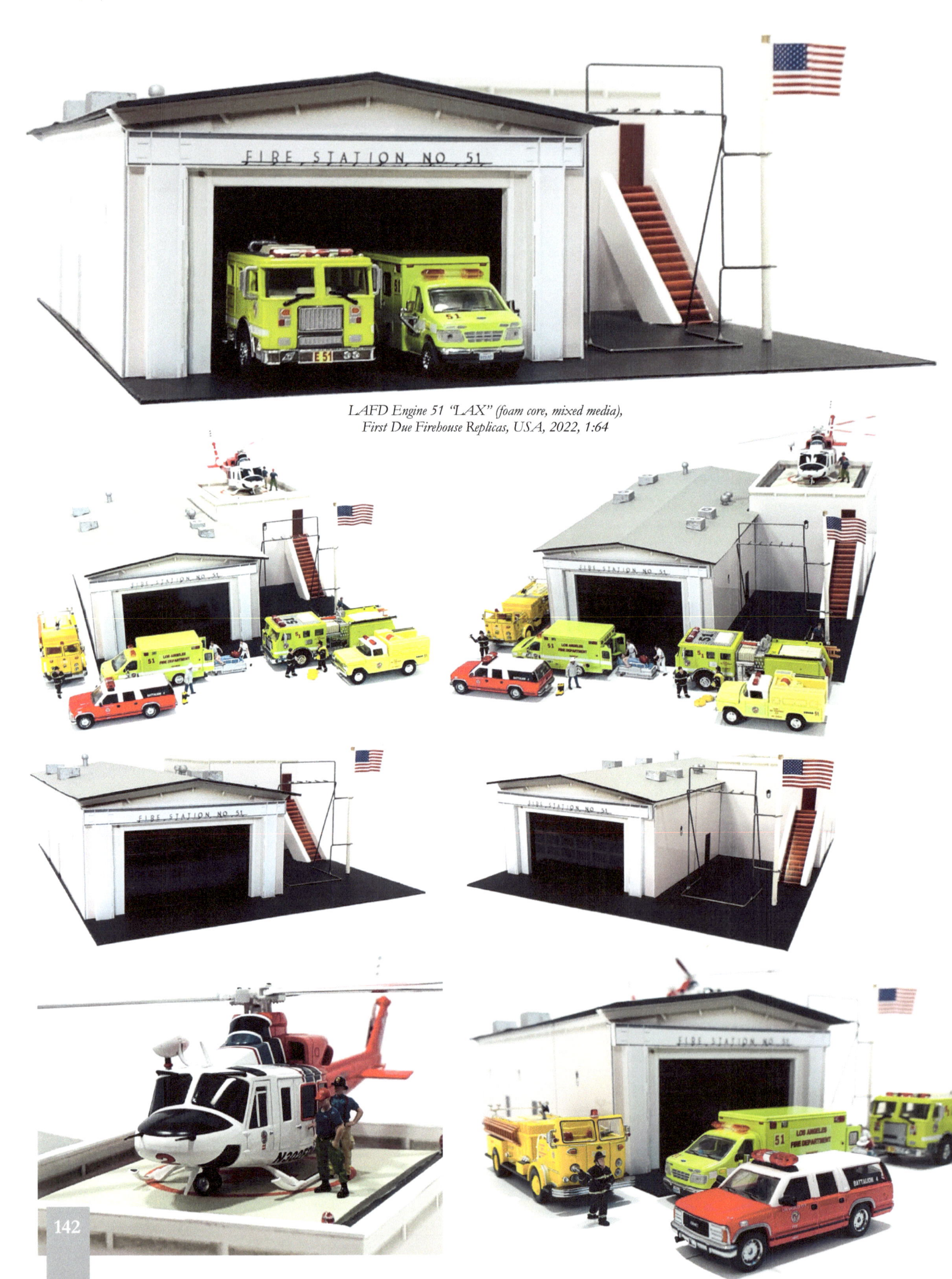

*LAFD Engine 51 "LAX" (foam core, mixed media),
First Due Firehouse Replicas, USA, 2022, 1:64*

LAFD Engine 51 "LAX"
First Due Firehouse Replicas #22

Release Date: August 2022

Taken from the booklet included with the firehouse replica:
Code 3 produced their first die-cast models in April of 1997. This series consisted of five Seagrave pumpers representing Los Angeles Fire Department (LAFD) Engine Companies 18, 39, 51, 88, and 90. The models were only sold through various retail outlets and toy stores and were an immediate hit with collectors. Lime green Engine 51 was the most sought-after model—the other four releases were all painted traditional red.

LAFD Fire Station 51 is located directly on the tarmac of Los Angeles International Airport (LAX)—the twenty-second release from **First Due Firehouse Replicas.**

Los Angeles Fire Station 80, 1956

LAFD Fire Station 51 is one of three fire stations situated on the property of Los Angeles International Airport, the others being Station 80 (ARFF) and Station 95 (engine/lightforce/hazmat/ambulance). The building was constructed in 1956 and became Fire Station 51 in 1985.

Since Station 51 and 80 are located within the fenced area of the airport, FAA requirements mandate these apparatus be painted lime green (Engine 51 is the only lime green pumper in LAFD's fleet). Station 51, 80, and 95 are all part of LAFD's West Bureau.

LAFD Engine 51 was organized in 1924. Their first firehouse was located at 817 North Steward Avenue, and they responded from this location until disbanded in 1967. The company was reorganized in 1985 at the former quarters of Engine 80 at Los Angeles International Airport.

Engine 80 was first organized in 1941. Their original firehouse was located at 5905 W. Imperial Highway. They moved into their brand-new firehouse at 10435 South Sepulveda Boulevard in 1956. Due to significant growth at the airport, a new larger Fire Station was constructed in 1985, and their previous quarters became Fire Station 51.

Location: 10435 South Sepulveda Boulevard, Los Angeles, CA

Years in Service:
as Fire Station 80: 1956-1985
as Fire Station 51: 1985-present

Companies Quartered:
Engine 51 (organized 1924, quartered 1985–present)
Engine 80 (organized 1941, quartered 1956–1968, 1979–1985)
Paramedic Rescue Ambulance 51
Cycle Team 51 & 251 (medical bicycle teams in the terminals)

Apparatus Quartered:
Engine 51 (Seagrave, Code 3 #02450-0051, 1997)
Pumper 80 (Crown, Code 3 #12951 sold as set with Engine 18, 2000)
Ambulance 51 (Ford E350, customized Code 3)
Battalion 4 (GMC Suburban, Code 3 #12400-0004, 1998)
Air Ops 2 & Helipad (Bell 412 Helicopter, Code 3 #12601, 2001)
Squad 51 (Ford F-250, Racing Champions with custom decals)

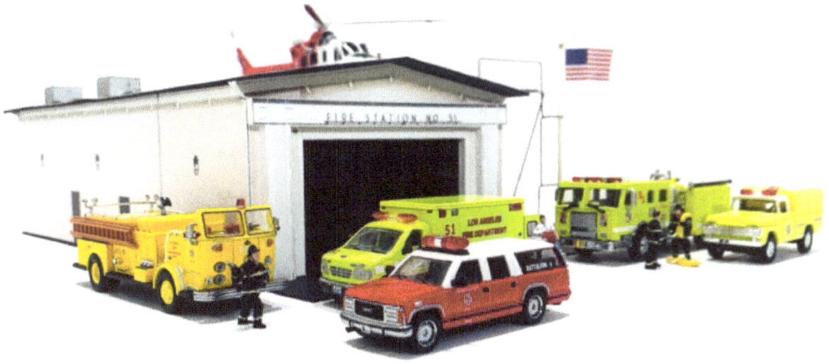

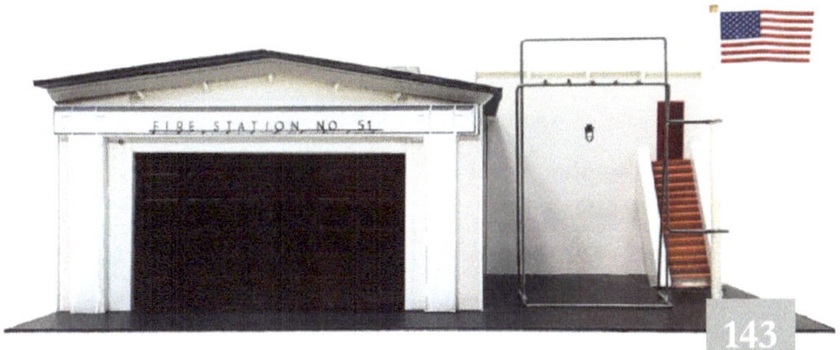

SFFD Engine 3/Truck 3
First Due Firehouse Replicas #21

Release Date: July 2022

Taken from the booklet included with the firehouse replica:
Code 3 produced a detailed replica of San Francisco Fire Department Engine 3, an American LaFrance Eagle pumper, in 2007. They also replicated an American LaFrance 900 series tiller truck for SFFD Truck 4, the same model operated by Truck 3. A printed sheet of unit numbers is included with the firehouse to assist in converting this existing model. These companies, based in the Tenderloin District, are consistently two of the busiest in the nation—the twenty-first release from **First Due Firehouse Replicas**.

Engine/Truck 3's three-story firehouse is located at 1067 Post Street and was constructed in 1974. For many years Engine 3 was in the 9,000-10,000 calls-per-year range—the advent of medical outreach teams has helped to soften the call load. The area is densely populated with many large hotels and apartment buildings, along with a large homeless population on the streets.

SFFD Engine 3/Truck 3 were once again rated the busiest companies in the United States in 2023

SFFD Engine 3/Truck 3 (foam core, mixed media), First Due Firehouse Replicas, USA, 2022, 1:64

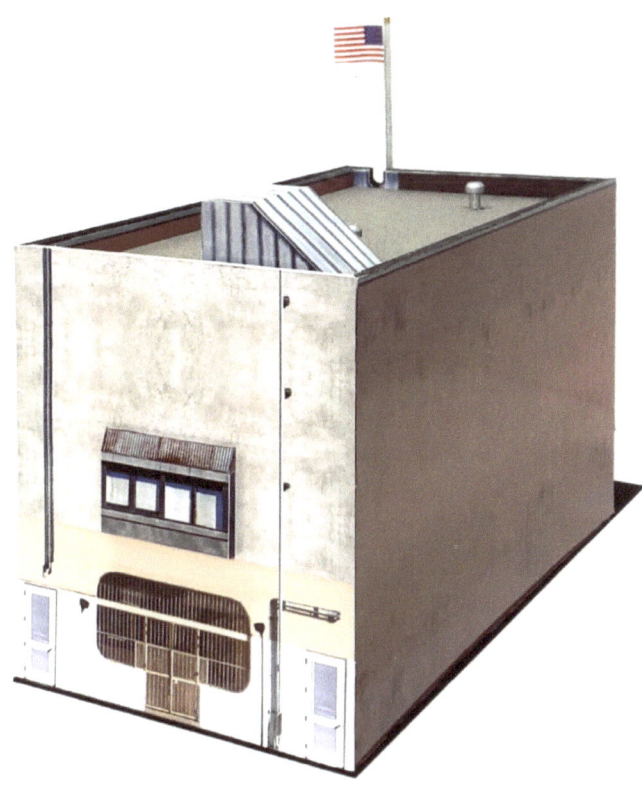

<u>Location:</u> 1067 Post Street, San Francisco, CA

<u>Years in Service:</u> 1974–present

<u>Companies Quartered:</u>
Engine 3 (organized 1866, quartered 1974–present)
Truck 3 (organized 1874, quartered 1974–present)

<u>Apparatus Quartered:</u>
Engine 3 (American LaFrance Eagle, Code 3 #12145, 2007)
Truck 3 (American LaFrance 900, Code 3 with custom decals)

Engine Company 3 was established December 3rd, 1866 and was first assigned to Sutter Street (south side) between Jones and Leavenworth Streets at the former quarters of Volunteer Engine Co. No. 7. In 1872 the company was relocated to 1632 14th Avenue South (Oakdale Avenue), the former quarters of the South San Francisco Volunteer Fire Department.

Truck 3 was established in 1874 and was originally assigned to the quarters of Hose Co. No. 5 at 1421 Market Street. Both Engine and Truck 3's quarters were destroyed in the earthquake and fire of 1906.

The San Francisco Fire Department maintains 48 engine companies, 20 truck companies, 2 rescue squads, and 3 fireboats. There are 48 fire stations, including 3 at San Francisco International Airport. Engine and Truck 3 are part of the 4th Battalion/3rd Division.

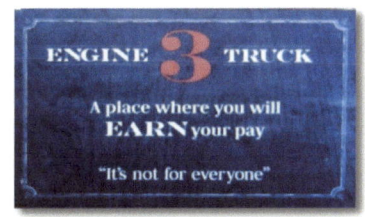

SFFD Engine 15/Truck 15
"Towering Inferno"/"Ocean's 15"
First Due Firehouse Replicas #24

Release Date: September 2022

SFFD Truck 15 appearing in The Towering Inferno movie

Taken from the booklet included with the firehouse replica:
Code 3 produced a replica of San Francisco Fire Department Truck 15 (a Seagrave tractor-drawn aerial) in October 2005 to celebrate its appearance in the famous 1974 movie *Towering Inferno*. This special release of 5,000 units included the replica along with a DVD of the award-winning movie starring Steve McQueen, Paul Newman, and Fred Astaire.

Together Engine 15 and Truck 15 (known as *"Ocean's 15"*) protect the Ingleside District of the city of San Francisco—the twenty-fourth release from **First Due Firehouse Replicas**.

San Francisco Fire Department's *"Towering Inferno/Ocean's 15"* firehouse opened in 1957 directly adjacent to San Francisco City College. As well as the college, Fire Station 15's first due area includes numerous small businesses and homes in the Ingleside and Westwood Park neighborhoods. Original inhabitant Engine Company 38 moved out in 1973, and Engine 15 moved in to join Truck 15 and Battalion 9 at this busy Ocean Avenue location. These three companies have been quartered here ever since.

<u>Location:</u> 1000 Ocean Avenue, San Francisco, CA

<u>Years in Service:</u> 1957-present

<u>Companies Quartered:</u>
Engine 15 (organized 1885, quartered 1973–present)
Truck 15 (organized 1923, quartered 1957-present)
Battalion 9 (organized 1918, quartered 1957-present)

<u>Apparatus Quartered:</u>
Engine 15 (Seagrave K-Type Pumper, Del Prado with custom decals)
Truck 15 (Seagrave, Code 3 #12967 sold with bonus DVD, 2005)
Battalion 9 (Ford Crown Victoria, Johnny Lightning #333-02, 2002)
SFFD Turbo Chief (American LaFrance Pumper, Corgi #51503, 2001, 1:50)
SFFD Turbo Chief (70th Anniversary Seagrave, Corgi Fire Heroes #90012, 2002, 1:72)
SFFD Engine Co. 1 Water Tender (1915 Ford Model T, Corgi Classics #C864-3, 1986, 1:43)

Andy Silvestri, the son of a retired firefighter, painted the historically-themed mural on the upper front facade in 1999. It features three horses pulling a steam fire engine and a firefighter carrying a ladder into a burning grocery store.

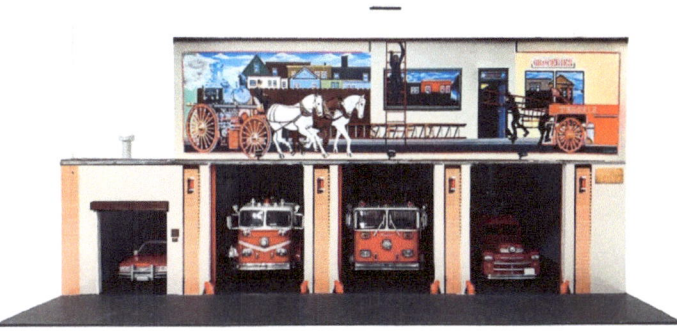

SFFD Engine 15/Truck 15 "Towering Inferno"/ "Oceans's 15"
(foam core, mixed media), First Due Firehouse Replicas, USA, 2022, 1:64

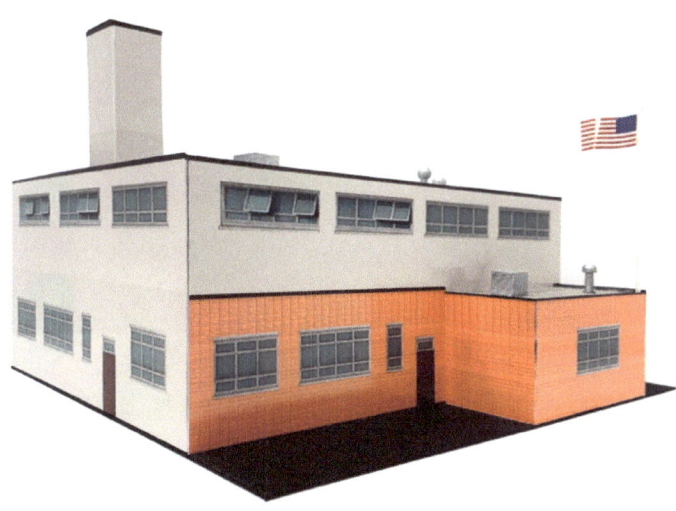

Honolulu Engine 5/Ladder 5 "Kaimuki"
(foam core, mixed media),
First Due Firehouse Replicas, USA, 2022, 1:64

Honolulu Engine 5/Ladder 5 "Kaimuki"
First Due Firehouse Replicas #25

Release Date: October 2022

Taken from the booklet included with the firehouse replica:
Code 3 produced replicas of Honolulu Fire Department Engine 5 in December 1997 and Ladder 5 in May 1998 (both Seagrave models). These companies are quartered together in the historic Kaimuki Fire Station which includes Diamond Head in its first due area. This is our first model representing the Honolulu Fire Department, and the twenty-fifth release from **First Due Firehouse Replicas**.

The Honolulu Fire Department (the 10th largest department in the United States) is unique in that all 44 fire stations are named as well as numbered. The names indicate the location on the island that each firehouse protects.

The original Kaimuki fire station is a two-story reinforced concrete structure with a stucco veneer designed by G. R. Miller in the Spanish-Mission style. The building was erected in 1924 and is still in use today. The structure includes a hipped roof of red tile and a tall hose tower which rises from the center of the rear of this box-like building.

The second story of the building has three sets of three jalousie windows. Originally these were casement, but in 1968 jalousies were installed in the majority of Oahu's operational fire stations. The only other exterior alterations involve the removal of light fixtures which once flanked the front doorways, and the removal of a round arched trellis which stood between the two doorways.

<u>Location:</u> 971 Koko Head Avenue, Kaimuki, Honolulu, HI

<u>Years in Service:</u> 1924-present *(rear addition completed in 1996)*

<u>Companies Quartered:</u>
Engine 5 (quartered 1924-present)
Ladder 5
Rapid Response Vehicle 5

<u>Apparatus Quartered:</u>
Engine 5 (Seagrave, Code 3 #02454, 1997)
Engine 5 (Crown, Code 3 with custom decals)
Ladder 5 (Seagrave, Code 3 #12660, 1998)
Rapid Response Vehicle 5 (Chevrolet, Greenlight with custom decals)
Tanker 5 (International Workstar, Greenlight with custom decals)
Fire Chief (Dodge Monaco, Greenlight with custom decals)
Waikiki Beach Patrol Lifeguard (Volkswagen Bus, Greenlight #58050, 2021)

The firehouse was completed in 1924 at a cost of $29,478. In 1992, an extensive renovation project to house a modern engine and ladder company began. The rear extension includes a long two-bay apparatus section and two dormitories with locker room facilities on the second floor. Engine Company 5 and Ladder Company 5 moved into their expanded and renovated quarters in October 1996. The project cost a total of $2,300,000.

The original station is on the National Historic Registry and has been restored to its initial condition. Located at the head of Koko Head Avenue (the major cross street in the Kaimuki district of Honolulu) with the summit of the Pu'u O Kaimukī Park volcano as a backdrop, the station presents a dramatic vista.

The Honolulu Fire Department was founded in 1851 and consists of a combination city-county department protecting the entire island of Oahu. The island is divided into five battalions which include 44 fire stations covering 604 square miles.

Original Kaimuki Fire Station

Bernard's Fire Station (Berlin, Germany) has been producing firehouse replicas and a variety of other scale buildings for over 25 years. Owner and master designer/builder Bernard Kunze creates molds to produce his highly-detailed hand-painted resin firehouses. These high-quality hard to find firehouses include removable roofs, functioning roll-up apparatus bay doors, realistic front aprons, and numerous other small details. For more information visit www.bfs-modelle.de.

FDNY Engine 231/Ladder 120 "Watkins Street" Bernard's Fire Station #21116

Taken from a Code 3 Collectibles flyer:
FDNY Engine 231 is quartered at the same firehouse as Ladder 120. This model of a traditional FDNY engine has official markings and the world-renowned Fire Department of New York paint scheme. This replica engine has a realistic weathered hose and a detailed pump panel.

This is an amazing model of FDNY Seagrave Aerialscope Ladder 120. You can see the Superman logo painted on the ladder board, as well as other strategic places on the rig. The cattle horns on the front of the truck are a tradition and are passed on to each new ladder truck. Ladder 120 is located at the same firehouse as item #12835 Seagrave Engine 231. This replica fire truck has an extending ladder, 3 sets of working stabilizers, and official FDNY logos and graphics.

<u>Location:</u> 107/109 Watkins Street, Brooklyn, New York, NY

<u>Years in Service:</u> 1905-present

<u>Companies Quartered:</u>
Engine 231 (organized 1892, quartered 1905-present)
Engine 232 (organized 1966, quartered 1966-1971)
Ladder 120 (organized 1905, quartered 1905-present)
Battalion 34 (quartered 1905-1906)
Battalion 44 (organized 1906, quartered 1906-1995, 1996-present)
Battalion 44-2 (organized 1965, quartered 1965-1969)
Battalion 58 (quartered 1969-1971)
Squad 4 (organized 1955, quartered 1955-1956)

<u>Apparatus Quartered:</u>
Engine 231 (Seagrave, Code 3 #12835, 2005)
Ladder 120 (Seagrave Aerialscope, Code 3 #12737, 2005)
Battalion 44 (GMC Suburban, Code 3 #12821 from Battalion 44 Box Set, 1999)

FDNY Engine 231/Ladder 120 "Watkins Street"
(hand-painted resin), Bernard's Fire Station, Germany, 2021, 1:64

FDNY Rescue 1 "Outstanding" (New)
Bernard's Fire Station #21105

FDNY Rescue 1 was organized on March 8, 1915 at the quarters of Engine 33 in the Bowery neighborhood of New York City. In 1973, they moved into the previous quarters of Engine 2 at 530 West 43rd Street in Hell's Kitchen where they continue to service the New York City borough of Manhattan.

Rescue 1's firehouse was destroyed in 1985 by a fire in a neighboring warehouse—the company was out on a call when building collapsed onto their quarters. The unit relocated to the quarters of Engine 34 until 1989 when construction of their present firehouse was completed. The old distinctive apparatus bay door was saved and relocated to the back of the new firehouse.

In 2002, five new rescue trucks designed by Rescue 1's captain Terry Hatton (who died on 9/11) were incorporated into the department's fleet with his characteristic exclamation "Outstanding" printed on the front of Rescue 1's truck. The subsequent 2007 Pierce had the same inscription with "T.H." added next to the motto. In 2005, the section of West 43rd Street between Tenth and Eleventh Avenues where the company's firehouse is located was named Terence S. Hatton Way.

Rescue 1 celebrated their centennial on March 8, 2015.

Location: 530 West 43rd Street, Manhattan, New York, NY

Years in Service: 1989-present

Companies Quartered:
Rescue 1 (organized 1915, quartered 1989-present)

Apparatus Quartered:
Rescue 1 (HME/Saulsbury, Code 3 #12703, 1998)
Rescue 1 (Emergency-One, Code 3 #12695, 2004)

FDNY Rescue 1 "Outstanding" (New)
(hand-painted resin), Bernard's Fire Station, Germany, 2021, 1:64

FDNY Rescue 2 "The Bulldog" (Old)
(hand-painted resin), Bernard's Fire Station, Germany, 2021, 1:64

FDNY Rescue 2 "The Bulldog" (Old)
Bernard's Fire Station #21113

Taken from a Code 3 Collectibles flyer:
Rescue Company 2 of the FDNY is certainly one of the most famous fire companies in the entire world. Since their organization on March 1, 1925, ninety-two of their members have been awarded individual medals for valor. In addition, the company itself has been given fifty-three-unit citations for acts of valor.

Rescue 2 was first organized in the quarters of Engine Company 210 at 160 Carlton Avenue, Brooklyn, NY. On October 22, 1929, they moved to the former fire department headquarters building at 365 Jay Street, which they shared with Water Tower 6.

They moved back to the quarters of Engine 210 at 160 Carlton Avenue on May 1, 1946, and remained there until July 26, 1985, when they moved to their quarters at 1472 Bergen Street, Brooklyn. They were the only occupants of that firehouse, which was formerly the quarters of Engine Company 234 and later Fire Salvage 1. After spending 34 years at the 126-year-old building on Bergen Street, Rescue 2 moved into their brand-new firehouse on November 14, 2019 (see page 106).

Rescue Company 2 is one of seventeen company-sized units in the FDNY's Special Operations Command, the others being Rescue Companies 1, 3, 4, 5, Squad Companies 1, 8, 18, 41, 61, 252, 270, 288, Marine Companies 1, 6, 9, and HazMat Company 1. In 2005, Rescue 2 responded to 3,531 alarms, of which 933 were workers.

The 1991 Mack Rescue, which carries FDNY registration number MR9101, resulted in the 19-foot Saulsbury body, originally mounted on a 1982 American LaFrance tilt-cab and chassis and carrying FDNY registration number AR8201, being removed and placed on a new 1991 Mack model MC688C tilt-cab cab and chassis. It was originally assigned to Rescue 2, with the original American LaFrance chassis, in January 1982. After receiving the new cab and chassis, it was used mainly as a spare rescue, however, it was assigned to Rescue 2 in February 1995 and served there until they received their new 1996 HME/Saulsbury rescue in April 1997. It then became a HazMat vehicle, however, did return to Rescue 2 following the destruction of the 1996 HME/Saulsbury on 9/11/01. Rescue 2 received their current apparatus, a 2002 Emergency-One/Saulsbury rescue in August 2002.

MR9101 was converted at the FDNY Shops in 2004 to be a Collapse Rescue Unit, first as Collapse Rescue 2, then Collapse Rescue 1, and later as Collapse Rescue 5. The equipment carried by the five Collapse Rescues (one per borough and a part of Special Operations Command), are normally operated by the members of the five Rescue Companies.

Location: 1472 Bergen Street, Brooklyn, New York, NY

Years in Service:
as Engine 234: 1893-1979
as Salvage 1: 1979-1985
as Rescue 2: 1985-2019

Companies Quartered:
Engine 234 (organized 1893, quartered 1893-1979)
Salvage 1 (organized 1972, quartered 1979-1985)
Rescue 2 (organized 1925, quartered 1985–2019)
Battalion 38 (quartered 1948-1977)

Apparatus Quartered:
Rescue 2 (HME/Saulsbury, Code 3 #12821-0002 from Battalion 44 Box Set, 1999)
Rescue 2 (Emergency-One, Code 3 #12694, 2002)
Rescue 2 (Mack MR, Code 3 #12554, 2006)
Rescue 2 (Mack R600, Solido Toner Cam II with custom decals, 1:60)

Twin Whistle Sign & Kit Company (Arden, North Carolina) has manufactured products for hobbyists, collectors, and model railroaders since 1992. Owner/designer/builder Allen Goethe has created an impressive selection of firehouses and fire accessories in numerous scales. Check out their full line of models at www.twinwhistle.com.

FDNY Squad 18 "South of the Park"
Twin Whistle Sign & Kit Company

Taken from Code 3 promotional material:
Squad 18 was organized on July 1, 1998 at 132 West 10th Street in lower Manhattan, and replaced Engine 18 that was disbanded that day. Engine 18 was originally organized on September 14, 1865 and replaced volunteer Guardian Engine 29. In 2002, they responded to 2,612 alarms of which 1,804 were working fires.

Location: 132 W 10th Street, Manhattan, New York, NY

Years in Service: 1891-present

Companies Quartered:
Engine 18 (organized 1865, quartered 1891-1998)
Squad 18 (organized 1998, quartered 1998-present)
HazMat Tender 18 (organized 1998, quartered 1998-2001, 2002-present)
Boat Tender 4 (organized 1901, quartered 1901)
Mobile Education Unit (quartered 1970-1971)

Apparatus Quartered:
Squad 18 (Seagrave, Code 3 #12656, 2003)

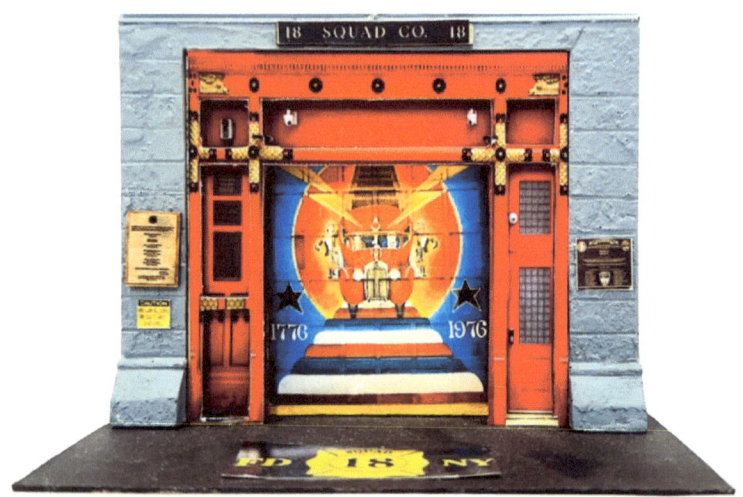

FDNY Squad 18 "South of the Park" (laser cut basswood), Twin Whistle Sign & Kit Company, USA, 2021, 1:64

*Other **Twin Whistle** Firehouse Releases:*

FDNY Engine 5 "14th Street Express," 1:64
FDNY Engine 249 "Camp Rogers Rats," 1:64
FDNY Engine 286/L135 "Myrtles Turtles," 1:64

FDNY Squad 61/Battalion 20
"Taking in a Job Near You"
Twin Whistle Sign & Kit Company

Taken from Code 3 promotional material:
Formerly known as Engine 61, Squad 61 became a squad company on July 1, 1998, at 1518 Williamsbridge Road in the northeastern section of the Bronx. The original Engine 61 was organized on February 1, 1896 in the quarters of Engine 1 of the Williamsbridge Volunteer Fire Department. The chiefs of the 20th battalion are also located in these quarters. They responded to 2,646 alarms in 2002, of which, 1,749 were working fires.

Differing in design and appearance from previous Seagrave pumpers of recent years, Squad 61's Commander II has a slightly longer and roomier cab configuration and has an enhanced HVAC system. It is equipped with a Detroit Diesel Series 60 engine, a Waterous 1,000 g.p.m. pump, and a 500-gallon water tank. After delivery, the apparatus was retrofitted with several large metal boxes over the cab and sides to carry the additional equipment used by a squad. This work was done by the FDNY **Fleet Services Division**, who also retrofitted the apparatus with different style warning lights.

The most unusual features of this particular apparatus are the large patriotic murals painted on the cabinet areas on both sides of the vehicle. This was a donation from Seagrave—this is one of only a few FDNY units to have this distinctive look. It differs from the murals on the side of the 2001 Seagrave rear mount Ladder 10.

Location: 1518 Williams Bridge Road, The Bronx, New York, NY
Years in Service: 1929-present
Companies Quartered:
Engine 61 (organized 1896, quartered 1929-1998)
Squad 61 (organized 1998, quartered 1998-present)
Battalion 20 (organized 1903, quartered 1930-2003, 2004-2012, 2012-2016)

Apparatus Quartered:
Squad 61 (Seagrave, Code 3 #12654, 2003)
Squad 61 (Seagrave "Tribute to 9/11," Code 3 #121814, 2008)
Battalion 20 (GMC Suburban, Code 3 with custom decals)

FDNY Squad 61/Battalion 20
"Taking in a Job Near You"
(laser cut basswood),
Twin Whistle Sign & Kit Company,
USA, 2021, 1:64

*Other **Twin Whistle** Firehouse Releases:*
FDNY Squad 252 "In Squad We Trust," 1:64
FDNY Squad 288/HazMat 1 "Fortuna Favet Fortibus, 1:64
FDNY Rescue 1 "Outstanding" (Old), 1:64

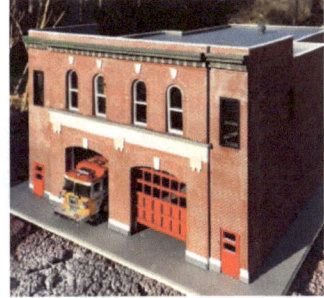

FDNY Rescue 4/Engine 292
"Winfield Cougars"
Twin Whistle Sign & Kit Company

Location: 64-18 Queens Boulevard, Queens, New York, NY

Years in Service: 1914-present

Companies Quartered:
Rescue 4 (organized 1931, quartered 1931-present)
Engine 287-2 (quartered 1914-1918)
Engine 292 (organized 1918, quartered 1918-present)
Bridge Chemical Unit (quartered 1944-1950)
Foam Apparatus Unit 81 (organized 1965, quartered 1965-1972)
Hazardous Materials Unit (organized 1965, quartered 1982-1984)

Apparatus Quartered:
Rescue 4 (HME/Saulsbury, Code 3 #12707, 2000)
Rescue 4 (Emergency-One, Code 3 #12692, 2004)
Engine 292 (Seagrave, Code 3 #12302-0292, 1998)

Taken from Code 3 promotional material:

The firehouse which is quarters to Rescue 4 and Engine 292 is located at 64-18 Queens Boulevard in the Winfield section of Queens. The Neo-Georgian design was the work of architects Dennison, Hirons & Darbyshire. Construction took place from November 12, 1913 through October 29, 1914.

Rescue 4 has Popeye in their logo and Engine 292 is known as the "Winfield Cougars."

FDNY Rescue 4/Engine 292 "Winfield Cougars" (laser cut basswood), Twin Whistle Sign & Kit Company, USA, 2021, 1:64

*Other **Twin Whistle** Releases:*

Hose Tower Kit, 1:64
New Jersey Fire Tower, 1:64

While in production, **Swiss Dog Studios** created numerous firehouses, skyscrapers, and other buildings from 2017 to 2022. Their replicas were available as pre-built models or in kit form in numerous scales and were constructed of laser-cut basswood.

Chicago-Style Four-Bay Firehouse
Swiss Dog Studios

Swiss Dog Studios (Woodstock, Illinois) created this 1:64 scale **Chicago-Style Four Bay** firehouse in 2021—it was assembled from a kit. The eight apparatus bay doors (four in front, four in rear) slide up on interior plastic rails and are held in the open position with magnets.

The building design is based on a generic working firehouse you would find in the city of Chicago in the early to mid 1900s. This replica was sold as both two-bay and four-bay versions. The example shown here is quarters to a collection of Chicago Fire Department O'hare International Airport replicas.

<u>Chicago Fire Department Apparatus Quartered:</u>
Ladder 63 (Pierce Platform, Code 3 #12909, 1999)
Ladder 63R (E-One Platform, Code 3 #12939, 2004)
Crash Truck 655 (Oshkosh, Code 3 #12150, 1999)
HMMWV Fire Pumper 7 (Hummer, Corgi Fire Heroes, 2003)
Helicopter & Helipad (Bell 412, Code 3 #12605, 2006)
Battalion 13 (Ford F-150, Greenlight #67050-E, 2024)
Command Vehicle (LDV, Code 3 #12532, 2003)
(not included with firehouse)

Two-Bay version of the Swiss Dog's Chicago-Style Firehouse

Chicago-Style Four-Bay Firehouse (laser cut basswood), Swiss Dog Studios, USA, 2021, 1:64

Los Angeles County
Engine 51/Squad 51 *"EMERGENCY!"*
Iconic Replicas Shelf-Size
EZ-Assembly Kit #50-0520

Release Date: December 2023

This 1:50 scale firehouse was released in December 2023 by **Iconic Replicas** (Boca Raton, Florida) to display their recent replicas of LA County Ward LaFrance Ambassador Engine 51, Dodge 300 Squad 51, and the latest Crown Engine 51 release.

The Iconic Replicas *EMERGENCY!* firehouse was sold by **Awesome Diecast** unassembled in the box along with a double-sided sheet of instructions. Prints resembling the real firehouse were applied to the plastic walls which were then cut out (as there are slight overcuts on the inside of the material)—so this model is not 3D-printed or made from a mold. The walls and exterior beams come with double-sided tape to attach them together.

The solid one-piece plastic apparatus bay door slides up and into the firehouse on a pair of plastic rails, there is no rear door. The plastic front, side, and rear pedestrian doors all open. The kit includes a colorful flexible pad base made of a thin foam/rubber kind of material which is a nice addition.

Note—while the Iconic Replicas 1:50 scale replica of Squad 51 fits nicely inside the firehouse, the Engine 51 replica does not (with the apparatus bay door closed). *Firehouse dimensions are 18" x 10" x 6¼" (apparatus bay is only 6" deep).*

This firehouse is a very nice addition to the world of diecast fire collecting, and I applaud Iconic Replicas for their recent releases—I wish more companies would make detailed fire apparatus models and firehouses. It will stand tall (if not as deep) with my other *EMERGENCY!* firehouses which bring fond memories of the TV show that got so many of us interested in the fire service. *Update: Iconic Replicas released 1:87 scale versions of their LA. County EMERGENCY! Fire Station 51, Engine 51, and Squad 51 in December 2024.*

Location: 2049 E. 223rd Street, Carson, CA

Apparatus Quartered:
Engine 51 (Ward LaFrance Ambassador, Iconic Replicas #50-0393, 2023, 1:50)
Squad 51 (Dodge 300, Iconic Replicas #50-0338, 2022, 1:50)

Awaiting Delivery:
Engine 51 (Crown, Iconic Replicas #50-0544, 2025, 1:50)

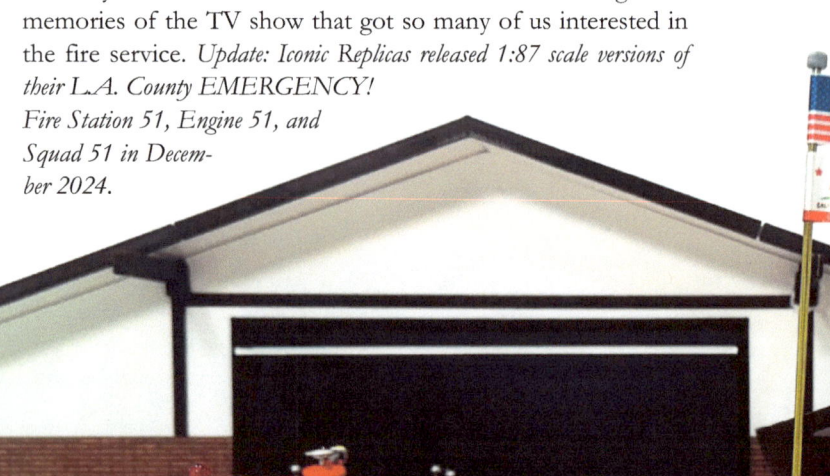

Los Angeles County Engine 51/Squad 51 "EMERGENCY!" (plastic), Iconic Replicas, USA, 2023, 1:50

APPENDIX: MISCELLANEOUS FIRE DEPARTMENT MODELS

The diverse fire department-related models contained in this appendix were created by a very talented group of artists. Hopefully their creations will provide inspiration for your own projects.

If you would like to have your own firehouse replicas considered for inclusion in future editions of this book, please post them to my Facebook group or contact me at andrew @andrewbenzie.com.

We begin with a ten-part article I originally posted online called *Building a Firehouse Replica*. Over a two-month period, through these posts I detailed the process involved to select, design, and build a **First Due Firehouse Replica**.

Building a First Due Firehouse Replica by Andrew Benzie

Part 1: Selecting a Firehouse/Sketching a Plan

The first step in building a **First Due Firehouse Replica** begins with selecting a suitable firehouse to replicate. My focus is making replicas for existing 1:64 scale models which were replicated by Code 3 Collectibles (from 1998 to 2011), so this article will focus on building a replica of a unique firehouse in Manhattan which is home to FDNY Engine 9, Ladder 6, and Satellite 1—the **Chinatown Dragonfighters**.

I selected this firehouse in part because I love the history of the houses from New York City—and based on Code 3 Collectible's releases, clearly they did as well. I also chose this building as I thought with its unique "mesh" second floor covering it would make for an interesting and challenging building to replicate. It also didn't hurt that I have owned a Code 3 model of FDNY Engine 9 since it was released in April 1998… I still remember finding it at a local KB Toys store.

Unfortunately, Code 3 never released models of Ladder 6 or Satellite 1, so this firehouse replica will require some reworking of existing units. For Ladder 6, I decided to renumber my existing Seagrave Tractor-Drawn Aerial lettered for "Bureau or Training" model. For Satellite 1, my friend Nghia Takeshi (in Viet Nam) designed, 3D printed, and hand-painted a wonderfully detailed 1:64 replica of this unit for me.

FDNY Engine 9, Code 3 Collectibles, 1998, 1:64

FDNY Engine 9/Ladder 6 "Chinatown Dragonfighters" firehouse in Chinatown, Manhattan

Part 1 *(cont'd.)*

Once I had my plan of which firehouse to make and what units to house inside, it was time to get started with an overall sketch of the master plan. I always try to make my replicas as accurate as possible, but sometimes in order to build scale models one must make small alterations or simplifications for a variety of reasons. This building has a number of different planes on the front which required a few hours of 3D brain-pondering in order to figure out how to recreate it most successfully in 1:64 scale. Until I see the final assembled replica—like you—I'm somewhat in the dark as to what it will actually look like. That's part of the fun of this craft.

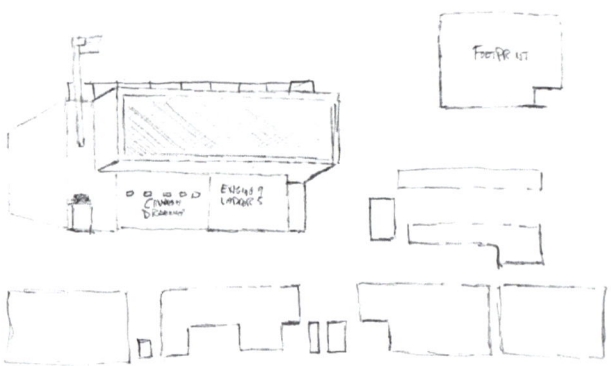

Part 2: Re-Numbering FDNY Ladder 6

The first step I take when converting a Code 3 model is to gather as many photos of the target apparatus as I can. In this case, since FDNY's number "6" is the same as an upside-down "9," all I had to do was take photos of my existing Code 3 model's Engine 9 numbering, flip the "9" upside down, scale in Photoshop, and print replacement signage for Ladder 6.

Once I had my "6," I then created new 1:64 scale graphics for both rear side-door numbers, the front bumper number, and the rear tiller box number. For the ladder sign, I used a photo of the real truck which required scaling and color adjustments which I performed in Photoshop.

For both Ladder 6 and Engine 9, I created the "Chinatown Dragonfighters" upper windshield graphics as well as the gold dragons located on the grills. Notice how the grill dragons face each other when they are parked in the firehouse. These are the interesting kinds of details I would only discover by going through the process of creating a replica like this.

Note: All First Due Firehouse Replicas which require renumbering of Code 3 Collectibles models include a high-quality poster printed sheet of replacement graphics with each purchase.

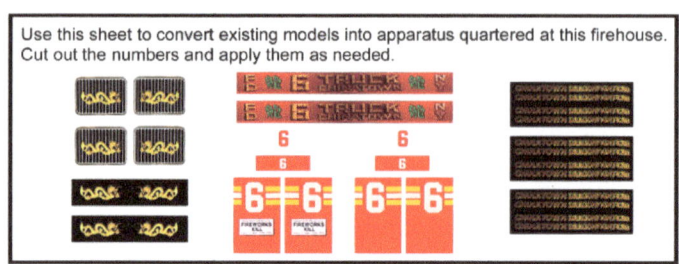

Part 3: Assembling the Firehouse Graphics

The third step in creating our 1:64 scale replica of FDNY Engine 9/Ladder 6/Satellite 1 involves creating the artwork for the exterior firehouse walls. This process includes the gathering of numerous photos of the real building, the resizing of the images into 1:64 scale, and finally the merging of the images into one piece of printable artwork.

This can be a rather tedious process which involves paying great attention to a variety of small details (such as the bay doors, the entry doors, any memorials, etc.), which each on their own may not seem too important, but together they really make the replica stand out on the display shelf.

Once I have gathered a sufficient number of photos, I merge them all into one Photoshop file and then begin sorting through everything to find the best shots of each part of the building. The Photoshop file I build is intentionally created with each element floating independently in its own "layer" in order to easily adjust, merge, or separate the parts for printing as necessary.

Part 4: Manipulating Firehouse Graphics

In many cases, simply using photographs of the exterior of a firehouse to create a replica doesn't work very well due to shadows, power lines, pedestrians, parked cars, and a variety of other factors that fall into play. I usually end up (as I did for this replica) having to recreate the walls—in this case using a black granite slab pattern for the lower floor, and a light-colored brick pattern for the walls of the upper floors. However, to achieve the most realism, all the imagery I create is based directly on real photographs of each firehouse.

Once I have my basic wall shapes and textures created in Photoshop, I then add back in the real photographic elements of all the fine details including company names, doors, windows, lighting, gutters, and any memorials that might be present. Through this process I can ensure my firehouse replicas include photographically accurate details of the real firehouse yet lack the problematic issues contained in the original photos.

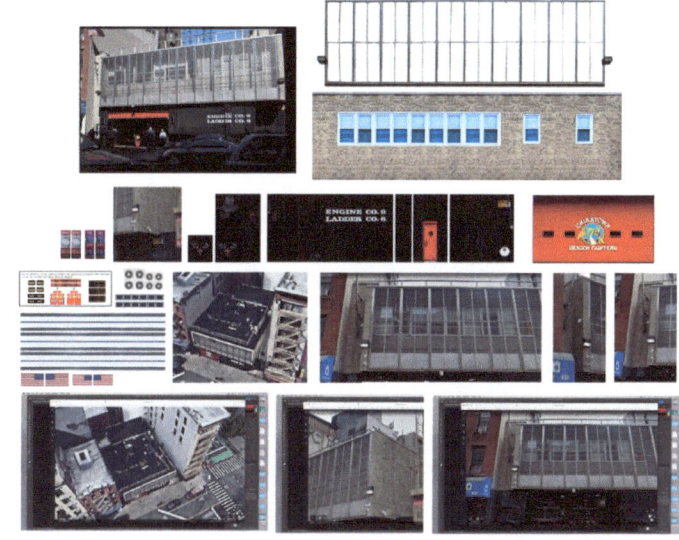

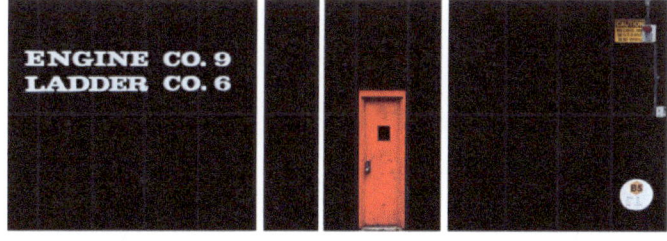

163

Part 5: Assembling a Mockup Replica

Before I print the high-resolution poster-quality prints for final production of each new firehouse replica I produce, I print out low-resolution prints on my home printer and assemble a mockup replica to ensure the parts fit together as intended. Since my home printer only prints 8.5 x 11-inch sheets I usually have to print the walls in sections, cut them out, then tape them together to form the sample wall segments.

After many hours of pre-production work, the taping of these wall segments together is the first time I actually get a glimpse of what the final replica will look like. During this phase I check all walls are sized correctly, fit as planned, and faithfully represent each firehouse in scale. Any final adjustments to the design are made during this process.

At this time, I also always double-check the apparatus bay entryways are large enough to fit the apparatus models which will be quartered at the firehouse. Keep in mind the well-known carpentry rule—"measure twice, cut once."

This firehouse has a unique design with a "screen" covering the exterior of the second floor. To replicate the screen I decided to use a roll of aluminum window screen material.

Part 6: Prepping Exterior Firehouse Parts

After making any changes necessary to the final artwork (based on viewing our previous mockup replica), I sent the files to the print shop to make high resolution 300 dpi glossy color prints. Once I receive the graphics, I will apply these prints to the walls, cut them out, and begin final assembly of the firehouse replica.

While I wait for the prints to be made, there are a number of other items which can be prepared so the assembly process goes faster. Items I prepare and pre-paint include the garage doors (and various parts to make them function), air conditioning units (for both the windows and roof), various railings, vents, pipes, bollards, flags, and flagpoles.

I also use this time to prepare the informational booklet I include with each of my firehouse releases. In this case for this replica of FDNY Engine 9's firehouse, I also spent time preparing the unique aluminum "mesh" screen which will cover the exterior of the second floor.

In the final photo below, you can see the prints have arrived all neatly rolled up.

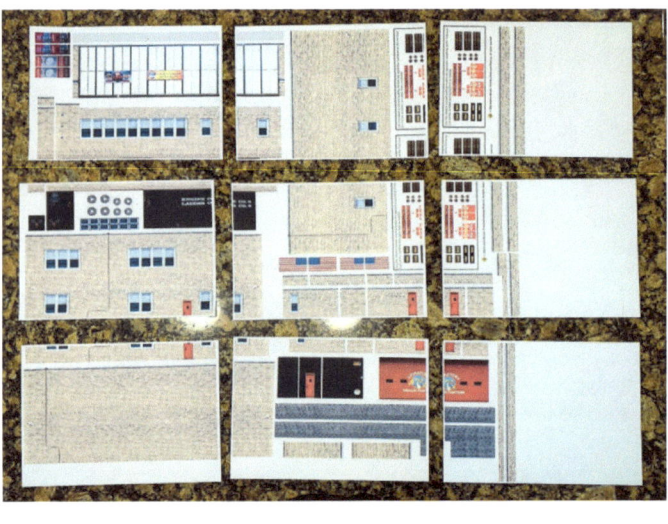

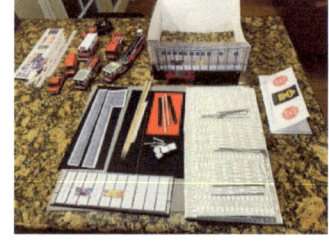

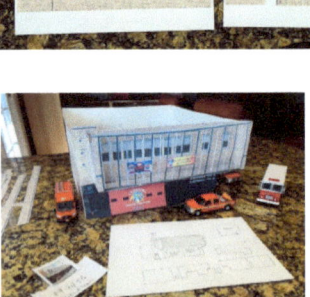

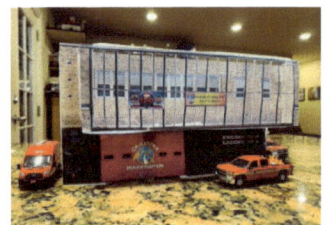

Part 7: Preparing Walls for Assembly

Now I have received the glossy high-resolution prints from the printer, I'm ready to prepare the walls for final assembly. To save on printing costs, for my Photoshop file I assemble all printed parts as close together as possible. In this case I was able to keep all the parts within a two-square-foot print.

The next step is to cut out the individual parts and match them to foam core board sections I have pre-prepared. This is also a good time to gather the previous elements I created (AC units, vents, flag, railings, planter, etc.).

To produce exact 90° and 45° cuts for the walls, I use a professional-grade matte cutter which I have altered to cut foam core boards. This step is crucial for achieving perfect joins at the corners of each replica. In the case of this firehouse—again, the upper "screen" area requires extra work by hand to prepare. Now all the parts have been prepared we are finally ready to assemble this firehouse replica.

Part 8: Assembling the Firehouse

During the next step, I'm finally starting to get an idea of what the finished replica will look like. Just like in real building construction, once all the parts are prepared and on site the framing actually goes quite quickly. This is where all the detailed work of preparing all the angles and cuts of the walls will pay off.

I always test the walls have been correctly prepared by first assembling them loosely together with masking tape. Once I'm satisfied everything fits well, I use white glue to attach the rear wall to the baseboard. From there I usually work forward by attaching the side walls, then the front of the facade (which has already been fitted with the working apparatus bay doors). I use masking tape to make sure the joins are all tight, then allow everything to set overnight.

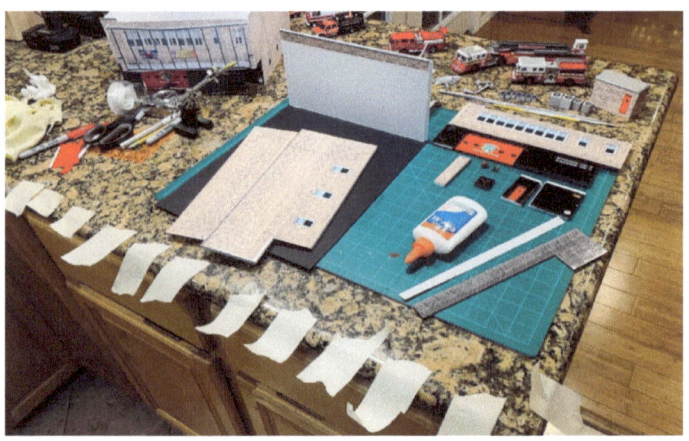

Part 9: Installation of Roof, Facade, Flag

Now the walls have been completed, the final step in building this firehouse replica is to add the facade, roof, and any other exterior elements. This firehouse has a unique "screen" facade covering nearly the entire second floor—to replicate this design I first created accurate scale artwork in Photoshop, then printed, cut out, and mounted the prints over a section of aluminum window screen material.

For the roof, I cut out a sheet of pre-colored board and added various vents, AC units and the roof stairway access area. I made the railing out of bamboo skewers which I spray-painted grey. The flag holders are made of reworked paperclips and allow the flag to be removed for shipping. The yellow bollards and flowers complete the very sharp looking facade of this lower Manhattan firehouse.

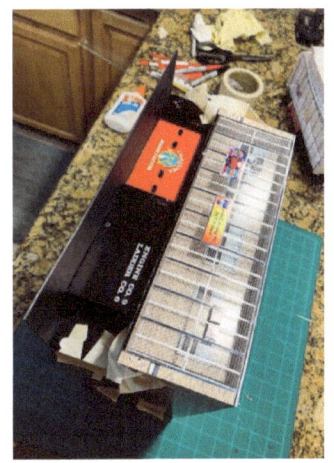

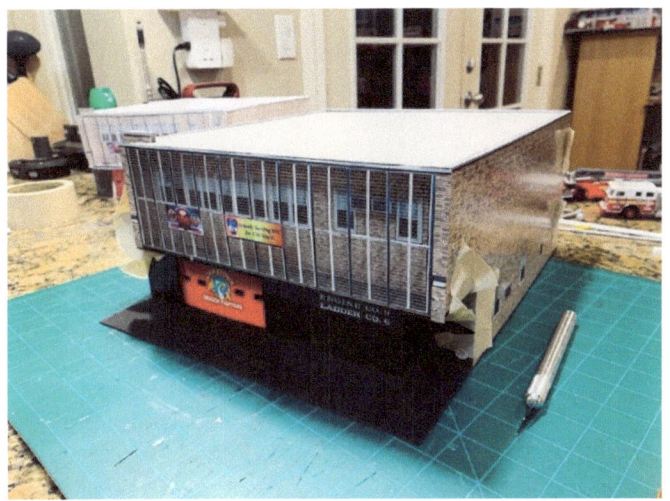
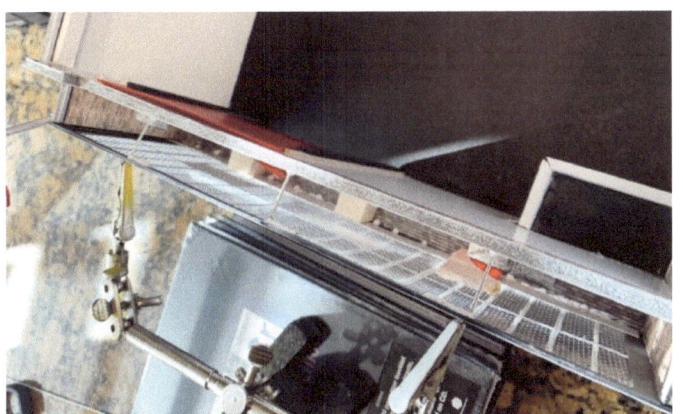

Part 10: Photography/Website/Promotion

The final step in the process is to share the replica with fellow collectors. To take photos, I built a simple lightbox out of foam core boards which I loosely tape together so I can easily break it down when not in use. I use two overhead lights and two photography lights mounted to a makeshift tripod I can move around to capture the best lighting for each shot.

For the scene itself, I use the appropriate Code 3 (and other) apparatus models quartered at each firehouse arranged with various 1:64 scale American Diorama firefighter figures (and accessories) as well as American flags produced by Code 3 in 2009 as part of their Old Glory Flag Assortment Set #12564.

I usually take 50 to 100 photos which I edit in Adobe Photoshop. I then select the best ten to fifteen shots to be used for promotion. I build a webpage for each firehouse replica I create—and along with the best of these photos, the webpage includes the same information which I wrote for the booklet along with other information including the release date, dimensions, features included, pricing, and details on the apparatus quartered at the firehouse. When possible, I also include links to related books and videos.

To see the best of the FDNY E9/L6/SAT1 photos I took, see page 78-79 of this book and the webpage I created at www.ModelFireEngines.com/fdny-e9.html.

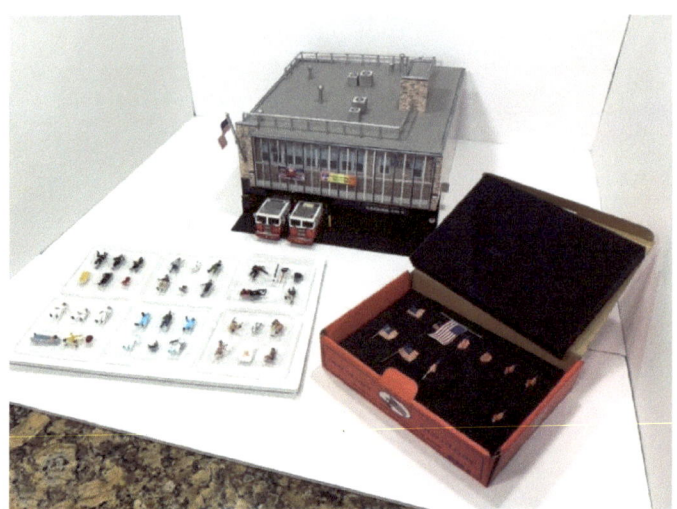

FDNY Engine 9/Ladder 6 "Chinatown Dragonfighters" (foam core, mixed media), First Due Firehouse Replicas, USA, 2023, 1:64

Assorted Firehouse Replicas
by Rip Van Winkle Hose Company/Bill Craven

Long-time collector Bill Craven created this series of foam-core firehouse replicas under the name **Rip Van Winkle Hose Company** in the 1990s, 1:50-1:64 scale.

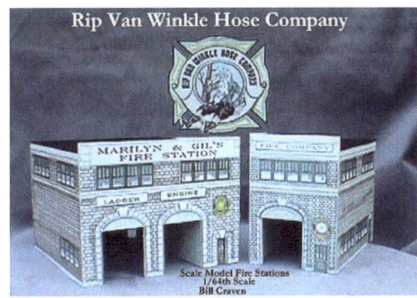

Town of Mamaroneck Fire Department
by Tony Mirande

Firefighter Tony Mirande built this beautiful 1:64 scale replica of the **Town of Mamaroneck Fire Department** located in Larchmont, New York (Westchester County) in 2022. This is a very special firehouse for Tony as he was a captain here in 1984, and his father Tony Sr. was fire chief in 1953. The replica is constructed of styrene walls with a foam core base—the memorial bell is scratch built.

Town of Mamaroneck Fire Department (foam core/styrene), Tony Mirande, 2022, 1:64

Plans are in the works to create replicas of the current apparatus on duty

Town of Mamaroneck Fire Department, 1950s

Town of Mamaroneck Fire Department, 1990s

The real firehouse located at 205 Weaver Street was designed by the John Russell Pope architectural firm in 1922—it was completed in June 1923. The original building included only the two center apparatus bays, the two side bays were added during the building's reconstruction in 1994.

The two Tonys proudly serving, c.1968, 2020

1:87 Scale Firehouse Replicas
by Jeff Noyes

My friend Jeff Noyes has an impressive collection of 1:87 scale firehouse models. The firehouses shown here are from **AHM**, **Life-Like**, **Swiss Dog Studios**, **Twin Whistle Sign & Kit Company**, **Walthers Scene Masters**, and **Woodland Scenics**.

Fire Station, Engine No 3/Ladder No 5 (plastic), Woodland Scenics, 1980s, 1:87

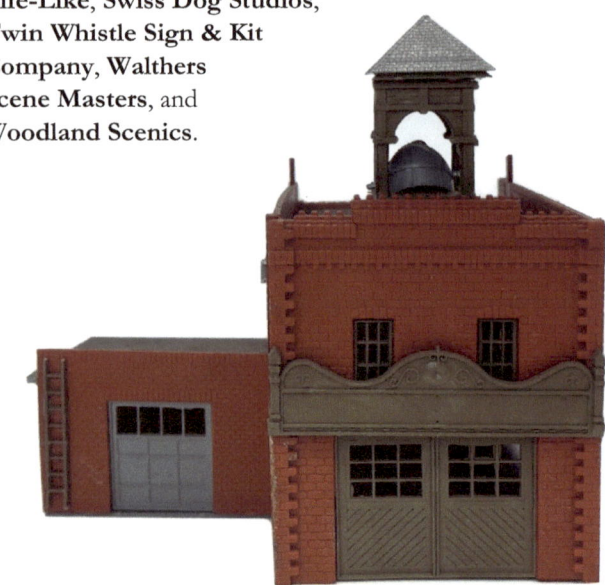

AHM Firehouse (plastic), 1980s, 1:87

Los Angeles County Fire Station #127 (#51 "EMERGENCY!") (laser cut basswood), Swiss Dog Studios, 2021, 1:87

Volunteer Fire Co. (plastic), Life Like Trains, 1980s, 1:87

Heljan Fire Station (plastic), Walthers Scene Masters, 1980s, 1:87

FDNY Ladder 8 "Ghostbusters" Firehouse (hand-painted resin), Twin Whistle & Sign Company, 2020s, 1:87

Two-Bay Fire Station (plastic), Walthers Scene Masters, 2012, 1:87

Two-Bay Fire Station (plastic),
Walthers Scene Masters, 2012, 1:87

Fire Department Repair Shop (plastic),
Walthers Scene Masters, 2013, 1:87

Fire Department Headquarters (plastic),
Walthers Scene Masters, 2010s, 1:87

Fire Department Drill Tower (plastic),
Walthers Scene Masters, 2010s, 1:87

FDNY LEGO Firehouse Replicas
by Cyrille Verhaeghe

Through great imagination and creativity, Cyrille Vrhaeghe (a professional firefighter in Paris, France) created these realistic **FDNY** firehouse replicas entirely out of **LEGO** blocks.

THE STATELY DUANE MANOR 🇺🇸
100 DUANE ST MA

■	7
■	1
□	B1

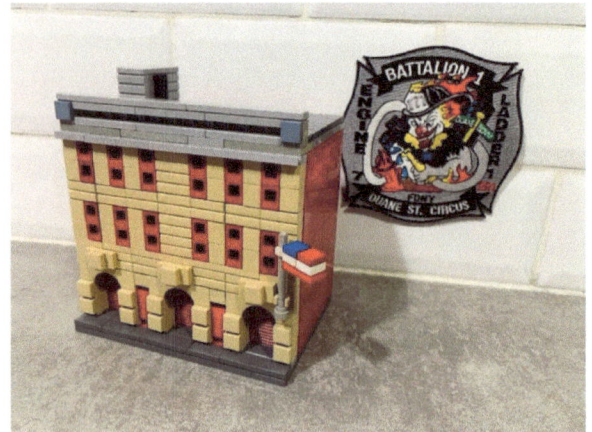

DRAGON 🐉 FIREFIGHTERS
75 CANAL ST MA

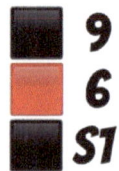

■	9
■	6
■	S1

TEN HOUSE 🇺🇸
124 LIBERTY ST MA

■ 10
🟧 10

FORT PITT 🇺🇸
25 PITT ST MA

■ 15
🟧 18
⬜ B4

KEEP BAY 🇺🇸
234 EAST 29 TH ST MA

■ 16
🟧 7

HELL'S KITCHEN 😈
440 W 38TH ST MA

■ 34
🟧 21

PRIDE OF MIDTOWN 🎭
782 8TH AVE MA

■ 54
■ 4
□ B9

THE CINQUANTACINQUE 🇮🇹
363 BROOKE ST MA

■ 55

FIRE 🐶 FACTORY
1365 5TH AVE MA

■ 58
■ 26

HARLEM ZOO 🦍
111 W. 133RD ST MA

■ 59
■ 30

THE LOST WORLD 🦖
120 W 83RD ST MA

■ 74

ANIMAL HOUSE
2175 WALTON AVE BX

■ 75
■ 33
□ B19

RED HOOK 🪝
31 RICHARDS ST BY

■ 202
■ 101
□ 32

TIN HOUSE GANG 🤖
25 ROCKAWAY AVE BY

■ 233
■ 176
□ FC2

JAMAICA 🇯🇲
153-11 HILLSIDE AVE QU

■ 298
■ 127
□ B50

🐙 AVE N
6405 AVE BY

■ 323

GHOSTBUSTERS 👻 TRIBECA
14 N MOORE ST MA

■ 8

RESCUE 1️⃣
530 W 43 ST MA

■ 1

🚢 FIREFIGHTER 2 ⚓
305 FRONT STREET SI

 9

GREENWICH VILLAGE 🌳
132 W 10 TH ST MA

SQ 18

MORRIS PARK 🇺🇸
1518 WILLIAMS BRIDGE RD BX

 61
B20

RICHMOND HILL 🇺🇸
121 ST   QU

 270
D13

FDNY LEGO Headquarters
by Jimmie Martinez

Firefighter Jimmie Martinez' love for **LEGOs** led him to design and build this fictitious 11-bay firehouse as a tribute to the **FDNY** firefighters lost on 9/11. This impressive structure contains between ten and twelve thousand elements and was under construction for three years.

As Jimmie's collection grew the firehouse continued to expand, only to be stopped by a lack of available shelf space. Interior features include apparatus bays, kitchen, dormitories, bathroom, and recreation room.

Apparatus Quartered:
Engine 34 (American LaFrance, Code 3 #12139, 2005)
Engine 231 (Seagrave, Code 3 #12835, 2005)
Engine 1 (Seagrave, Code 3 #12838, 2006)
Squad 1 (Seagrave, Code 3 #12657, 2003)
Brush Fire Support Unit 2 (Freightliner, customized Code 3)
Rescue 2 (Emergency-One, Code 3 #12694, 2004)
HazMat 1 (HME/Saulsbury, Code 3 #12705, 2003)
Truck 26 (Seagrave, Code 3 #12855, 2004)
Truck 160 (Baker Aerialscope 75' Tower Ladder, Code 3 #12730-0160, 2000)
RAC 4 (Ford E-350, Code 3 #12068, 2002)
Battalion 1 (GMC Suburban, customized Code 3)

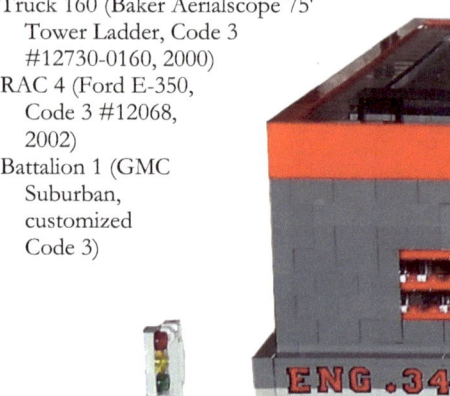

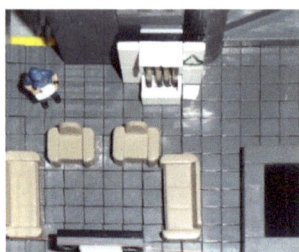

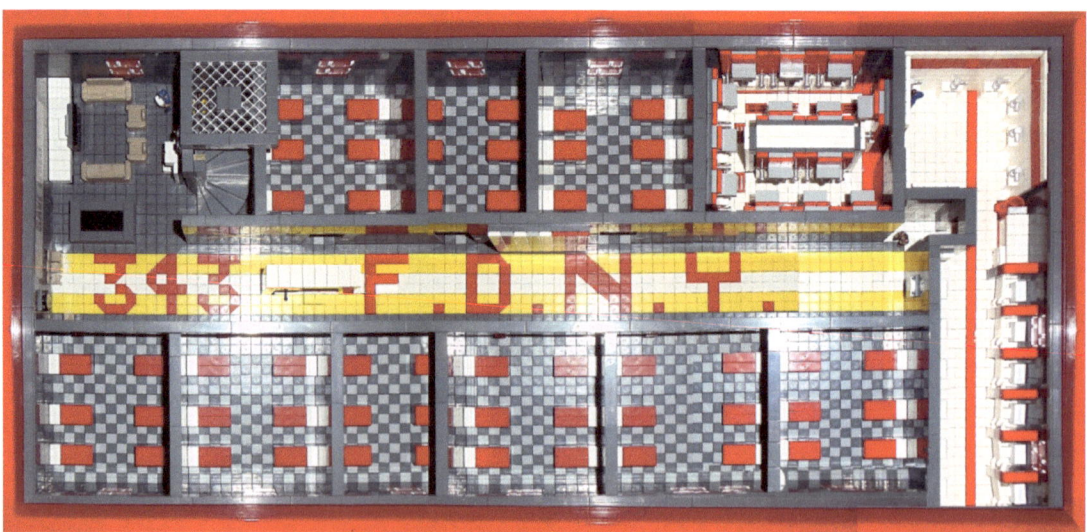

The upper floor features the dormitories, recreation room, and bathroom

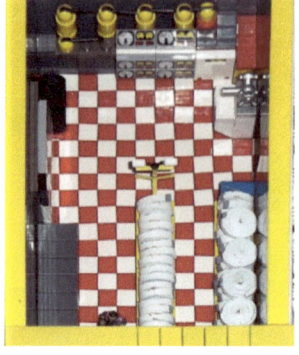

FDNY Fire Department Headquarters (LEGO), Jimmie Martinez, 2012, 1:64

The ground level features the large eleven-bay apparatus floor, a storage room, dining room, and kitchen

Los Angeles County Engine 51/Squad 51 *EMERGENCY!* LEGO Fire Station
by Jimmie Martinez

Location: 2049 E 223rd Street, Carson, CA

Years in Service: 1966-present

Apparatus Quartered:
Engine 51 (Ward LaFrance, Code 3 #12391, 2002)
Squad 51 (Dodge 300, Code 3 #13940, 2001)
Parade Engine 51 (1934 Dennis, customized Lledo)

Like so many of us, for Jimmie Martinez the *EMERGENCY!* television show was a driving factor which led him to pursue a career in fire/EMS. Over a span of three years Jimmie created this incredibly detailed replica of Fire Station 51 out of 16,000 **LEGO** pieces. Both the interior and exterior have been recreated of this real-life firehouse which is still in operation today.

Los Angeles County Engine 51/Squad 51 EMERGENCY! Fire Station (LEGO), Jimmie Martinez, 2015, 1:64

"This creation stands as a tribute to not only the firehouse, but the ER staff at Rampart General—the producers, director, and writers all have a locker." —Jimmie Martinez

183

Firehouse Dioramas
by Frank Moebius

Frank Moebius is an amazing artist and photographer from Germany who specializes in 1:64 scale dioramas. Vehicle models are by **Code 3 Collectibles** and **Greenlight Collectibles**.

Mack Fire Engine Assembly Plant
by Cary Murray

Cary Murray built this beautiful **Mack Fire Apparatus Assembly Plant** and matching model firehouse diorama in HO

scale. The structures are built on two separate modules which can be linked together via railroad tracks. These scenes represent the construction, shipping, and service of Mack fire trucks. The firehouses protect the fictional Walnut City, PA (Conrail era).

FDNY Fleet Services "The Shops" Facility
by Andrew Benzie/First Due Firehouse Replicas

Build Date: October 2021

First Due Firehouse Replicas diorama of **FDNY Fleet Services/Building Maintenance Division "The Shops"** building is our most ambitious project to date. Over one-hundred hours were put into replicating numerous vehicles as well as the interior and exterior of this extraordinary facility.

The Fire Department of New York Fleet Services building is a remarkable facility which has been keeping the nation's largest fire department in service for nearly 75 years. Inside the building resides a team of 350 dedicated workers in charge of the maintenance and repair of every single vehicle in service with the FDNY (including fire engines, trucks, tower ladders, rescues,

Main entrance to the shops at 48-58 35th Street, Queens, New York: "NO vehicles are to enter shop. Obtain clearance from office. By order of the Chief in Command"

FDNY Fleet Services "The Shops" Facility (foam core, mixed media), Andrew Benzie/First Due Firehouse Replicas, USA, 2021, 1:64

FDNY Ladder 125, "Tonka Truck" departing the shops

hazmat units, ambulances, chief and staff cars, service and fuel trucks, and dozens of spare vehicles).

The Long Island City Shops is in effect an enormous garage, with fire department rolling stock in various stages of rebuilding and repair neatly arranged along both sides. FDNY Buildings Maintenance Division is also located at this facility. This unit is responsible for the upkeep and maintenance of the city's 218 firehouses (including electricity, communications, plumbing, masonry, etc.).

In 1948, the Fleet Services Division moved into its vast new building at 154 Hunters Point Avenue (between 34th and 35th streets) in Long Island City, where it operates one of the most unique, and certainly the largest enterprise of its kind to be found in the nation's fire service.

The building itself is unusual in architecture (known as the Z-D system of Monolithic Construction) and was erected under the immediate supervision of Bernard J. Farrell, resident engineer of the Department of Public Works, and Robert Zabrowski, resident engineer for the Roberts & Schaefer Company, owners of the "Z-D" system.

It was the first of its kind in New York and is said to be "as near fireproof as science and a fire-conscious fire department could build." An important feature from a structural standpoint is the lack of posts, columns or supports of any kind on the main floor. This tremendous uninterrupted floor area is covered by a 3½ inch thick curved slab roof, suspended from arches on 35-foot centers. The shell structure is a multi-radius pipe sector of enormous rigidity which serves as a beam between the supporting columns.

The height of the entire building is two stories (32 ft.) and consists of three shells—a large one in the center and smaller ones on either side. The roof will carry a snow load of 40 lbs. per square foot. The towering antenna provides radio communication throughout the City.

It should be noted this main shop facility (for heavy duty apparatus) is not the only FDNY repair facility. Separate shops facilities are maintained in Queens for ambulance/light-duty vehicles. Fleet Services also has an apparatus storage facility in Brooklyn.

The rear of our FDNY Fleet Services replica

*Custom-built Mack Granite tow truck towing
disabled Ladder 49 to the Shops for repairs*

*Various FDNY Buildings Unit vehicles
parked at the shops*

The interior of the facility is equipped with numerous workstations outfitted with two and four-post lifts along with an assortment of professional-grade mechanical tools. At any given time 40 to 50 FDNY vehicles are waiting to be checked, serviced, or repaired.

When a new piece of FDNY apparatus arrives from a manufacturer, the Fleet Services Division is responsible for performing a thorough testing process before acceptance. This is a formidable job considering every item must be checked on hundreds of new units every year.

Among the special equipment housed here are four coal forges, a gas-fired furnace, a 200 lb. triphammer, an 800 lb. steam hammer (and various power saws, punches, and shears), a motor repair shop, a machine shop (with lathes, milling machines, grinders, shapers, planers, and drill presses), and paint-spray rooms for painting, stripping, and lettering the apparatus.

The shop contains over $4 million worth of Seagrave, Ferrara, and KME spare parts—everything, from truck transmissions, pumps, electrical parts, and tires is neatly stowed away in storage racks. Every part is labelled and registered. Complete aerial ladder assemblies are also stored onsite. If repairs are needed, crews will swap out the entire ladder—the ladders are then sent back in batches to the original builders to be refurbished.

<u>Location:</u>
154 Hunters Point Avenue
48-58 35th Street *(Fleet Services Division)*
48-34 35th Street *(Buildings Unit Division)*
Long Island City, Queens, NY

<u>Years in Service:</u> 1948-present

<u>Companies Quartered:</u>
Fleet Services Division
Buildings Unit Division

Spare parts are neatly stored throughout the shops

Features Include:
- black base with 2-inch apron
- removable roof
- 4 apparatus bay doors
- 1 loading bay door
- 2 flags/flagpoles
- 1 two-post lift by Mijo
- 2 four-post lifts by Greenlight
- 9 four-post lifts by M2 (widened to accept most Code 3 Collectibles models)
- 23 die-cast figures by American Diorama
- 50 die-cast models by Code 3 Collectibles, DCP/First Gear, ERTL, Greenlight, Hot Wheels, M2, Majorette, PlayArt, Racing Champions, and Winross
- printed firehouse fact sheet booklet

Just like the real facility, our 1:64 scale replica of FDNY Fleet Services building is jam-packed full of apparatus waiting to be serviced. Numerous Fleet Services vehicles are also quartered at this location.

Displayed along with our replica are two officers' vehicles, two field service vehicles (which do minor repairs off-site), a tire unit and a fuel tanker (which also work in the field), and a spare pumper. A variety of tow trucks also reside here, including our custom-built replica of FDNY's beautiful 2019 Mack Granite wrecker.

An assortment of Buildings Unit Division vehicles is also quartered at this location. Included in our diorama are two Chevrolet pickups, a Ford pickup and sedan, two Ford Transit Vans (Buildings Unit and Plant Ops versions), and a Chevy Silverado stake truck.

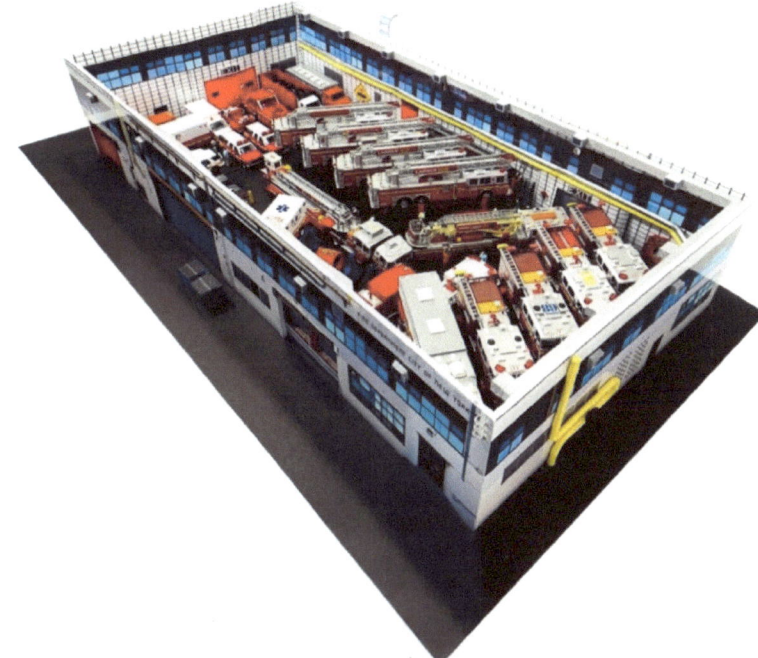

FDNY Fleet Services "The Shops" Facility, First Due Firehouse Replicas, 2021, 1:64

FIRST
DUE
F.D.N.Y.
AMBULANCE
FDNY
FIRE

TOWER LADDER
FIRE

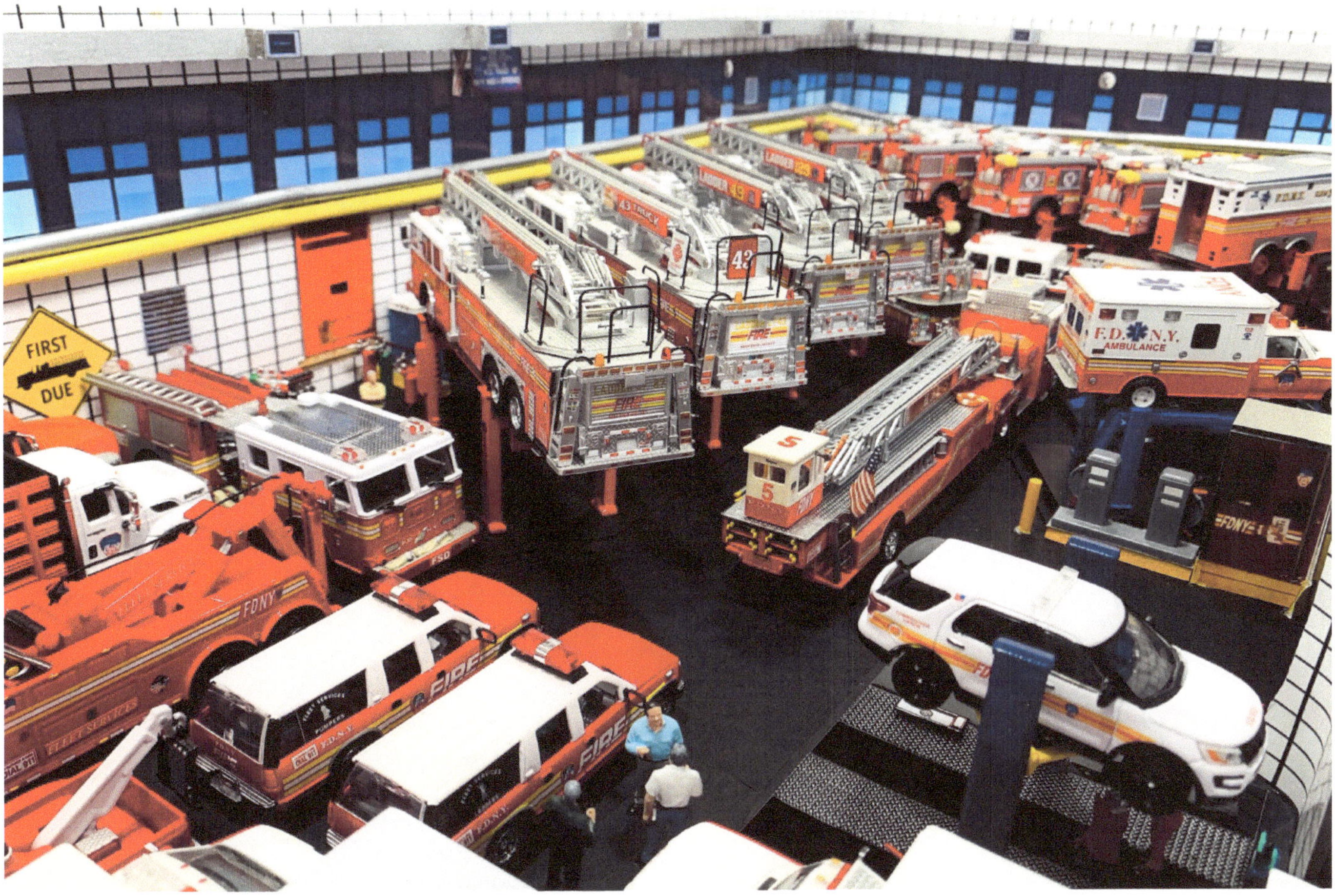

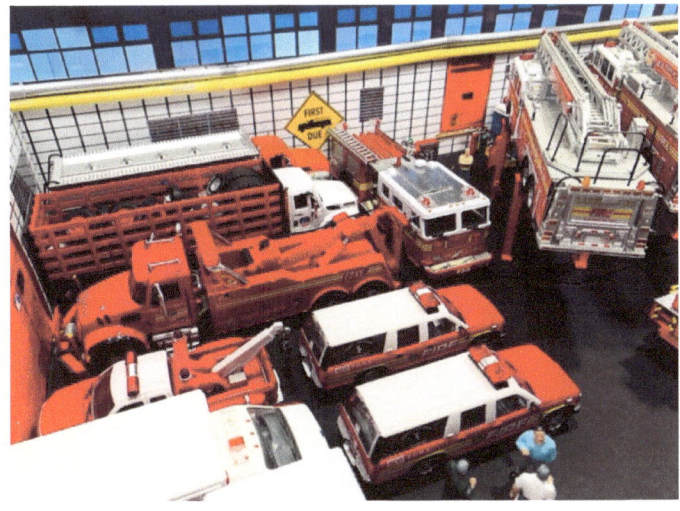

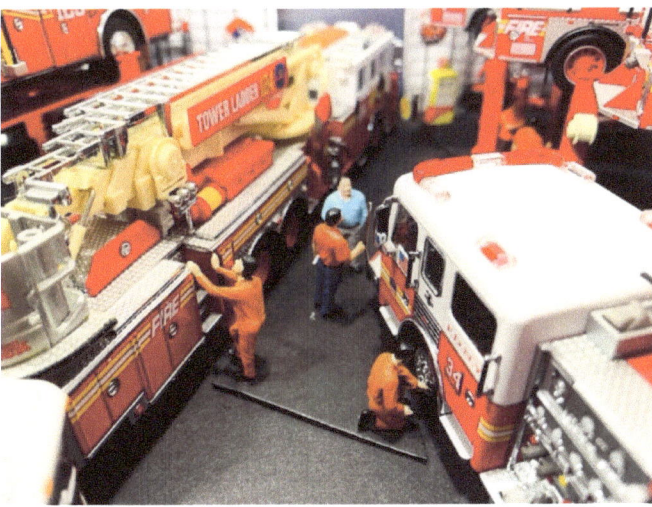

INDEX

PART ONE:
MODEL FIRE STATION TOYS

American Diorama 4 Bay Fire Station	48
Arcade Engine Co. No. 99	1
Boley Dept. 1-87 First Alarm Fire Station	44
Boley Dept. 1-87 First Alarm Fire Station (Prototype)	45
Corgi Classics Model Fire Depot	32
Corgi Juniors Coastal Rescue Station	35
Corgi Juniors Fire Station Set	34
Dinky Toys Fire Station Kit	6
Fleetwood Toys "*EMERGENCY!*" Firehouse	17
Funrise City Force Center Fire Station (1:64/1:32)	50
Galoob Micro Machines Blaze & Roar Fire Station	43
Galoob Micro Machines City Scenes Fire Station	42
Galoob Micro Machines Double Action Fire Station	43
Galoob Micro Machines Fire & Rescue Playset	43
Galoob Micro Machines Fire Dept.	43
Galoob Micro Machines Firehouse City	43
Galoob Micro Machines Travel City Firehouse	43
Hot Wheels City Super Loop Fire Station	41
Hot Wheels Downtown Fire Station Spinout Playset	41
Hot Wheels Firefighter Sto & Go	40
Hot Wheels Planet Micro Urban Firefighting Scene	41
Hot Wheels Raceway Fire Station	40
Hot Wheels Rescue Center	40
Hot Wheels Spin City Fire Station Spinner Tower	41
Hot Wheels Sto & Go *Baywatch* Rescue Station	41
Hot Wheels Sto & Go Emergency Station	40
Hot Wheels World Fire Station w/Elevator	40
Hot Wheels World Fire Station w/Pop Up Flames	40
Hubley Fire Dept. Fire Apparatus Scale Models	1
Ives Fire Engine House	1
Keystone Fire Department and Burning Building	2
Kingsbury Fire Station 8	1
LEGO Blaze Brigade	19
LEGO Engine Company No. 9	18
LEGO Fire Brigade	18
LEGO Fire Control Center	19
LEGO Fire House	18
LEGO Fire House-I	19
LEGO Fire Station (X3)	18
LEGO Fire Station (X6)	19
LEGO Fire Station with Fire Truck	19
LEGO Firefighter's HQ	19
LEGO Flame Fighters	19
LEGO *Ghostbusters* Firehouse Headquarters	19
LEGO Winter Village Fire Station	19
Lionel Fire Station	36
The Lucky Toys Joy Town Fire Station	5
Majorette Creatix Rescue Station	27
Majorette Firefighter Firehouse	27
Majorette/Jada Creatix Rescue Station	27
Majorette Majokit Emergency Center Set	26
Majorette Majokit Fire Station Construction Playset	26
Majorette Mini Majo-Kit Fire Brigade	27
Marx Automatic Fire House	1
Marx Fire House	3
Marx General Alarm Fire Department Headquarters	1
Matchbox Action Drivers Fire Station Rescue	13
Matchbox Big MX Complete Fire Rescue Site	11
Matchbox Car•Go Fire Station	12
Matchbox Emergency Station	10
Matchbox Fire & Rescue Center	12
Matchbox Fire Station (Green Roof)	9
Matchbox Fire Station (Red Roof)	8
Matchbox Fire Station Adventure Set	13
Matchbox Fire Station with Auto-Motion Features	12
Matchbox Fire Station Take-Along Playset	13
Matchbox Go! Action Rescue Town	13
Matchbox Hero City Fire Station Playset	13
Matchbox Motor City Electronic Rescue Station	12
Matchbox Motor City Fire Station	13
Matchbox Pop Up Adventure Set Fire Rescue	13
Matchbox Pop Up Adventure Set Fire Station	13
Matchbox Roll 'n Rescue Fire Station	13
Matchbox World's Smallest Fire Station Mini Playset	12
Mettoy Joytown Firehouse	5
Model Power Fire Department	37
Model Power Fire House	37
M.T.H. Operating Firehouse (Grey/Red)	36
Parker Brothers/Pastime Products Fire House	16
Plasticville Fire House Kit (O/HO)	3
Road Champs Fire-House Playset	46
Siku Volvo F12 Transporter w/Fire Station	30
SIKUWorld Fire Station	31
SIKUWorld Fire Station Set	31
Solido Jeu de Société Party Game	29
Starlux Caserne de Pompiers (for Solido models)	28
Starlux Centre de Secours (for Solido models)	29
Starlux City Intervention Set	29
Tomica Electro Fire Station	20
Tomica Fire Station	21
Tomica Fire Station	24
Tomica U-Mate Fire Station	22
Tomica U-Mate Fire Station	23
Tomica U-Mate Hospital	22
Tomica Hypercity Rescue Fire Station	25
Tomica Kabaya Fire Station and Hospital	24
TomyTec Diorama Collection Fire Station	25
Tonka Big Fire Department Playset	39
Tonka Builder Playset Fire Engine House	39
Tootsietoy Fire Station	14
Tyco US1 Electric Trucking Fire Station	38
Wyandotte Toytown Fire Dept.	4

PART TWO: FIREHOUSE REPLICAS

Boston E24/L23 "Grove Hall"	62
Boston E30/L25	124
Buffalo E2/L9/B56	116
Burning Building and Firefighter Figures	72
Chicago E17/L46 *Backdraft*	66
Chicago E18 "Devil Dogs"	126
Chicago E42/T3/S1 "Iron Ring"	128
Chicago E78/A6 "The Pride of Wrigleyville"	68
Chicago E113	130
Chicago E124/T38 "Hole In the Wall Gang"	132
Chicago-Style Four-Bay Firehouse	159
Denver E3 "Pride of the Points"/"Eye of the Storm"	134
Hose Tower Kit	158
How to Build a Firehouse Replica	161
LAFD E18 "Knollwood"	138
LAFD E39/T39/B10 "The Big House"	140
LAFD E51 "LAX"	142
Los Angeles County E51/S51 *EMERGENCY!*	70
Los Angeles County E51/S51 *EMERGENCY!*	160
Los Angeles County E51/S51 *EMERGENCY!* LEGO Firehouse	182
FDNY E1/L26 "Midtown Madness"	74
FDNY E5 "14th Street Express"	156
FDNY E7/L1/B1 "Duane Street Circus"	76
FDNY E9/L6/SAT1 "Chinatown Dragonfighters"	78
FDNY E10/L10 "The Tenhouse"	54
FDNY E40/L35 "The Cavemen"	80
FDNY E58/L26 "Fire Factory"	82
FDNY E59/L30 "Harlem Zoo"	84
FDNY E73/L42 "La Casa Caca"/"La Casa Elefante"	86
FDNY E75/L35/B19 *Animal House* (Old) Valiant Service Edition	88
FDNY E75/L35/B19 *Animal House* (New)	90
FDNY E82/L31 "La Casa Grande"	56
FDNY E160/R5 "The Hillbillies"/"Blue Thunder"	110
FDNY E201/L114/B40 "Emerald Isle"	92
FDNY E207/L110/B31/Super Pumper System "Tillary St. Tigers"	94
FDNY E231/L120 "Watkins Street"	150
FDNY E235/B57 "The Eye of Bed-Stuy"	58
FDNY E242 "The Pride of Bayridge"	96
FDNY E249 "Camp Rogers Rats"	156
FDNY E273/L129 "The Mouse House"	98
FDNY E286/L135 "Myrtles Turtles"	156
FDNY E292/R4 "Winfield Cougars"	158
FDNY L8 *Ghostbusters*	100
FDNY L79/B22 "North Shore Truckin'"	60
FDNY S1 "The One and Only"	102
FDNY S18 "South of the Park"	156
FDNY S61/B20 "Taking in a Job Near You"	157
FDNY S252 "In Squad We Trust"	157
FDNY S288/HazMat 1 "Fortuna Favet Fortibus"	104
FDNY S288/HazMat 1 "Fortuna Favet Fortibus"	157
FDNY R1 "Outstanding" (Old)	157
FDNY R1 "Outstanding" (New)	152
FDNY R2 "The Bulldog" (Old)	154
FDNY R2 "The Bulldog" (New)	106
FDNY R3 "Big Blue"	108
FDNY R4/E292 "Winfield Cougars"	158
FDNY R5/E160 "Blue Thunder"/"The Hillbillies"	110
FDNY Rescue Company 3D Patch Set	72
FDNY EMS Station #19 "University Heights"/ "Da Boogie Down Bronx"	89
FDNY Fleet Services "The Shops" Facility	188
FDNY LEGO Firehouses	174
FDNY LEGO Headquarters	180
Firehouse Dioramas	184
Honolulu E5/L5 "Kaimuki"	148
Mack Fire Engine Assembly Plant	186
New Jersey Fire Tower	158
Oceanic VFDNY H&L Co. No.1 E1/BFU1	112
Old Glory American Flag Assortment	73
1:87 Scale Firehouses	172
Orlando E2/L2 "The Pride of Parramore"	136
Philadelphia E50/L12 "Northern Knights"	122
Rip Van Winkle Hose Company	169
SFFD E3/T3	144
SFFD E15/T15 *Towering Inferno*/ *Ocean's 15*	146
Syracuse Fire Station 1	118
Town of Mamaroneck Fire Department	170
Washington, D.C. E10/L13 "House of Pain"	64
West Haverstraw Hose Co#2 E23/R23 "House of Blues"	120
Yonkers E313/T73 "Far East"	114

Chicago Fire Department Engine 42/Truck 3/Squad 1 "The Iron Ring" apparatus bay doors

BIBLIOGRAPHY

A Photographic Journey Through the Firehouses of the Fire Department City of New York by Paul Hashagen and Larry Woodcock, 2014

Classic Miniature Vehicles Made in Germany by Dr. Edward Force, 1990

Code 3 Collectibles Collectors Guides, flyers, website (*screenshots*)

Code 3 Firetrucks website

The F.D.N.Y. Super Pumper System by John A. Calderone, 1985

Feuerwehrmodelle by Thomas Herminghaus, 1987

FHNY: Fire House New York: A Pictorial History of Firehouse Architecture in the City of New York by Brian McCaffrey, 2002

Firefighting Toys 1940s-1990s by James G Piatti and Sandra Frost Piatti, 2005

First Due Firehouse Replicas website

The History of American Firefighting Toys by Charles V. Hansen, 1990

How New York Keeps Its Fire Apparatus Rolling, Fire Engineering Magazine, August 1947

Miniature Emergency Vehicles by Dr. Edward Force, 1985

Model Fire Engines: Conrad by Andrew Benzie, 2017

Model Fire Engines: Siku by Andrew Benzie, 2017

Model Fire Engines: Tomica by Andrew Benzie, 2017

The Siku Story by Ulrich Biene, 2014

Siku-Sammlerkatalog RAWE 2003 by Wilfried Raschke and Manfred Weise, 2003

Siku.de website, catalogs, dealer brochures

TocaraTomy.co.jp website, catalogs

Tomica 40th Anniversary Guide, 2010

Tomica 1,000 Collection (Book 2), 2005

About the Figures
The 1:64 scale die-cast metal firefighting figures seen throughout this book were produced by **American Diorama** (americandiorama.com) as part of their **Mijo Exclusives** series. The 1:50 scale metal figures (pages 96-97, 127) are by **Corgi Classics**.

Special Thanks
Thanks to Bill Craven, Jimmie Martinez, Tony Mirande, Frank Moebius, Cary Murray, Jeff Noyes, and Cyrille Verhaeghe for their contributions to the **Appendix**. Thanks to my proofreaders, especially John A. Calderone (editor of *Fire Apparatus Journal* magazine) for confirming, correcting, and adding to the information provided in this book. And extra thanks to all the members of my Facebook group, I appreciate your interest and input. And of course, a huge thanks to you for purchasing this book—please spread the word around the firehouse kitchen table!

ABOUT THE AUTHOR

Author Andrew Benzie began collecting model emergency vehicles in the 1970s when his grandparents gave him his first Corgi and Dinky toy fire engines. Andrew currently lives in the San Francisco Bay Area where he runs a design/book publishing company and plays bass and drums with several local bands.

andrew@andrewbenzie.com

- - - - - - - - - - - - - - -

andrewbenzie.com
modelfireengines.com
andrewbenziebooks.com

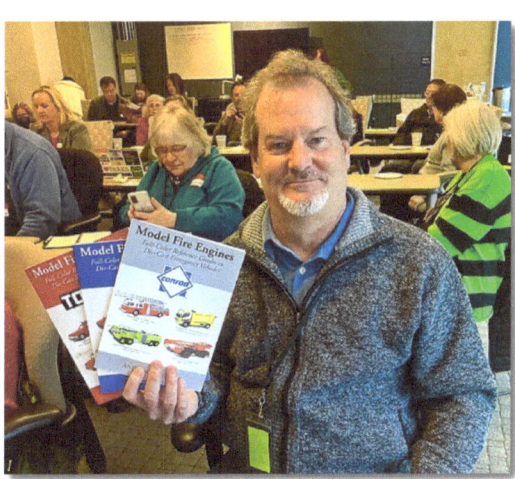

OTHER BOOKS IN THE SERIES

If you enjoyed this book and would like to see more books published in this series, please consider leaving a positive review on Amazon, it really helps. We hope you will consider exploring the other titles in our *Model Fire Engines* series of books. Until our next book, happy collecting!

for information about updates, new releases and other books in this series:
www.ModelFireEngines.com

Model Fire Engines
Full-Color Reference Guides to Die-Cast Emergency Vehicles

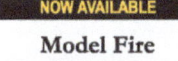

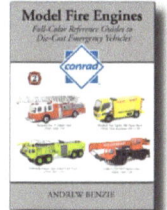
Model Fire Engines: Conrad

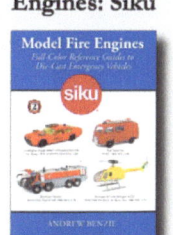
Model Fire Engines: Siku

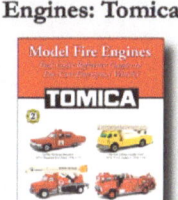
Model Fire Engines: Tomica

all books available at:
www.ModelFireEngines.com
amazon
and other bookstores

More titles coming soon.
Join mailing list: www.ModelFireEngines.com

CORGI · CODE 3 · HOT WHEELS
LLEDO · MAJORETTE · MATCHBOX